UTILITARIANISM AND
DISTRIBUTIVE JUSTICE

Utilitarianism and Distributive Justice

Jeremy Bentham and the Civil Law

P. J. KELLY

CLARENDON PRESS · OXFORD
1990

Oxford University Press, Walton Street, Oxford OX2 6DP
Oxford New York Toronto
Delhi Bombay Calcutta Madras Karachi
Petaling Jaya Singapore Hong Kong Tokyo
Nairobi Dar es Salaam Cape Town
Melbourne Auckland
and associated companies in
Berlin Ibadan

Oxford is a trade mark of Oxford University Press

Published in the United States
by Oxford University Press, New York

British Library Cataloguing in Publication Data
Kelly, Paul
Utilitarianism and distributive justice: Jeremy Bentham
and the Civil Law.
1. Justice. Theories of Bentham, Jeremy, 1748–1832
I. Title
179
ISBN 0–19–825418–0

Library of Congress Cataloging in Publication Data
Kelly, P. J. (Paul J.)
Utilitarianism and distributive justice: Jeremy Bentham and the
civil law/P. J. Kelly
Includes bibliographical references.
1. Law—Philosophy. 2. Utilitarianism. 3. Bentham, Jeremy,
1748–1832—Contributions in law. I. Title.
K334.K45 1990 340'.1–dc 90–35278
ISBN 0–19–825418–0

Typeset by Cambrian Typesetters, Frimley, Surrey
Printed in Great Britain by
Biddles Ltd.
Guildford and King's Lynn

For
Anne, Thomas, and Ruth

Acknowledgements

IN writing this book I have incurred a number of debts, both general and specific. I owe a considerable debt of gratitude to my parents for the understanding and support they have shown over many years. I have also benefited from the continued advice and encouragement of my earliest teachers: Susan Mendus, John Horton, and Peter Nicholson who first introduced me to Political Philosophy.

This book began as a Ph.D. dissertation supported by an ESRC-linked studentship with the Bentham Project at University College London between 1984 and 1987. I am grateful to them for their financial support. My greatest single debt is to Professor Fred Rosen, the General Editor of the *Collected Works of Jeremy Bentham*, and the director of the Bentham Project, who acted as my thesis supervisor. Without his enthusiasm and advice at all stages of writing, this book would not have been completed. My own work has been greatly influenced by his writings on Bentham's Political Philosophy, and while we may not agree on all points I have learned a great deal more from his scholarship than this work illustrates. Not least, he has shown that one does not have to be a Benthamite in order to think seriously and sympathetically about Bentham as a Political Philosopher. I was fortunate to have as my thesis examiners Professor Maurice Cranston and Professor A. J. M. Milne, both of whom gave me detailed comments on how it might be improved. I am especially grateful to Professor Gerald Postema whose own book on Bentham has been the focus of many of my own arguments; I can only hope that my own criticism of his work does justice to its depth and subtlety. Whatever merits my argument possesses is in no small measure due to Professor Rosen and Professor Postema; needless to say, whatever defects remain are my responsibility alone.

The Bentham Project in preparing a new definitive edition of the works of Jeremy Bentham has become the centre for a considerable resurgence of interest in all aspects of Bentham's life and thought. I have been fortunate in that my attachment to the project has put me in touch with many scholars working in a number of disciplines with whom I have been able to discuss Bentham. It is not possible to mention everyone from whom I have learned something, neither is it possible to recall all those who have contributed in some way to the formulation of my own interpretation. However, a number of scholars deserve special mention. From those working on Bentham at the same time as me I have learned much. Janet Semple graciously agreed to read and comment on a late manuscript version of this work and has contributed greatly to its improvement. Many conversations with Dr A. D. Dube have enabled me to develop my own ideas and learn from his and I am grateful to him for allowing me access to his work. Professor William Twining discussed my own interpretation and that of Gerald Postema with me thus clarifying my own ideas and saving me from much misunderstanding. I have also benefited at a late stage from the written comments of Professor David Lieberman; these have saved me from many infelicities. From my colleagues on the Bentham Project I have learned a great deal more during many conversations with Dr Stephen Conway and Dr Philip Schofield than they realize. Though under-funded and undervalued the Bentham Project has provided an enviable working environment, and I am grateful to all who have made it so. As well as those already mentioned, I would like to add Jane Haville and Dr Cyprian Blamires. Although I am unlikely to have persuaded them on all points, I have learned much from Professor John Dinwiddy, Professor Douglas Long, Professor Robert Fenn, Marco Guidi, James Crimmins, and Don Jackson. I would also like to thank my editor Richard Hart for his enthusiasm and diligence in seeing this book to publication.

I have enjoyed the assistance of a number of institutions in writing this book. I am indebted to the Librarian and staff of University College London, and am grateful for permission to quote from the Bentham Manuscripts in their possession. Similarly, I am grateful to the Librarian and staff of the British Library and to the Keeper of manuscripts for permission to quote from Bentham Manuscripts in their possession. I would also like to thank the Athlone Press and Oxford Unversity Press for permission to quote from the published volumes of the new *Collected Works of Jeremy Bentham*.

Finally, I would like to thank my wife Anne, who not only supported me in writing this book, but also read and corrected countless drafts of the work from its earliest inception as a series of seminar papers in 1985. Without her support this and much else besides would not have been possible, and it is to her and our two children Thomas and Ruth that I dedicate this book.

P.J.K.
The Bentham Project
University College London
October 1989

Contents

Abbreviations

BL Add. MSS   Bentham manuscripts in the British Library

Bowring   *The Works of Jeremy Bentham Published under the Superintendence of his Executor, John Bowring* (11 vols., Edinburgh, 1838–43)

(CW)   The Collected Works of Jeremy Bentham, general eds., J. H. Burns, J. R. Dinwiddy, and F. Rosen (London and Oxford, 1968–)

IPML   Jeremy Bentham, *An Introduction to the Principles of Morals and Legislation*, ed. J. H. Burns and H. L. A. Hart (London, 1970)

OLG   Jeremy Bentham, *Of Laws in General*, ed. H. L. A. Hart (London, 1970)

UC   Bentham manuscripts in University College London Library: UC xxx, 21 = box 30, p. 21

1

Introduction

THE standard criticism of utilitarian theory in the recent literature is that it cannot provide an adequate account of individual rights and entitlements, and therefore fails to accord due respect to persons. This criticism is not new, but has recently been given a significant restatement in the writing of John Rawls.[1] Rawls argues that utilitarian moral theory adopts the model of individual prudential rationality as the framework for rational social choice. Therefore, just as the individual agent can discount various present satisfactions in favour of future well-being, so it is argued the utilitarian legislator or the impartial spectator can discount the interests of some individuals in favour of the interests of others.[2] Against this Rawls argues that individual agents are unique autonomous sources of value which cannot be discounted against one another. Underlying his argument is an intuitive belief in the moral priority of persons and their rights over any conception of social welfare or well-being. Consequently, Rawls argues that utilitarian moral theories cannot make sense of distributive justice because they are concerned with maximizing overall benefits irrespective of how they are distributed. Thus if the benefit to be distributed by the legislator is liberty, a utilitarian might have to concentrate maximum liberty in the hands of a minority and consign the rest to slavery because that is the condition which maximizes happiness. Such a consequence is contrary to the received understanding of liberalism because it fails to take account of individual rights to liberty. Even in those cases where the utilitarian calculation does favour the equal distribution of liberty, this can only be contingent upon existing circumstances. In alternative circumstances a utility calculation could result in the reduction of liberty for a particular minority. Rawls's point is that at best utilitarianism can only accord a subordinate status to basic moral rights.

The resurgence of interest in the problems of utilitarianism that has developed following Rawls's work is illustrated by the proliferation of a series of deontological theories of justice which aim to provide a foundation

---

[1] Rawls is still refining his theory of distributive justice; see e.g. 'Kantian Constructivism in Moral Theory', *Journal of Philosophy*, 77 (1980), 515–72. However, the classic expression of his theory remains *A Theory of Justice* (Oxford, 1972). See also 'Two Concepts of Rules', *Philosophical Review*, 64 (1955), 3–32, 'Justice as Fairness', *Philosophical Review*, 67 (1958), 164–94, 'Distributive Justice', in P. Laslett and W. G. Runciman (eds.), *Philosophy, Politics and Society*, 3rd ser. (Oxford, 1967), and 'Distributive Justice: Some Addenda', *Natural Law Forum*, 13 (1968), 51–71.   [2] Rawls, *A Theory of Justice*, p. 28.

for basic moral rights without having to rely on consequentialist reasoning.[3] As these deontological theories have been the main focus of liberal thought in recent years, they have inevitably had some influence on the interpretation of previous political theorists. The measure of a liberal political theory which gives a significant role to the protection and extension of liberty becomes the role of moral rights within that theory. Consequently, utilitarian theories have been described as essentially illiberal,[4] with at best only a secondary role for liberal values such as freedom, equality, and autonomy. Moral rights have become the paradigmatic feature of contemporary liberal thought, and this appears necessarily to preclude Bentham from the canon of liberal political thinkers because of his avowed hostility to natural moral rights.[5]

The relevance of this deontological critique of utilitarianism to the interpretation of Bentham's thought is not to difficult to discover. Rawls's target is an idealized version of utilitarian theory, but it is meant to encompass the thought of all the major utilitarian thinkers: Sidgwick, Mill Edgeworth, and Bentham.[6] Clearly Rawls thought that Bentham's act-utilitarianism embodies the general defects which he identifies in utilitarian theory. And his critique of a utilitarian model of practical reasoning is reflected in the writings of some who are more closely concerned with explaining the structure of Bentham's argument. Thus H. A. Bedau argues[7] that Bentham's act-utilitarian theory is unable to account for moral rights which are at the heart of a theory of justice, and for equality which is the basic distributive principle of those rights. Parekh[8] also argues that Bentham's moral theory cannot make provision for the notion of equal moral agency and the entitlements that are derived from it. Goldworth and Werner also reflect these criticisms of Bentham, arguing that his theory is

---

[3] The most significant deontological theories of justice after Rawls's are: R. Nozick, *Anarchy, State and Utopia* (Oxford, 1974), R. Dworkin, *Taking Rights Seriously* (London, 1977), and B. Ackerman, *Social Justice in the Liberal State* (New Haven, Conn., 1980). It is somewhat ironic that those theories of justice developed by Rawls and others in response to utilitarian theories should be described as deontological. The word was first coined by Bentham in the *Westminster Review* (6 (1862), p. 448), and it was certainly not intended to be contrasted with utilitarianism.

[4] A. Ryan (ed.), *John Stuart Mill and Jeremy Bentham: Utilitarianism and other Essays* (Harmondsworth, 1987), 31–2.

[5] Bentham's attack on natural rights is most famously stated in his *Anarchical Fallacies* (Bowring, ii. 489–534); it also appears in 'Of the Levelling System', printed as an appendix to the 'Principles of the Civil Code' (Bowring, i. 358–604), and 'Pannomial Fragments' (Bowring, iii. 217–21). Despite Bentham's critique of declarations of rights, it will be argued in Ch. 3 that this hostility to natural rights does not translate easily into a critique of contemporary rights theories. Indeed it is suggested in this work that he provided a utilitarian theory of moral rights within his theory of distributive justice.

[6] Rawls, *A Theory of Justice*, pp. 22–3, and 32.

[7] H. A. Bedau, 'Justice and Classical Utilitarianism', *Nomos*, 6 (1963), 284–305.

[8] B. Parekh, 'Bentham's Theory of Equality', *Political Studies*, 18 (1970), 478–95.

unable to accommodate distributive principles and individual entitlements.[9] The theoretical rejection of utilitarianism which is embodied in these deontological theories is also reflected in the work of Bentham scholars whose purpose has not been the philosophical reconstruction of his moral thought. Thus Bahmueller uses Bentham's Poor Law writings as a paradigm of the defects of his utilitarian philosophy precisely because they reflect the sacrifice of the liberty of a minority to the common good. Bahmueller argues on the evidence of these writings that Bentham sacrifices a real commitment to the values of liberty and independence to the utilitarian virtues of efficiency and control.[10] Long,[11] another recent critic, has argued that Bentham's reliance on security in place of liberty rules out any significant commitment to the liberal values of autonomy and diversity. Instead, Long argues that his reliance on security reflects the ideas of coercion and control, which, according to many critics, are paradigmatic of his legal theory. The fact that ostensibly historical interpretations of Bentham's thought reflect the contemporary rejection of utilitarianism raises important methodological questions which range beyond the scope of my argument. However, given that Bentham was one of the founders of modern utilitarianism, it is not surprising that the interpretation of his writings should be influenced by the contemporary understanding of utilitarian moral theory. This is a regrettable outcome to the extent that historically utilitarianism does not refer to a single unequivocal theory, but rather to a family of more or less closely related theories. Writers as diverse as Hutcheson, Hume, Godwin, Paley, Bentham, J. S. Mill, F. Y. Edgeworth, and Sidgwick are all described as utilitarians, though beyond that they have little in common. Hume and Paley are rule-utilitarians. Godwin is perhaps the only writer who has taken to its logical extreme the notion of a global utility calculation. Bentham, J. S. Mill, and Sidgwick represent developed utilitarian theories employing indirect strategies, but even these differ significantly on important issues.

By focusing my discussion of Bentham's theory of distributive justice on Rawls's criticisms of utilitarian theory I hope to illustrate just how Bentham was aware of many of those difficulties in utilitarian theory. Thus, instead of opening myself to criticism on the grounds of adopting an unhistorical conversational style of reading Bentham, this strategy will show just how far, in respect of distributive justice, utility, and rights, Bentham was contributing to debates which are still going on, though in an ever more technical manner. It is precisely in the Civil Law writings that Bentham addresses many of the difficulties that are still at the centre of contemporary

---

[9] A. Goldworth, 'The Meaning of Bentham's Greatest Happiness Principle', *Journal of the History of Philosophy*, 7 (1969), 315–21, and 'The Sympathetic Sanction and Sinister Interest in Bentham's Utilitarianism', *History of Philosophy Quarterly*, 4 (1987), 67–78; also L. Werner, 'A Note about Bentham on Equality and about the Greatest Happiness Principle', *Journal of the History of Philosophy*, 11 (1973), 237–51.

[10] C. F. Bahmueller, *The National Charity Company* (Berkeley, Calif., 1981), 1–11, and 201–17.   [11] D. G. Long, *Bentham on Liberty* (Toronto, 1977).

discussions of utilitarian theory. To claim that this is imposing concerns on Bentham's thought which are alien to his intentions is to fail to take seriously the extent to which distributive questions preoccupied Bentham in the Civil Law writings—a fact which is further illustrated by their alternative description as Distributive Law writings.

The contemporary philosophical critique of utilitarianism is important for Bentham scholarship because it lends support to the received understanding of his moral and political thought.[12] The received interpretation of Bentham has its classic statement in Halevy's *Growth of Philosophic Radicalism* (1928). One of the main themes of Halevy's monumental study is to show how Bentham's utilitarianism undermined his commitment to liberal values, and thus put him outside the liberal tradition. This line of criticism is continued in the work of many recent Bentham scholars such as L. J. Hume in *Bentham and Bureaucracy* (1981), D. G. Long in *Bentham on Liberty* (1977), and C. F. Bahmueller in *The National Charity Company* (1981), as well as articles by Parekh and Himmelfarb. None of these works involves any sustained discussion of Bentham's moral theory yet all assume that his utilitarianism undermines any possible connection with the liberal tradition. The contemporary deontological critique of utilitarianism tends to support the received interpretation, by precluding utilitarianism as a foundation of liberalism, and by emphasizing moral rights and liberties as the paradigmatic features of an adequate liberal theory. A further reason for using contemporary discussion of utilitarianism and distributive justice as a focus for developing an interpretation of Bentham's position, is that in showing the theoretical resources that he employed in order to accommodate such supposed difficulties, it will be possible to undermine this unargued first premiss of the received interpretation and to show that Bentham's utilitarianism can be reconciled with liberalism. Both the received interpretation and the contemporary philosophical critique of utilitarianism obscure the important role utilitarian theory played in the emergence of the liberal tradition.

More recently there has been a reaction within utilitarian theory to the criticisms epitomized by Rawls and the claims of the deontological theories of justice.[13] A number of important works have been published which show

---

[12] The received interpretation of Bentham's moral thought refers to the crude act-utilitarian theory embodied in the works of Parekh, Bedau, and others. This is to be distinguished from the more general received interpretation of Bentham's thought which is embodied in Halevy's *The Growth of Philosophic Radicalism* (London, 1928), and L. J. Hume's 'Revisionism in Bentham Studies', *Bentham Newsletter*, 1 (1978), 3–20, and *Bentham and Bureaucracy* (Cambridge, 1981), which emphasizes the distinction between Bentham's political theory and liberalism.

[13] See the writings of R. M. Hare, *The Language of Morals* (Oxford, 1952), *Freedom and Reason* (Oxford, 1963), and *Moral Thinking: Its Method, Levels and Point* (Oxford, 1981). Also see D. H. Regan, *Utilitarianism and Co-operation* (Oxford, 1980), R. B. Brandt, *A Theory of the Good and the Right* (Oxford, 1979), D. Parfitt, *Reasons and Persons* (Oxford,

how utilitarianism can accommodate liberal values and can provide accounts of distributive justice. Of more particular interest than this resurgence within utilitarian theory is the way it has also influenced the interpretation of the classical utilitarians. J. S. Mill has been the chief beneficiary of this resurgence of interest—there is now a large literature of revisionist interpretations of his moral and political thought.[14] However, while the thought of J. S. Mill has enjoyed a renaissance, Bentham has fared less well.[15] There is a recent trend within Bentham scholarship to provide a more sympathetic understanding of Bentham as a philosopher and moral theorist which is not premised on his necessary antagonism to the liberal tradition. This is particularly clear in the writings of H. L. A. Hart,[16] but recently it has also found expression in works by Harrison,[17] Rosen,[18] and Postema.[19] All of these writers have made a significant contribution to the understanding of Bentham's political philosophy. None of these works is specifically concerned with his political morality; consequently there is still no systematic revisionist account Bentham's moral theory.

There are two reasons why Bentham has fared less well than J. S. Mill in light of the recent trend towards revisionism in utilitarianism studies. Firstly, Bentham studies have continued to concentrate on the 'historic' as opposed to the 'esoteric' Bentham.[20] The 'historic' Bentham is the social reformer and projector who was known for his Panopticon Prison scheme. The 'esoteric' Bentham is the writer who composed the massive collection of manuscripts now in the possession of University College London. The works of the 'esoteric' Bentham include his major contribution to legal theory, *Of Laws in General*, the complete text of which has only recently been published as part of the new *Collected Works of Jeremy Bentham*. However, alongside his unpublished writings ought to be included many of

1984), and J. Griffin, *Well-Being* (Oxford, 1986). The best outline of recent developments in utilitarian theory is J. Griffin's 'Modern Utilitarianism', *Revue Internationale de Philosophie*, 36 (1982), 331–75.

[14] See in particular F. R. Berger, *Happiness, Justice and Freedom* (Berkeley, Calif., 1984), J. Gray, *Mill on Liberty: A Defence* (London, 1983), and D. Lyons, 'Mill's Theory of Morality', *Nous*, 10 (1976), 101–20, 'Human Rights and the General Welfare', *Philosophy and Public Affairs*, 6 (1977), 113–29, 'Mill's theory of Justice', in A. I. Goldman and J. Kim (eds.), *Values and Morality* (Dodrecht, 1978), 1–20, and 'Benevolence and Justice in Mill', in H. B. Miller and W. H. Williams (eds.), *The Limits of Utilitarianism* (Minneapolis, Minn., 1982), 42–70.

[15] There is the basis for a revisionist interpretation of Bentham's moral and political theory in a number of papers by H. L. A. Hart, recently published in his *Essays on Bentham* (Oxford, 1982). Sadly, Hart has chosen not to develop many of his insightful comments into a more systematic interpretation of Bentham's moral thought. Instead he has chosen to confine his attention to Bentham's theory of sovereignty and his philosophy of Law.

[16] Hart, *Essays on Bentham*.

[17] R. Harrison, *Bentham* (London, 1983).

[18] F. Rosen, *Jeremy Bentham and Representative Democracy* (Oxford, 1983).

[19] G. J. Postema, *Bentham and the Common Law Tradition* (Oxford, 1986).

[20] The thesis of the 'two Benthams' is to be found in J. R. Dinwiddy, 'Bentham and the Early Nineteenth Century', *Bentham Newsletter*, 8 (1984), 15.

the works which though published failed to make any public impression. In this second category can be included *An Introduction to the Principles of Morals and Legislation* (1789), which is still taken as the basic text of his moral theory. The reason for including this among Bentham's 'esoteric' writings is best described by J. B. Schneewind in his major study of nineteenth-century English moral theory:

His *Introduction to the Principles of Morals and Legislation* in the original edition of 1789 had only a very small sale, and was not reprinted until 1823. His ethical theory is ignored by most of the periodicals, and is simply not discussed in the philosophical literature. The Scottish philosophers attack Paley's version of utilitarianism, or occasionally Hume's, but never Bentham's. Mackintosh's historical *Dissertation on the Progress of Ethical Philosophy*, written for the *Encyclopaedia Britannica* in 1830 contains a long chapter entitled 'Bentham', but Bentham is hardly discussed in it, although it is admitted that no sketch of 'ethical controversy in England' would be complete without a reference to him. He is treated not as a philosopher but as the ideologist of a small and rather fanatical political group; . . . Bentham had a moral philosophy, and Bentham was famous, but Bentham was not famous for his philosophy. It was not until the middle of the 1830s that he began to be taken seriously as philosopher by philosophers. For the change John Stuart Mill and William Whewell were largely responsible.[21]

Bentham wrote much but published relatively little, and what he did publish in the field of moral theory had no immediate influence; he was better known as a reformer, and this label has remained with him to this day. Therefore, while J. S. Mill is now treated as a political philosopher of the first order, Bentham is still regarded as a second-rate one, whose mind was always diverted by practical details and reform projects.

The second reason that Mill has fared better than Bentham in the recent revisionist trend in utilitarian scholarship is connected with the first. Bentham published little on moral theory in his life, and what he did publish was largely ignored. However, as Schneewind points out, when Bentham eventually achieved recognition as a philosopher, this was largely as a result of J. S. Mill. This is doubly unfortunately because during the 1830s Mill was reacting against Bentham and 'Benthanism', so the philosopher Bentham that Mill draws attention to is the familiar crude act-utilitarian of the received interpretation. Therefore, it has become an unacknowledged premiss of the revisionist interpretation of J. S. Mill that he is an interesting and subtle thinker to the extent that he abandoned 'Benthamism'. This ignores the fact that in the development of his own utilitarian theory in the 1850s and 1860s Mill came to a substantial reconciliation with much of his Benthamite heritage. The basic difference between Mill and Bentham is that whereas the character of Mill's utilitarian theory can be derived from two short works, Bentham's is spread through a variety of writings, many still in

---

[21] J. B. Schneewind, *Sidgwick's Ethics and Victorian Moral Philosophy* (Oxford, 1977), 129–30.

manuscript form. Consequently, the focus of much of my argument will be on the 'esoteric' Bentham, in that it will rely largely on unpublished Civil and Distributive Law manuscripts. It is in these Civil and Distributive Law writings that Bentham developed his utilitarian theory of distributive justice; they therefore have a significant role in determining the character of his utilitarian political morality.

The main objective of this work is to develop a response from Bentham's thought to the two basic themes covered in this introduction. Firstly, I will argue that Bentham had a developed a utilitarian theory which embodied a theory of distributive justice, and this enabled him to take seriously liberal values such as liberty, equality, and independence. Secondly, the development of this theory of distributive justice provides part of the material for a revisionist interpretation of Bentham's moral theory. The defence of this theory in the remainder of the book will not only show that Bentham was concerned with the problems of developing a utilitarian moral theory as the basis of his projects for social and legal reform, but also that Bentham's utilitarian theory already provided much of the material required by J. S. Mill in the development of his utilitarian theory nearly thirty years after Bentham's death. While there is insufficient space in this work to explore the extent to which Mill was influenced by Bentham's theory of justice, it will be argued that in certain crucial respects Bentham's theory surpasses that of J. S. Mill.

The argument of this work is intended to demonstrate that Bentham not only had a utilitarian theory of justice, but also that it accommodates the liberal values of liberty, equality, and personal inviolability, and therefore that his utilitarian theory is not subject to the substantial criticisms raised by Rawls and others. This involves explaining how Bentham can provide a substantial commitment to distributive justice within the specification of his theory of utility. It is relatively easy to justify liberal rights within a utilitarian framework on the grounds that they provide the maximum of social well-being. However, these arguments can at best provide a contingent justification for these values and rights because it always remains possible that the discovery of new information about the components of individual well-being and the structure of society will provide the grounds for a utilitarian distribution that does not reflect the equal provision of those rights. Hart argues that one of the reasons that Bentham did not attempt to describe utilitarian entitlements as the basis of rights is that:

the content of such utilitarian entitlements would fluctuate with changing circumstances and have none of the stability over time and consequent availability as guides for action both for the right-holder and others who are strongly associated with the notion of rights where the notions is employed.[22]

---

[22] Hart, *Essays on Bentham*, p. 86.

The second part of this work argues that Bentham's use of the concept of expectation enabled him to construct a utilitarian theory of justice that employed individual entitlements in the specification of his theory rather than arguing that these are contingent means of securing the direct pursuit of utility. Expectations are given such a significant role with his political morality because they provide the framework within which individuals form and pursue their own conceptions of well-being. I will argue that Bentham did not advocate the direct pursuit of utility because the legislator was not in a position to make direct utility calculations and also that he could not pursue a direct act-utilitarian policy and provide a secure pattern of expectation which is a necessary condition of the conception of welfare that the direct utility calculation would aim to maximize. The formation of expectations is a function of formal regularities in behaviour that result from fixed social practices and rules. The most important source of these exceptations is the legal system.

The basic concern of Bentham's theory of justice is securing a pattern of expectations which enables each individual to secure his own conception of well-being. The second component of social well-being which is at the centre of Bentham's theory of justice is the provision of subsistence. The provision of subsistence is best secured through the provision of security of expectation because this enables each individual to secure his own subsistence through productive labour. However, for those who are unable to secure their own subsistence as a result of structural disadvantages, the legislator must guarantee the provision of the means of subsistence. Subsistence provides the material conditions of interest formation and realization because it guarantees continued existence; it is both a material condition of expectation, and in an economically developed society it is a consequence of a secured pattern of expectations. It is also argued that the provision of subsistence is ultimately connected with the maintenance of security because without a basic guarantee of subsistence individuals have an incentive to undermine security if they have no other means of sustaining such a basic component of well-being.

The concern for security of expectations and the provision of the minimum conditions of subsistence are developed into two principles which form the basis of Bentham's theory of distributive justice. The 'security-providing principle' is a formal principle which determines that pattern of expectations which the legislator ought to secure in legislation and upon which the codifier ought to premiss his utilitarian code. The 'disappointment-preventing principle' is Bentham's substantive principle of justice. It determines the ways in which the legislator may act in realizing an ideal utilitarian set of rules, while accommodating the expectation utilities which are derived from an existing system of rules. Because the right to property is the basic source of expectation underlying the 'security-providing principle' the substantive principle of justice is largely concerned with extending access to property as the primary material condition of interest formation and realization, while protecting those expectations which are derived from the existing distribution of property rights.

Bentham's identification of property and property rights as the basic source of expectation, and therefore the primary condition for the formation and satisfaction of individual conceptions of well-being explains the emphasis he places on maintaining the security of property. The reliance on property as the primary source of expectation, and consequently its role as a condition of personal continuity and coherence connects his discussion of property and its role within a theory of justice with some contemporary libertarian theories which also advocate security of property as the basic task of distributive justice.[23] However, Bentham also had a substantial commitment to the equal distribution of property as a means of realizing the pattern of expectations prescribed by the 'security-providing principle'. It has been argued by some commentators[24] that Bentham only had a weak commitment to equality because of the importance he attached to security of expectation, and therefore, to stability of property. The 'disappointment-preventing principle' enables the Benthamite legislator to pursue a policy of the substantial equalization of property holdings while also respecting the pattern of expectations embodied in the existing distribution of property.

Bentham's concern with the importance of secured expectation illustrates how far his own theory was from a crude act-utilitarianism, and emphasizes the importance of rule-governed social interaction in determining both individual and social well-being. Whatever the ultimate merits of Bentham's theory of justice, on this last point he has made a significant contribution to the development of utilitarian theory, and one that has largely been ignored by previous commentators.

The two principles which form the basis of the theory of distributive justice are developed in separate chapters in the latter part of this work. It begins with two chapters devoted to some of the claims raised by the received interpretation of Bentham's moral theory. The first chapter is a discussion of his psychological theory and theory of motivation. Here it is argued that Bentham did not claim that all men directly or consciously pursue only pleasure, but rather that he used the concepts of pleasure and pain as the basis of a causal account of motivation. Although a sensation-based account of welfare has been largely reflected by contemporary utilitarians, it does at least have the consequence of locating the subject of those sensations at the centre of moral theorizing, in a way that preference-utilitarian theories cannot do without difficulties. The chapter also considers the role of egoism within Bentham's psychological theory, and

---

[23] See Nozick, *Anarchy, State and Utopia*, F. A. Hayek, *The Constitution of Liberty* (London, 1960), and *Law, Legislation and Liberty* (3 vols., London, 1973–9), and J. Hospers, *Libertarianism* (Los Angeles, Calif., 1971). The role of property within distributive justice is also discussed in A. Buchanan, 'Distributive Justice and Legitimate Expectations', *Philosophical Studies*, 28 (1975), 419–25.   [24] See Goldsworth, Werner, and Parekh.

how far he attempted to develop a precise mathematical calculus of pleasure and pain.

The second chapter explores the role of pleasure and pain within Bentham's concept of utility. The chapter will consider whether Bentham committed the 'naturalistic fallacy', and discuss his justification of the principle of utility. Also to be considered in Chapter 2 is how far Bentham intended the principle of utility to function as a direct source of obligations, and how this question is related to defending him against the criticisms of Rawls and the deontologists. The conclusion is drawn that Bentham does not fit easily into the categories of indirect or direct utilitarianism, and that the true character of his theory of utility can only be discovered by going beyond the standard sources of his moral theory: *An Introduction to the Principles of Morals and Legislation*, *A Fragment on Government*, *Constitutional Code*, and *Deontology*.

The main portion of this book is, however, devoted to the development of the theory of distributive justice found in the unpublished Civil and Distributive Law writings. Many of these are contemporary with *An Introduction to the Principles of Morals and Legislation*, and show that Bentham was developing a utilitarian theory which did not simply rely on the legislator or individual agent making direct utility calculations. Instead it is argued that he developed a theory of utilitarian entitlements based on the necessary conditions of interest formation and realization. These four chapters within which the theory of distributive justice is developed deal successively with security, expectation and liberty, subsistence, abundance and equality, the 'security-providing principle', and the 'disappointment-preventing principle'. The first two of these chapters concern the four components of social well-being, and the remaining two chapters address the development of the two principles which enable the utilitarian legislator to pursue these objectives.

Although this work is not concerned directly with Bentham's economic writings, the fact that Bentham's theory of distributive justice determines the balance between security of property and equality has important implications for understanding the character of his economic theory. This is because Bentham's theory of justice provides the framework of rights and titles on which his political economy is premissed. While Bentham's political economy shares much with classical *laissez-faire* theory, his theory of justice is not based on a crude economic conception of social relationships. Therefore, Bentham can consistently adopt positions that are described as 'collectivist,'[25] and yet maintain a substantial commitment to economic liberty.

[25] See J. B. Brebner, 'Laissez-faire and State Intervention in Nineteenth Century Britain', *Journal of Economic History* (suppl.), 8 (1948), 59–73, A. V. Dicey, *Lectures on the Relation between Law and Public Opinion in England during the Nineteenth Century* (London, 1905), and F. Petrella, 'Benthamism and the Demise of Classical Economic *Ordnungspolitik*', *History of Political Economy*, 9 (1977), 215–36.

The concluding chapter will show just how far Bentham was able to accommodate liberal values such as liberty, equality, and personal inviolability within his theory of distributive justice. It will be argued that the pattern of rights which are prescribed by the utilitarian theory of distributive justice enjoys a priority because those rights provide the framework of an ordered social reality within which individual practical reasoning can take place. This priority is not merely contingent because it is based on a straightforward utility calculation, but is necessary because it embodies the conditions of personal continuity. Thus, given the condition of human nature and the world, the basic liberal values of liberty, independence, and equality are necessary components of the utilitarian good. This is a broad outline of Bentham's answer to the charge that utilitarian theory can only give a contingent role to fundamental moral values.

It might still be objected, however, that while Bentham addresses a number of distributive questions in the Civil Law writings, they do not amount to a full theory of justice, as there is no discussion of either need or desert in the distribution of titles. There is also the problem raised against Mill's theory of justice, namely by focusing attention on the violation of rules and moral rights as the concern of justice one tends to see all cases of wrong-doing as acts of injustice.[26] Bentham's theory is not as open to this form of criticism as Mill's, because although Bentham still focuses attention on rules and conventional rights, sanctioned by the principle of utility through the 'security-providing principle', his concern in these writings is primarily with the distribution of rights and titles in the Civil Code, and this captures the distributive element in the concept of justice. The violation of these rights and titles would, therefore, be acts of injustice, and this may lead to the slightly curious result of murder being described as unjust, a locution which while true certainly does not do justice to the enormity of the crime. However, it would make a lot more sense to describe a legislator who failed to acknowledge such rights and titles as acting unjustly, for failing to accord those rights which constitute the conditions of personal inviolability would be a failure of distribution. As for considerations of merit and desert, there is some considerable scope for incorporating these within an utilitarian framework. However, they would not function as values independently of their utilitarian justification.

There are two main areas in which this work departs from previous accounts of Bentham's moral and political theory, firstly in terms of the extensive reliance on previously unpublished manuscripts, and secondly in the use of this material to overturn some of the basic premises of the received interpretation. The main body of the argument is based on Bentham's Civil and Distributive Law manuscripts, which he returned to a number of times throughout his life. Consequently, they reflect a continuing

[26] A. Quinton, *Utilitarian Ethics* (London, 1989), p. 74.

theoretical concern with the problem of the distribution of rights and titles within utilitarian theory.

Though his return to these problems at different periods is no doubt dictated by difficulties he faced in developing other parts of his moral and social theory, there is, nevertheless, a surprising continuity of conception and argument. Bentham's use of the 'disappointment-preventing principle' from the late 1820s onwards certainly marks a development within his thought. However, it will be argued that the substance of this principle can be found in manuscripts that are derived from the 1780s. Given this substantial continuity within the Civil Law writings, I have not attempted a chronological study of these writings, but have assumed this underlying continuity of position in the course of developing my argument. The question of why Bentham chose to return to the Civil Law at different times is best answered in terms of circumstances external to his theory rather than in terms of a substantial change or development in his philosophical position. The majority of the manuscripts referred to in this work have not previously been published. Others have been included in works such as 'Principles of the Civil Code' and 'Pannomial Fragments' which were constructed by the editors for the Bowring edition of the *Works of Jeremy Bentham*. Throughout I have used my own transcriptions of these manuscripts and have only used the Bowring texts when there is sufficient manuscript evidence for the authenticity of the passage cited. The use of these manuscripts not only provides new information about Bentham's moral theory, but also provides a new perspective from which to approach his utilitarianism.

The Civil Law writings illustrate that an adequate interpretation of his utilitarianism must range more widely than the standard texts such *An Introduction to the Principles of Morals and Legislation* and *A Fragment on Government*. The subsequent arguments will demonstrate that Bentham's political morality as more complex than the received interpretation suggests, and that a significant portion of it is developed in his Civil Law writings. This is all the more interesting given that J. S. Mill wrote that: 'It is with regard to [what is the foundation of all] the Civil Code, that he has done least, and left most to be done.'[27] Mill's remark is partly justified by the fact that Bentham published very little of his thoughts on the utilitarian distributive principles underlying the Civil Code. In part I have taken Mill's claim as the key to understanding Bentham's political morality by arguing that the Civil Law writings provide the framework upon which he built his political morality. However, it is clear that I disagree with Mill that Bentham contributed least to the development of a utilitarian Civil Code. It is beyond the scope of my arguments to show just how far Mill's theory of

---

[27] J. S. Mill, *Essays on Ethics, Religion and Society*, ed. John M. Robson (Toronto, 1969) (The Collected Works of John Stuart Mill, x), 497.

justice was influenced by Bentham's writings on the Civil Law. Nevertheless, this influence has not gone unnoticed by recent Mill and Bentham Scholars.[28]

Having placed Bentham's Civil Law writings at the centre of my argument it is possible to provide a sympathetic reconstruction of Bentham's position which both exposes the weakness of the received interpretation, and provides scope for advancing beyond the work of Harrison, Hart, Postema, and Rosen. In developing this argument I have drawn on both recent scholarship in Mill and Bentham studies, and recent philosophical work on the theory of liberalism and utilitarianism. I do not intend to advance the unhistorical claim that Bentham engaged in a direct dialogue with contemporary writers such as Rawls. However, he was the first to develop a recognizably modern utilitarian theory, and consequently was one of the founders of an important tradition of political and legal theory within which much of the contemporary work on liberal moral theory is to be found. Therefore, while utilitarianism and rights theory has become ever more refined and technical, many of the basic problems which concern contemporary utilitarian and non-utilitarian moral theorists are the same as those which concerned Bentham and Mill.

Finally, while it is clear that the effectiveness of this argument will reflect on the adequacy of the Rawlsian account of utilitarianism, and his attempt to draw a clear and uncontroversial distinction between deontological and teleological moral theories,[29] it is *not* my direct intention to advance this argument as part of a more general attempt to defend utilitarianism or consequentialism as an adequate basis for morality and practical reasoning.

---

[28] See S. Hollander, *The Economics of John Stuart Mill* (2 vols., Oxford, 1985), 602–76, J. C. Rees, *John Stuart Mill's* On Liberty (Oxford, 1985), and F. Rosen, 'Bentham and Mill on Liberty and Justice', in F. Rosen and G. Feaver (eds.), *Lives, Liberties and the Public Good* (London, 1987).

[29] For a recent discussion of Rawls's contrast between deontological and teleological theories see W. Kymlicka, 'Rawls on Teleology and Deontology', *Philosophy and Public Affairs*, 17 (1988), 173–90.

2

Psychological Hedonism and the Basis of Motivation

AT the beginning of *An Introduction to the Principles of Morals and Legislation*[1] Bentham describes how mankind is placed 'under the governance of two sovereigns masters, *pain* and *pleasure*.' In this famous passage he indicates that his philosophy is premissed on his psychological theory. This psychological theory explains the conditions within which the legislator has to work in order to secure the maximum of social well-being. By providing an account of the way individuals act, the legislator is able to determine the encouragements and punishments needed to bring those actions into conformity with the requirements of duty. Bentham's reliance on law as the primary means of ordering social interaction already suggests that there is no necessary conformity between the dictates of duty and ordinary human motivations. Therefore, if the legislator has to co-ordinate individual purposive action with the requirements of justice he needs to understand the sources of human motivation. Bentham's psychological theory plays a crucial role in his thought, by explaining the causes of action, and by instructing the legislator how he is to constrain particular types of action.

By identifying pleasure and pain as the basic explanatory concepts of his theory of motivation, Bentham adopts a hedonistic psychology. However, Bentham's psychological hedonism has been the subject of much of the unfavourable criticism that his theory has received; it has also been the cause of much confusion. The received interpretation of Bentham's theory[2] maintains that the ultimate goal of all action is the pursuit of pleasure.

---

[1] *IPML*, (CW), p. 12.

[2] The received interpretation is derived from the standard work on Bentham, E. Halévy's *The Growth of Philosophic Radicalism*, trans. M. Morris (London, 1972). A modified version is found in L. J. Hume, 'Revisionism in Bentham Studies', *Bentham Newsletter*, 1 (1978), 3–20, and *Bentham and Bureaucracy* (Cambridge, 1981). Other works which reflect aspects of the received interpretation include B. Parekh, 'Bentham's Justification of the Principle of Utility', in id. (ed.), *Jeremy Bentham: Ten Critical Essays* (London, 1974), 'Bentham's Theory of Equality', *Political Studies*, 18 (1970), 478–95, and J. B. Stearns, 'Bentham on Public and Private Ethics', *Canadian Journal of Philosophy*, 5 (1975), 583–94. Parekh's papers reflect the direct act-utilitarian understanding of Bentham's moral theory. However, on the question of psychological theory his position differs from that of Halévy, in that he acknowledges the role of non-egoistic motives. He also presents a historical theory of the role of non-egoistic motives in the pursuit of social well-being. See Parekh's Introduction to *Jeremy Bentham: Ten Critical Essays* (loc. cit.).

Parekh wrote that according to Bentham 'by the very constitution of his nature man desires nothing but pleasure'.[3] This criticism has been taken up by recent revisionist commentators on J. S. Mill.[4] They argue that Bentham's simplistic psychological hedonism is one of the aspects of his thought that Mill explicitly rejected following his abandonment of Benthamism, and indeed this is one of the premisses of many revisionist accounts of Mill.[5] Fred Berger reflects the received interpetation of Bentham's theory when he argues that the claim that persons always act from a desire for pleasure can with plausibility be attributed to Bentham.[6] Despite this willingness to argue that Bentham accepted the direct pursuit of pleasure as the ultimate end of action, these recent Mill scholars have been quick to point out that it is an implausible view and one that Mill did not hold.[7] The first part of this chapter will explain the function of pleasure within Bentham's psychological theory, and how far he committed the errors attributed to him in recent Mill scholarship.

Another difficulty with Bentham's theory of motivation arises from the confusion of psychological hedonism with psychological egoism. It is a major premiss of the received interpretation of Bentham's thought that he was a psychological egoist, and argued that each person will prefer his own interest to that of others.[8] David Lyons, who argues for a revisionist account of Bentham's ethical theory, refers to the argument which maintains that psychological hedonism is a specific form of psychological egoism 'on the assumption that the pleasures one seeks and the pains one tries to avoid are always one's own.'[9] Despite the distinction of being the most discussed interpretation of Bentham's thought, Lyons's general

---

[3] Parekh, 'Bentham's Justification of the Principle of Utility', *Ten Critical Essays*, p. 103.

[4] See F. R. Berger, *Happiness, Justice and Freedom* (Berkeley, Calif., 1984), J. Gray, *Mill On Liberty: A Defence* (London, 1983), and D. Lyons, 'Mill's Theory of Morality', *Nous*, 10 (1976), 101–20, 'Human Rights and the General Welfare', *Philosophy and Public Affairs*, 6 (1977), 113–29, 'Mill's Theory of Justice', in A. I. Goldman and J. Kim (eds.), *Values and Morals* (Dordrecht, 1978), 1–20, and 'Benevolence and Justice in Mill', in H. B. Miller and W. H. Williams (eds.), *The Limits of Utilitarianism* (Minneapolis, Minn., 1982), 42–70.

[5] A significant exception to this trend is provided by S. Hollander, *The Economics of John Stuart Mill* (2 vols., Oxford, 1985), 602–76. Hollander presents a detailed interpretation of Mill's rejection of Benthamism in the early years following his mental crisis in 1826. However, Hollander also shows how Mill came to be reconciled to many of Bentham's arguments when he developed his defence of utilitarianism in *On Liberty* (1859) and *Utilitarianism* (1863). Hollander's interpretation is similar to that of an earlier historian of economic thought, J. Viner. Viner wrote that: 'The intellectual history of Mill is in large part a history, first of faithful discipleship, then of rebellion from and finally of substantial return to the Benthamite set of doctrines' ('Bentham and J. S. Mill the Utilitarian Background', in *The Long and View and the Short* (Glencoe, Ill., 1958), 306).

[6] Berger, *Happiness, Justice and Freedom*, p. 13.   [7] Ibid.

[8] Halévy, *The Growth of Philosophic Radicalism*, p. 466.

[9] D. Lyons, *In The Interest of The Governed* (Oxford, 1973), 69. Lyons, however, argues that Bentham did not adopt a strictly egoistic view of human motivation. He writes: 'I believe it is also true that Bentham's hedonism was not meant to have such [egoistic] implications and probably had none at all' (p. 70).

argument has been criticized and rejected by most subsequent scholars.[10] Nevertheless, this claim that psychological hedonism is simply one form of egoism is reflected throughout the discussion of Bentham's psychological theory. The first part of this part of this chapter will address the relationship between hedonism and egoism, and by discussing each concept separately I will argue that while there is a tendency towards an egoistic explanation of action within Bentham's theory of motivation, psychological hedonism and egoism are not synonymous. Furthermore, despite this practical tendency towards egoism, it will be argued that Bentham's psychological hedonism is a variety that does not entail egoism nor is it premissed on a prior commitment to psychological egoism as Halévy has suggested in his *The Growth of Philosophic Radicalism* (1972).[11]

The remainder of this chapter is concerned with the meaning of Bentham's utilitarian calculus,[12] and how far he intended this to ground a precise 'Political Arithmetic'.[13] The standard view of Benthamite man is one of a rational calculator who weighs up the expected pleasure of any course of action in accordance with the model described in chapter 4 of *An Introduction to the Principles of Morals and Legislation*. Against this received interpretation I will argue that Bentham was aware of the difficulties of establishing a precise utilitarian calculus. He substituted these calculations of the value of subjective experience with objective calculations using money as the publicly accepted criterion of value. He also developed a series of empirical 'axioms of mental pathology' which provide the basis for his political morality and utilitarian theory of justice. It is these axioms which are the foundation of Bentham's legislative project, and not a series of direct utility calculations. The interpretation of Bentham's psychological theory in this chapter will provide part of the foundation for the subsequent arguments concerning his theory of distributive justice.

I

The 'two sovereigns' passage at the beginning of *An Introduction to the Principles of Morals and Legislation* is one of the best known in Bentham's works, and it has become the focus of the discussion of his psychological theory. He wrote:

Nature has placed mankind under the governance of two sovereign masters, *pain* and *pleasure*. It is for them alone to point out what we ought to do, as well as to

---

[10] The most substantial discussion of Lyons's book is J. R. Dinwiddy's 'Bentham on Private Ethics and the Principle of Utility', *Revue Internationale de Philosophie*, 36 (1982), 278–300. Other critical discussions of Lyons's thesis are to be found in Stearns, 'Bentham on Public and Private Ethics', R. Harrison, *Bentham* (London, 1983), 263–77, and F. Rosen, *Jeremy Bentham and Representative Democracy* (Oxford, 1983), 203–6.

[11] pp. 502–3.

[12] *IPML* (CW), pp. 38–41.

[13] Bowring, iv. 540.

determine what we shall do. On the one hand the standard of right and wrong, on the other the chain of causes and effects, are fastened to their throne. They govern us in all we do, in all we say, in all we think: every effort we can make to throw off our subjection, will serve but to demonstrate and confirm it. In words a man may pretend to abjure their empire: but in reality he will remain subject to it all the while.[14]

This passage illustrates that pleasure and pain are the basic explanatory concepts of Bentham's psychological and moral theories. They not only prescribe what we ought to do, but also what we shall do. This immediately questions the status of the claim at the heart of Bentham's psychological theory. Most recent commentators accept that Bentham's descriptive psychological theory was empirically based. However, if this empirical basis is supposed to include the claim that pleasure determines what 'we shall do', then this is inadequate because it is usually interpreted as implying that all men necessarily pursue pleasure.[15] As A. J. Ayer has argued, either the claim that all action is directed at pleasure is an empirical claim, in which case it is false, or else it is a tautology.[16] Ayer's criticism depends upon interpreting Bentham's psychological theory as a version of psychological egoism. Until psychological hedonism is disentangled from a strong version of egoism it will not be possible to understand Bentham's theory and its empirical basis.

Another important Bentham scholar, David Baumgardt,[17] has argued that the 'two sovereigns' passage has been given too much weight as an authoritative statement of Bentham's real position. He defends a more subtle interpretation of Bentham's psychological theory on the basis of other textual sources. He also argues that Bentham did not intend the 'two sovereigns' passage to be a definitive statement of his psychological or moral theoy, by drawing attention to Bentham's remark at the end of the passage, where he wrote: 'But enough of metaphor and declamation: it is not by such means that moral science is to be improved.'[18] According to Baumgardt this passage is not a precise statement of Bentham's position but was written for literary effect, and precision of expression was not the primary concern. However, Baumgardt's primary reason for distracting attention from the 'two sovereigns' passage was to defend Bentham against the charge that he committed the 'naturalistic fallacy', as G. E. Moore

---

[14] *IPML* (CW), p. 11.

[15] This is part of the received interpretation derived from Halévy; see n. 2, above.

[16] A. J. Ayer, 'The Principle of Utility', in G. W. Keeton and G. Schwartzenberger (eds.), *Jeremy Bentham and the Law* (London, 1948).

[17] D. Baumgardt, *Bentham and the Ethics of Today* (Princeton, NJ, 1952), 170. However, a recent commentator, L. J. Hume, has written that 'In describing pleasure and pain as our "sovereign masters" he [Bentham] was not indulging in showy rhetoric but was expressing his real understanding of the springs of human action' (*Bentham and Bureaucracy*, p. 66).

[18] *IPML* (CW), p. 11.

suggested.[19] The idea of pleasure and pain as the criteria of moral judgement will be one of the concerns of the next chapter.

While Baumgardt correctly drew attention to the caveat introduced at the end of the 'two sovereigns' passage, and warned against trying to deduce Bentham's psychological and ethical theories from this passage alone, this passage contains an important insight into the nature of his psychological theory.

The received interpretation of Bentham's psychological theory implies that all action is directed at the pursuit of pleasure or the avoidance of pain. This is based on passages such as the following where Bentham wrote: 'Pleasures and exemption from pain with their correlatives happiness and exemption from unhappiness, are the only ultimate ends, and of every sensitive being, the only ultimate ends of action.'[20] It is not clear whether this passage supports the claim that all action is directed at the pursuit of pleasure or the avoidance of pain, because it remains unclear what status Bentham intended to attach to the notion of 'ultimate ends' of action. These 'ultimate ends' could either be the conscious objects of action, in which case there would be support for the received interpretation, but equally they could mean the efficient cause of action, where they do not have to be the intentional objects of action at all. This question also raises the further problem of the status of Bentham's psychological hedonism. If this is understood as an empirical claim then the problems raised by A. J. Ayer create serious difficulties for Bentham's theory. If his hedonistic psychology is empirically based then it is easily falsifiable, by identifying a person whose ultimate object of action was not pleasure or the avoidance of pain. Yet it is unlikely that Bentham could have intended that his psychological theory was empirically based in this sense. However, if he intended that pleasure and pain are the 'ultimate ends' of action in the second sense as the final efficient causes of action, then this claim is not strictly empirical. This universe proposition cannot be verified by asking agents what is the basic motivation for their actions, because it implies that whatever conscious motivation they may adduce for acting, the final cause for that action is explainable in terms of pleasure and pain.

The best evidence that Bentham intended his psychological hedonism as a causal theory of action is provided by the 'two sovereigns' passage. Therefore, Baumgardt is too dismissive of this passage as an informative statement of the form of Bentham's theory. Here Bentham argues that: 'the chain of causes and effects, are fastened to their throne'.[21] This implies that they are the basic concepts of a causal theory of action. However, if this

---

[19] See G. E. Moore, *Principia Ethica* (Cambridge, 1903), 18. Moore's argument is adopted by recent commentators such as J. P. Plamenatz, *The English Utilitarians* (Oxford, 1966), and B. Parekh, 'Bentham's Justification of the Principle of Utility', *Ten Critical Essays*, p. 103.

[20] BL Add. MS 33550, fo. 63 (punctuation added).

[21] *IPML* (CW), p. 11.

theory is not empirical, what is Bentham's justification for adopting hedonism as the basis of his theory of motivation. If all action, whatever its express or conscious motivation, is caused by the perception of pleasure or pain, what is the point of Bentham's theory? To reduce the infinite variety of conscious motivation to the two efficient causes of action appears to deprive Bentham's psychological theory of any effective explanatory power. It does not enable the legislator to determine why some individuals find certain courses of action pleasurable and not others.

There is, however, a justification of Bentham's adoption of hedonism as the basis of his psychological theory, which is similar to his justification of the principle of utility as the sole criterion of moral judgement. In the case of moral judgement, Bentham argues that without some objective standard of moral judgement it would not be possible to bring to resolution real problems, because it would be impossible to frame those problems in a publicly accepted framework which enabled some measure of agreement about what should be done. He also argues that by adopting real entities such as pleasure and pain as the basic criteria for determining the meaning of moral discourse, and by showing that rival theories including the principles of 'asceticism' and 'sympathy and antipathy'[22] are unable to provide a public standard for moral discourse, the principle of utility is the only means of creating a publicly acceptable moral language. In the case of Bentham's theory of motivation, his object is to provide a basis for a science of legislation. This is premissed on the practical task of enabling the legislator to co-ordinate or constrain action in order to realize the maximum social well-being. To attain this end the legislator must be able to count on a basic uniformity of motivation irrespective of the conscious aims of all agents. The possibility of a legislative project requires a single causal theory of motivation which a legislator can apply in order to co-ordinate and constrain action. Thus the claim that pleasure and pain are the final causes of action is not an empirical one. However, this does not affect the overall empirical character of Bentham's psychological theory, as will be seen from the rest of this chapter.

Pleasure and pain are feelings or objects of sensation which Bentham describes as 'interesting perceptions'.[23] The reason that Bentham considers these as the efficient cause of action is his adoption of a Humean theory of motivation which maintains that reason cannot be the ultimate source of action. Hume argued in his two famous works *A Treatise of Human Nature*[24] and *An Enquiry Concerning Human Understanding*[25] that we have an indirect experience of the world. Our perceptions of the world form

---

[22] Ibid., p. 17.   [23] Ibid., p. 42.

[24] D. Hume, *A Treatise of Human Nature*, ed. L. A. Selby-Bigge, 2nd edn., rev. P. H. Nidditch (Oxford, 1978), 1–7.

[25] Id., *Enquiries Concerning Human Understanding and Concerning the Principles of Morals*, ed. L. A. Selby-Bigge, 3rd edn., rev. P. H. Nidditch (Oxford, 1979), 17–22.

impressions and ideas. An impression is the direct product of perception. Its weaker counterpart, which Hume describes as an idea, is the retention of an impression after perception in the processes of thinking and reasoning. The mind is, therefore, populated solely by ideas which have their origin in experience or through combination in the understanding. All reasoning is constrained by the raw material with which the understanding operates, namely ideas. Consequently, it must be about 'matters of fact' which consist of the combination of ideas according to specific rules, or else it involves consideration of numbers which are indirectly derived from impressions.

Thus, for Hume, and the tradition of British Empiricism which followed him, in which Bentham is included, there could be no rationalist account of action, because reason is solely concerned with facts and numbers. This does not, however, imply that reason has no part in determining among the various courses of action. It does not exclude a role for reason as a means of determining the best way of realizing the end of action; it simply means that the object or goal of action has no direct origination in the understanding. An individual's desires and preferences are not a matter of reasoning, though how these are attained and ordered is a matter of reason. Hume accounts for the source of action within his theory of the passions. Bentham relies on the theory of psychological hedonism to account for the basic motivation to act.[26]

Bentham's causal theory of action implies that any end whatever is caused by the pursuit of pleasure and the avoidance of pain. This is so irrespective of the conscious motivation of an agent, because pleasure and pain provide the original source of whatever motivation he may have. Therefore, far from

[26] Recent critics of psychological hedonism have argued that pleasure or pain cannot be the basis of action if these are analysed as sensations because pleasure and pain are not strictly speaking sensations at all. See A. Kenny, 'Happiness', *Proceedings of the Aristotelian Society*, 66 (1965), 93–102, A. MacIntyre, 'Pleasure as a Reason for Action', *Monist*, 49 (1965), 215–33, G. Ryle, 'Pleasure', *Proceedings of the Aristotelian Society* (suppl.), 28 (1954), 135–46. The subject is discussed most fully in J. C. B. Gosling, *Pleasure and Desire* (Oxford, 1969), 28–85.

Hart acknowledges in his essay 'Lecture on a Master Mind: Bentham' that the current understanding of the concept of pleasure is not as a distinct and identifiable sensation, but rather as an attitude towards an activity one is engaged in. Thus wishing to continue in the pursuit of the activity, being engrossed in it, and preferring its continuance to some other end, are all taken as part of the meaning of finding something pleasurable and not criteria of a distinct sensation. Hart wrote: 'The wish for prolongation of the activity or experience enjoyed; the resistance to interruption; the absorbed or rapt attention; the absence of some further end beyond the activity enjoyed—these are surely conceptually and not merely empirically linked with pleasure' (*Proceedings of the British Academy*, 48 (1962), 304). Gosling has, however, argued that these 'adverbial' views of pleasure are inadequate because there are circumstances in which it does make sense to describe pleasure as an identifiable sensation or feeling (Gosling, *Pleasure and Desire*, pp. 147–56). However, while much current philosophical writing appears to undermine the credibility of Bentham's attempt to base a legislative science on a psychological theory which sees pleasure and pain as sensations, one recent philosopher R. B. Brandt, has defended a version of utilitarianism based on psychological hedonism (*A Theory of the Good and the Right*, (Oxford, 1979).

constraining all human motivation to the direct pursuit of pleasure which would be contrary to the evidence of experience, Bentham is able to account for the variety of different motivations in terms of the efficient causes of pleasure and pain. Whatever an individual consciously desires is described as his interest, although Bentham does not restrict an individual's interest to his conscious desires or preferences. It is with interests that Bentham's empirical psychology is concerned. While all actions are caused by pleasure and the avoidance of pain, interests are as varied as the circumstances within which individuals find themselves. Bentham thought that there was a degree of uniformity of interests and that given the constitution of human nature there were certain things in the interests of all individuals. However, what these are remains an empirical question.[27] Individuals have basic interests in the provision of subsistence in order that they may survive. They also have an interest in security so that they can realize their substantive projects and engage in activities such as labour which serve as intermediate conditions of those projects. To a lesser extent but as a consequence of having an interest in security they also have an interest in abundance and equality, in so far as these are also a condition of extended security.

Each particular interest gives rise to a kind of pleasure. These can be simple pleasures such as those derived from food and drink, or else they can be more complex combinations of simple pleasures. Thus a complex goal or project can provide a whole variety of pleasures which become inter-connected. In the *Table of the Springs of Action*,[28] written in 1815 and published in 1817, Bentham attempted to provide a list of simple motives divided into classes, and to connect these classes of motives with a corresponding source of pleasure or pain. His intention was to provide the legislator with an analysis of actions in terms of simple motives and then show how these are connected to pleasures or pains. This would help the legislator identify the basic sources of motivation. Thus the motives of self-preservation and self-defence would be connected to pains of death and bodily suffering. When faced with certain threats the individual's motive is to act in self-defence. However, the efficient cause of his acting in self-defence is provided by the prospect of bodily suffering.

J. S. Mill was quick to point out that the whole notion of providing a comprehensive list of motives is curiously naïve. It is implausible to think that one could provide an exhaustive catalogue of all possible motives for purposive actions, because this list must be as numerous as the number of actions. There is in principle at least as many motives as there are actions and this number necessarily increases with every change in the circumstances of action. Mill wrote: 'motives are innumerable; there is nothing whatever

---

[27] The rest of the study is concerned with identifying those components of real interest which are essential in order for any individual to pursue his own goals or projects.

[28] *Deontology together with A Table of the Springs of Action and Article on Utilitarianism*, ed. A. Goldworth (CW), 74–115.

which may not become an object of desire or of dislike by association.'[29] Mill's criticism of the *Table of the Springs of Action* was written at a time when he was least sympathetic to Bentham's philosophical position. Despite the plausibility of Mill's criticism, Bentham's *Table of the Springs of Action* was not as ludicrous as he suggested. Bentham's aim was not to provide an exhaustive catalogue of all possible motives. He wanted to provide a practical classification of certain basic types of motivation in order to facilitate the legislator's task of constructing a utilitarian science of legislation rather than a complete and exhaustive catalogue of all possible motivations. Once the legislator was aware of the most basic simple motives, he could incorporate this information into the development of sanctions and legal rules. Therefore, the fact that it may prove practically impossible to complete the task of the *Table of the Springs of Action* should not count against its utility.

In so far as the individual agent does not directly pursue pleasure it is clear that Bentham's psychological hedonism is not premissed on egoism. The individual agent is consciously motivated by his conception of well-being, and his interest can be as varied as the number of possible motivations will allow. As an empirical judgement Bentham would accept Mill's claim that 'there is nothing whatever which may not become an object of desire'.[30] What individuals desire and what can constitute an interest is an empirical question. Therefore Bentham is not committed to the position that all action must be self-orientated, and this undermines the basis for claiming that his psychological theory is a version of psychological egoism.

Lyons has referred to the standard argument that psychological hedonism is a version of psychological egoism on the grounds that 'the pleasures one seeks and the pains one tries to avoid are always one's own.'[31] This is partly right, but does not provide any ground for egoism, because, while the pleasures that form the efficient cause of one's action are necessarily one's own, these can, nevertheless, cause actions which are not self-referring or are only indirectly self-referring. Thus, while an agent's project of protecting his family originates in the pleasure he will derive from their safety and security, his direct motivation is the non-self-referring goal of realizing that end.[32] Similarly, an agent can desire the pleasure of another and yet his action is still caused by the self-referring pleasure he derives from their

---

[29] J. S. Mill, 'Remarks on Bentham's Philosophy', *Essays on Ethics, Religion and Society*, ed. John M. Robson (Toronto, 1969) (The Collected Works of John Stuart Mill, x), 13.

[30] Ibid.   [31] Lyons, *In The Interest of the Governed*, p. 69.

[32] Parekh has argued that 'though no human being can ever escape himself, or that the source of man's action must be located in himself', this theory is, nevertheless, 'congruous both with the view that man is essentially a selfish creature who can pursue his own interest as well as with the view that he is an altruistic being who consistently subordinates his interest to those of others' (*Ten Critical Essays*, x).

good. The claim would only be justified if it were true that all individuals aim directly at their own pleasure, but this is not the case and is not implied by Bentham's psychological theory.

The egoistic interpretation of Bentham's psychological theory is further refuted by the fact that he acknowledges sympathy[33] and benevolence[34] as sources of pleasure. Though sympathy and benevolence can be self-referring in that benevolent actions for the good of others can give one pleasure, to argue that they can be reduced to a version of egoism is to undermine the explanatory force of the concept. Egoism as it is used both in psychological and ethical theory usually signifies self-regarding motivations. In an egoistic theory an individual's motives are confined to the pursuit of his own well-being, and his interests only incorporate those of others in so far as their interests correspond with his. Therefore, an egoistic theory of motivation rules out actions which are done solely for the benefit of others. However, psychological hedonism only implies that the cause of action be self-referring, that is that one's own pleasure provides the efficient cause of the action. This does not entail that the object of action or the agent's interest be self-regarding, for it is possible to derive pleasure from actions which are wholly other-regarding, such as caring for others. In the case of caring for others the object of action can be wholly other-regarding while the cause remains self-experienced pleasure. An egoistic theory cannot acknowledge the existence of other-regarding motivations without emptying the concept of any specific meaning.

Psychological hedonism differs from egoism in that it does not require that all interests be self-regarding. Bentham appears to have thought that as a matter of empirical fact most people were motivated by self-regarding or egoistic motives. However, this is an empirical judgement. He did not claim that other-regarding motivations were impossible, and he did not attempt to derive this egoistic conclusion from his psychological hedonism.

Baumgardt has argued that what individual agents aim at are not isolated entities of pleasure. They aim at activities and objects which have a 'hedonic tinge'.[35] This suggests that the sources of pleasure and pain are objective qualities in the world and that this 'hedonic tinge' provides the connection between actions and the causal motivations of individual agents. A 'hedonic tinge' is any property of an action or object which causes pleasure or the avoidance of pain. However, while these objective sources of pleasure are the properties of actions which result in their pursuit, not all individuals aim at the same ends or objects. Given that these sources of pleasure have a causal effect on action how is it that some individuals find pleasure in some actions while others do not? What is implied by Baumgardt and what Bentham intended is that at a basic level all individuals find pleasure in a certain class

[33] *Deontology* (CW), p. 84.
[34] *IPML* (CW), p. 44.
[35] Baumgardt, *Bentham and the Ethics of Today*, p. 178.

of objects. These are the simple pleasures such as those of food and drink and others such as bodily comfort. Thus, while an ascetic may forego many of the pleasures of the body in order to gain greater pleasures in the next world, it does not make sense to say that he does not have a natural inclination towards pleasures derived from food or bodily comfort, although he may well consider it virtuous to overcome these inclinations. These basic causes of action are the simple pleasures which Bentham lists in the *Table of the Springs of Action*. Though in many instances these basic sources of pleasure exist singly they also exist in combination with other sources of pleasure. These combinations of pleasure or complex pleasures form the basis of complex interest. Therefore in most cases individual agents are not motivated by simple pleasures, but pursue interests which are the source of a combination of pleasures.

There are of course circumstances in which an agent may directly pursue a certain type of pleasure as a conscious goal. Beyond the basic level of simple pleasures, agents are motivated by varying pleasures which they derive from the almost infinite variety of human action. Some derive pleasure from push-pin (a game resembling shove-halfpenny), others from poetry. Experience of the actions of others enables the agent to associate certain types of action with certain pleasures and the circumstances of the agent influence the extent of his experience. Therefore, differences in circumstances are partly responsible for the variety of interests, because they are responsible for the varied experience of pleasures. Similarly, circumstances affect sensibility, which is 'The disposition which any one has to feel such or such a quantity of pleasure or pain, upon the application of a cause of given force',[36] and sensibility is also a condition which affects the variety of interests. Bentham argued that: 'Pain and pleasure are produced in men's minds by the action of certain causes. But the quantity of pleasure and pain runs not uniformly in proportion to the cause; in other words, to the quantity of force exerted by such cause.'[37]

This difference in sensibility and circumstances accounts for the different interests that individual agents pursue. Therefore, given the circumstances of a person's sensibility they may find more pleasure in a certain type of activity than another who has different circumstances of sensibility. Unlike Mill, Bentham does not make the non-empirical claim that a certain class of higher pleasures will always be chosen by someone who has experienced both, because the circumstances of individual sensibility are ultimately inscrutable. An informed individual may yet find push-pin more pleasurable than poetry, despite having the education which enables him to appreciate poetry. For Bentham an individual determines between the various pleasurable options open to him by means of the quantity of pleasure derived from those respective options. Sensibility and circumstance

[36] *IPML* (CW), p. 51.   [37] Ibid.

ultimately determine what that person finds pleasurable at any given moment, but these can change because actions can themselves influence the agent's circumstances, and thus change the composition of his sensibility. The pleasure of expectation enables an agent to form long-term projects or life plans which provide considerable pleasure at a future date. The role of pleasures derived from expectation means that individual agents are not confined to the pursuit of immediate pleasures, and can build up complex patterns of interest. The pleasure of expectation provides the continuing efficient cause of actions which contribute to a long-term project. Though Bentham uses the word happiness as a synonym of pleasure[38] he also uses it as an achievement word signifying the attainment of pleasure within a given period of time. Thus he wrote: '*Happiness*' is a word employed to signify the sum of pleasures experienced during the quantity of time which is under consideration, dedication made or not made of the quantity of pain experienced during that same quantity of time.[39]

While this second sense of happiness does not imply the Aristotelian concept of *eudaimonia*, which many critics argue Mill tried to incorporate into his concept of happiness, it does nevertheless signify that Bentham did not imply that all action was the direct pursuit of immediate gratification.

The most significant problem facing hedonistic accounts of motivation arises from the fact that they separate the conditions of motivation from the object of action. The causal condition of motivation is the subjective experience of pleasure derived from the object of action, whereas the object can be anything that an agent desires. This has led many critics of hedonistic theories to argue that the artificial creation of the pleasurable sensation could be a substitute for the same pleasure derived from action. The problem is most acute in the case of utilitarian theories that are premissed on psychological hedonism, for it is then argued that because the consistent utilitarian is committed to the maximization of pleasurable states, he can also be committed to the requirement to produce those states, even by artificial means. Thus we have the arguments of Nozick[40] and Smart[41] who argue that given a machine which could produce the pleasurable sensation resulting from any experience whatever, without any further costs, a consistent hedonist would favour being plugged into the machine, and would enjoy artificial stimulation rather than taking a chance of pleasure in the real world, along with its attendant pains. Nozick argues that to choose being connected to such a machine is to opt out of our humanity:

Plugging into the machine is a kind of suicide. It will seem to some, trapped by a picture, that nothing about what we are like can matter except as it gets reflected in

[38] *Deontology* (CW), p. 87.
[39] BL Add. MS 33550, fo. 62.
[40] R. Nozick, *Anarchy, State, and Utopia* (Oxford, 1974), 42–5.
[41] J. J. C. Smart, 'An Outline of a Sytem of Utilitarian Ethics', in id. and B. Williams (eds.), *Utilitarianism: For and Against* (Cambridge, 1973), 19.

our experiences. But should it be surprising that what *we are* is important to us? Why should we be concerned only with how our time is filled, but not with what we are?[42]

The problem of the pleasure machine creates difficulties for Bentham's thought because his moral theory and legislative science are premissed on a hedonistic psychology. Parekh[43] has argued that Bentham's remark about the inmates of the Panopticon school—'Call them soldiers, call them monks, call them machines, so they are but happy ones, I should not care'[44]— supports the view that Bentham would not object to pleasure machines as a means of maximizing social well-being. This is, however, a piece of rhetoric and should not be given much weight in determining the character of Bentham's social theory.

A full reponse to this criticism would involve a consideration of Bentham's moral theory, and whether it provides a straightforward injunction to maximize pleasurable states. However, at the level of Bentham's psychological theory there is still a possible response to this criticism which avoids the counter-intuitive consequences of the pleasure machine. Bentham's hedonistic psychology does not claim that all individuals desire only pleasure or that pleasure is the sole object of action. Instead he argues that pleasure is the ultimate efficient cause of action, and that the pleasure derived from the various objects of action accounts for an individual's choice of a particular interest or goal. Therefore there is nothing in Bentham's psychological theory which entails that an individual agent would necessarily choose being connected to a pleasure machine in order to stimulate the pleasurable sensation derived from the object of action rather than simply pursue the object of action directly. The pleasure derived need not be the conscious goal of action so the possibility of the sensation of pleasure resulting from the action without all the other facets of experience need not prove at all attractive to the prospective agent. Furthermore, because individuals can pursue complex interests which are realized over long periods of time, there is some scope for arguing that the character of an individual's life can be of importance in determining his choice of objectives. This still has to be explained in terms of the efficient causes of pleasure and pain, but there is nothing in Bentham's theory which necessitates individuals being concerned simply with the direct pursuit of pleasurable experiences.

The notion of pleasures of expectation which plays such a significant role in Bentham's theory of justice provides a further proof that the direct pursuit of maximally pleasureable experiences are not the sole object of individual action. Pleasures of expectation provide the framework within which individuals can produce ordered life-plans which entail many of the values of a developed and cultivated character. They provide an explanation

---

[42] Nozick, *Anarchy, State, and Utopia*, p. 43.
[43] Parekh, 'Bentham's Theory of Equality', p. 495.
[44] Bowring, iv. 64.

of how Bentham's psychology can account for many motives such as thrift and industry which contribute to the formation of rational life plans, but which do not constitute immediate sources of pleasure. A conception of self which is concerned with personal character and the dimensions of a well-ordered life can be the ultimate object of an individual's hedonistic goals so long as Bentham's theory is not constructed in such a way that the immediate experience of pleasure is the sole human motivation. Pleasures of expectation provide this possibility because they incorporate a future dimension into determinations of individuals interest so that an individual can form a complex life-plan within a hedonistic framework.

Though Bentham's hedonistic principle is not empirically based, he did not wish his psychological theory to contradict the evidence of experience, and deny motivations which did exist. Therefore, Bentham did not maintain that individuals only sought immediate pleasure. Consequently, he would not have argued that all individuals would prefer the artificial stimulations of the pleasure machine instead of those pleasures derived from the pursuit and realization of complex interests. His intention in his psychological theory was to provide a causal explanation of all human motivations in order to construct a legislative science which facilitates the maximum of social well-being. The argument so far is in agreement with Lyons's claim that the most important part of Bentham's psychological theory was a hedonistic theory of causes.[45] I make the stronger claim that it is only in virtue of this prior hedonistic theory of causes that Bentham can also be said to have a hedonistic theory of goals. I have claimed that the conscious goal of action need not be the direct pursuit of pleasure. Therefore, it can only be the case that Bentham has a hedonistic theory of goals, if the 'hedonic tinge' of an action which accounts for its causal efficacy can also be described as the aim of action. However, given that the direct pursuit of pleasure need not be the conscious aim of action it is most appropriate to interpret Bentham's psychological hedonism as entailing only a hedonistic theory of causes, and confining the hedonistic theory of goals to the same category as psychological egoism, as a useful empirical generalization. Furthermore, it is only a hedonistic theory of causes that Bentham requires for the basis of his science of legislation.

While I have already argued that Bentham's psychological hedonism is not premissed on psychological egoism, there is, nevertheless, a significant tendency towards egoism is his thought. Most commentators have acknowledged the role of egoism as a premiss of Bentham's constitutional theory.[46] The notion of the 'duty-interest junction principle', which features in both revisionary and received interpretations of Bentham's thought, is founded on private egoism conflicting with a morality of public benevolence.

---

[45] Lyons, *In The Interest of the Governed*, pp. 71–2.
[46] Rosen, *Jeremy Bentham and Representative Democracy*, pp. 206–11.

This tendency towards egoism, embodied in the 'self preference principle' is most apparent in Bentham's *Constitutional Code*. He wrote:

Instructional

ART. 7.I. In all human minds, in howsoever widely different proportions—*self-regard*, and *sympathy* for others or say *extra-regard*, have place.

Instructional

ART. 8. II. But, in self-regard even sympathy has its root: and if, in the general tenour of human conduct, self-regard were not prevalent over sympathy—even over sympathy for all others put together—no such species as the human could have existence.

Instructional. Expositive

ART. 9. Take any two persons, A and B, and suppose them the only persons in existence—call them, for example, *Adam* and *Eve*. *Adam* has no regard for himself: the whole of his regard has for its object *Eve*. *Eve* in like manner has no regard for herself: the whole of her regard has for its object *Adam*. Follow this supposition up: introduce the occurrences, which, sooner or later, are sure to happen, and you will see that, at the end of an assignable length of time, greater or less according to accident, but in no case so much as a twelvemonth, both will unavoidably have perished.[47]

It has already been argued that Bentham's psychological theory was a hedonistic account of causes. This does not imply that pleasure is the sole conscious object of action nor that the pleasure that an agent may aim at must necessarily be his own. It is clear that Bentham did not intend to derive the 'self-preference principle' from his psychological theory, and this immediately raises the question of the status of the egoistic 'self-preference principle'.

Bentham's intention is difficult to identify in this case, for while he stated that 'the only interests which a man at all times and upon all occasions is sure to find *adequate* motives for consulting, are his own',[48] suggesting that man is generally self-interested, he also wrote:

This observation is of a piece with another observation equally trite concerning man in general, that he is never governed by any thing but his own interest. This observation in a large and extensive sense of the word interest (as comprehending all sorts of motives) is indubitably true: but as indubitably false in any of the confined senses in which upon such an occasion the word *interest* is wont to be made use of.[49]

---

[47] *Constitutional Code*, i, ed. F. Rosen and J. H. Burns (Oxford, 1983) (CW), p. 119.
[48] *IPML* (CW), p. 284.   [49] *OLG* (CW), p. 70.

Here Bentham acknowledged that an individual is solely concerned with his own interest only in those instances where interest is taken to cover all possible motivations. When the concept is given a more confined meaning referring only to self-regarding motivations it is clear that the contention of the 'self-preference principle' is false. Throughout Bentham's career, he acknowledged the existence of social and semi-social motivations such as sympathy and benevolence. Thus he could not have thought that individuals are motivated only by self-regarding interests. Given that he acknowledged sympathy and benevolence as among the social motives he cannot have intended the 'self-preference principle' to have been based on an empirical generalization, for by his own admission he acknowledged the existence of significant exceptions to this rule. Neither can he have intended to derive a principle of self-regard from the fact that pleasures are always self-referring, for this fact does not entail that those pleasures cannot be derived from non-self-regarding actions. A clue to Bentham's intention is to be found in a passage from the *Deontology* (CW), where he wrote:

To better his condition, to acquire for the future some means of enjoyment more than at present he is in possession of, is the aim of every man. Not perhaps in the character of a universal proposition, true: but for argument sake, be it so.[50]

This passage expresses some of the substance of the 'self-preference principle' in that it argues that every man is occupied with the self-regarding objects of bettering his condition and increasing his wealth and property. Bentham acknowledged that such a claim did not have the status of a universal truth, but he argued that for practical purposes this is a useful maxim for the legislator to remember. Bentham's intention was to provide a practical maxim for the legislator to apply in his institutional reforms. By adopting the view that man is essentially self-regarding, the legislator can construct institutions which take this into account, and direct this self-regard towards his own beneficial ends. A self-regarding functionary will not be assumed to follow the general interest, but will be assumed to have a selfish interest. As Bentham wrote in the *Constitutional Code* (CW):

whatsoever evil it is possible for a man to do for the advancement of his own private and personal interest ... at the expense of the public interest—that evil, sooner or later, he will do, unless by some means or other, intentional or otherwise, prevented from doing it.[51]

On the basis of this assumption the legislator can create institutional checks which prevent that functionary's selfish interest becoming a sinister interest that is in competition with the maximum social well-being. Bentham's position is similar to that of Hume, who argued that in politics 'every man ought to be supposed a *knave*, and to have no other end, in all

---

[50] *Deontology* (CW), p. 132.
[51] *Constitutional Code* (CW), p. 119.

his actions, than private interest.'[52] This interpretation of Bentham's 'self-preference principle' is similar to that presented by Harrison,[53] Postema,[54] and Rosen.[55] Each account varies in emphasis, but all accept that he adopted a version of strategic egoism.

There is a tendency towards egoism within Bentham's thought. However, it is not derived a priori from his analysis of the causes of action nor is it a strictly empirical generalization. Instead, he adopts egoism as a legislative strategy not only because he thought egoistic motives predominated over non-egoistic ones, but also because we cannot have any certainty in distinguishing those who are not self-interested from those who are. He wrote:

Instructional

ART. 12. To the above rule suppose there is this or that exception: still, with a view to practice, there might as well be none: forasmuch as by no criterion will it be possible, to distinguish the individuals in whose instance the exception has place, from those in whose instance the general rule has place: more especially when, as in the case of all Legislative arrangements of a general nature, the individuals in question are unassigned or unassignable.[56]

Bentham's stategic egoism does not imply the much stronger claim advanced by Halévy that Bentham 'considered the individual as elementally egoistic, and all the disinterested inclinations as so many transformations of this primordial egoism.'[57] Halévy's claims depend on an egoistic methodology[58] applied to Bentham's psychological hedonism on the basis that the

---

[52] D. Hume, 'Of the Independence of Parliament', in *Essays, Moral, Political and Literary*, eds. T. H. Green and T. H. Grose (2 vols., Oxford, 1963), 42.

[53] Harrison, *Bentham*, pp. 140–8.

[54] G. J. Postema, *Bentham and the Common Law Tradition* (Oxford, 1986), 385–9.

[55] Rosen, *Jeremy Bentham and Representative Democracy*, pp. 206–11.

[56] *Constitutional Code* (CW), pp. 119–20.

[57] Halévy, *The Growth of Philosophic Radicalism*, pp. 502–3.

[58] The most significant difference between the received interpretation presented by Halévy and the revisionist theory of Postema in his book *Bentham and the Common Law Tradition*, arises from the interpretation given to Bentham's individualist methodology. Halévy interprets Bentham's individualism as a version of egoism (see n. 57, above). He argues that all individual interests must be self-regarding. Postema on the other hand interprets Bentham's legal and constitutional theory as a means of supressing the selfish motivations of public functionaries in order that they can identify their interest with a public conception of the good. He sees Bentham's theory as a means by which social motivations may come to predominate rather than a means of coercing the self-regarding interest of each individual into a conception of the public good. Despite this he still recognizes Bentham's methodological individualism, which claims that the basis of value is within individual experience, and that public goods must be reducible to the good of the individuals which form the community.

There is also some scope for arguing that the basic difference between Postema's revisionist theory and L. J. Hume's modified version of the received interpretation (see n. 2 above) is the emphasis given to Bentham's individualism. Hume argues that towards the end of Bentham's career his methodological individualism became prescriptive. Hume borrows this notion from M. P. Mack's *Jeremy Bentham: An Odyssey of Ideas* (London, 1962), 10. This prescriptive individualism advocated the complete individualization of society, that is, the complete

pleasures which constitute the efficient cause of action are always those of the agent. However, it cannot be inferred from this that all motives are necessarily self-regarding, and, therefore, that human nature is primarily egoistic.

II

In the previous section it was argued that the individual agent determines between different possible motivations in terms of the amount of pleasure he associates with various options. I have used the term pleasure, as does Bentham, to refer to the sources of pleasure. Though Bentham writes of pleasures of expectation, of piety, benevolence, or of a good name, these are not distinct pleasures, but rather distinct sources of pleasure. Pleasure is a single sensation which is the efficient cause of action, but the sources of pleasure or that part of an action or the object of action, which provides its causal efficacy, are described by Bentham as pleasures. This means that the individual does not have to make qualitative distinctions between the various kinds of pleasure in determining a course of action. The individual agent's sensibility and circumstances will mean that he perceives qualitative distinctions in the various objects of action available. These qualitative distinctions are subjective in that they are a consequence of the agent's sensibility and circumstances. The only public distinctions between pleasures are differences of quantity.

Individual practical reasoning is ordinarily concerned with interests, and not with pleasures because they are the efficient causes of action, whereas interests are the objects of action. Therefore, the individual is concerned with the best way of realizing his interest. An individual's choice of project requires that he is able to determine the quantity of pleasure he expects to derive from an action or object. Similarly, if the legislator is to determine how to co-ordinate or constrain actions he must be able to determine the amount of pleasure or pain following from different actions. This implies the possibility of a public calculus of pleasures and it is the idea of this calculus which has dominated the interpretation of Bentham's psychological and ethical theories. Halévy has written that: 'pleasure and pain are susceptible of becoming the objects of a calculus, and a rational and

destruction of all social forces acting on the formation of individual conceptions of well-being. Hume and Mack argue that this individualization of society became the overall aim of Bentham's reform strategy.

Again Postema argues that Bentham was simply concerned with removing those institutions and practices which enabled sinister interests to flourish and instead to construct institutions which gave scope to the functionaries' non-self-regarding motives. Bentham's theory was not designed to reduce everything to individual entities. It was designed so that a conception of the public good could be developed which was more then the collection of individual self-regarding interests.

mathematical science of pleasure is possible.'[59] Bentham gives the impression that he advocated a rational and mathematical science of society based on the calculation of the value of pleasure derived from certain actions when he wrote of his 'political arithmetic'.[60] However, Bentham gives a misleading impression of the true nature of his science of legislation in such passages— he was acutely aware of the difficulty of providing an objective measure of subjective experience.

In chapter 4 of *An Introduction to the Principles of Morals and Legislation*, 'Value of a Lot of Pleasure or Pain, How to be Measured', Bentham reinforced the impression that he intended to construct a 'political arithmetic' as the basis for his legislative science. In this chapter Bentham identifies four circumstances which are to be considered by an individual agent in determining the value of a pleasure. These are: intensity, duration, certainty or uncertainty, and propinquity or remoteness.[61] To determine the value of a pleasure or pain to a group of individuals three more circumstances are added. These are: fecundity, purity, and extent.[62] Not all of these circumstances are appropriate to the measurement of pleasure as a sensation. The considerations of fecundity and purity refer, according to Bentham, to the tendency of acts to produce pleasures. The problem with this theory is that it does not enable the legislator to produce an objective determination of the value of a particular pleasure. This is because intensity and duration refer solely to subjective experience. The intensity of a pleasure will vary according to the sensibility of the particular individual under consideration; therefore, no objective value can be given to it. Bentham acknowledged the difficulty of providing a precise determination of subjective sensibility when he wrote:

To every man, by competent attention and observation the quality of his own sensibility may be made known: it may be known by the most impressive and infallible of all direct evidence, the evidence of a man's own senses.

To no man, can the quality of sensibility in the breast of any other man be made known by any thing like equally probative and unfallacious evidence.[63]

An individual can determine among various courses of action in accordance with the dimensions of pleasure and pain, but it does not follow that the legislator is able to use the same model in determining that individual's actions. The individual can make such distinctions, and determine the value of pleasure because the effect of a pleasure on his sensibility will be experienced, and therefore he can give it some degree of comparative weighting. This weighting is not a publicly accessible evaluation because the variation in feeling that is caused by differences in individual sensibility cannot be made accessible to others. Bentham writes:

[59] Halévy, *The Growth of Philosophic Radicalism*, p. 492.
[60] Bowring, iv. 540.   [61] *IPML* (CW), p. 38.
[62] *IPML* (CW), p. 39.   [63] *Deontology* (CW), p. 131.

Countenance, gesture, deportment, contemporary conduct at the time, subsequent conduct at other subsequent times—from each of these articles of circumstances, separately or collectively taken—indications much surer and [more] unambiguous may be deduced than from any such direct evidence as is or can be constituted and delivered by any verbal account given by him of his own feeling.[64]

But such a consideration of the behaviour of the individual agent will not provide the means for attaching a determinate value to his subjective experience. If the legislator is merely supposed to infer the subjective value of pleasure from the observable behaviour of individual agents he is faced with an enormous task. A further problem is that while observed behaviour gives some indication of subjective experience it gives no precise indication of the value of that experience. The legislator is, therefore, unable to distinguish between the subjective value of experience solely on the basis of observable behaviour.

This problem undermines the rest of Bentham's argument in *An Introduction to the Principles of Morals and Legislation*, chapter 4. The question remains as to the point of this chapter if it clearly does not provide an adequate means for determining the value of a pleasure or a pain. A clue to its purpose was provided by Bentham in the following passage where he wrote:

In all this there is nothing but what the practice of mankind, wheresoever they have a clear view of their own interest, is perfectly conformable to. An article of property, an estate in land, for instance, is valuable, on what account? On account of the pleasures of all kinds which it enables a man to produce, and what comes to the same thing the pains of all kinds which it enables him to avert. But the value of such an article of property is universally understood to rise or fall according to the length or shortness of the time which a man has in it: the certainty or uncertainty of its coming into possession: and the nearness or remoteness of the time at which, if at all, it is to come into possession.[65]

Bentham suggests that he is simply providing a description of the reasoning individuals go through when they determine the value of particular objects or decide upon a course of action. An individual can rationally decide upon his conception of interest by means of this procedure because he is able to determine the intensity and duration of certain pleasures on his particular sensibility. The problem of publicly measuring subjective states casts doubt on the possibility that this procedure could form the basis of a 'political arithmetic'. However, Bentham suggests that he thought it possible to derive precise calculations of the value of pleasure and pain from this procedure, despite the fact that he thought it need not be applied in every case of judicial decision-making.[66] In other works Bentham acknowledged the

[64] Ibid., p. 131.
[65] *IPML* (CW), p. 40–1.
[66] Ibid., p. 40.

difficulty to giving a precise determination of the value of subjective experience. In the 'Principles of the Civil Code' he used the notion of 'value in affection',[67] and in a later work incorporated into the 'Pannomial Fragments' he refers to 'idiosyncratical' value.[68] 'Value in affection' is used to refer to the subjective value an individual places on a particular object of property which cannot be given an objective value by means of the criteria of exchange. 'Idiosyncratical' value is also described as the subjective value that an individual places on an object over and above the exchange value of that object. 'Value in affection' is used to refer to objects which have a peculiar relationship to an individual property-holder, and which enjoy a special place in an individual's subjective experience. In the 'Principles of the Civil Code', Bentham wrote:

Things may be distinguished into two classes: those which have commonly only an intrinsic value, and those which are susceptible of a value in affection . . . To the second may be referred a pleasure-garden, a library, statues, pictures, collections of natural history. As to objects of this kind the exchange ought never to be forced: it is not possible to appreciate the value that the feeling of affection may give them.[69]

Part of Bentham's overriding concern for the protection of property is based on the notion of 'value in affection'. This is because the legislator is unable to measure precisely the pain resulting from direct interference with property; therefore, he cannot make a provision that will offset the cost. Beyond the problem of finding some means of compensating for the pain arising from violated property rights, the notion of 'idiosyncratical value' suggests that some values which are derived from imaginative identification with the objects of property are not susceptible to conversion. Thus an object which has formed part of the lifetime work of an individual might be incalculably valuable to that person, and no amount of money could compensate for its loss.

This notion of 'idiosyncratical values' introduced into Bentham's thought some very radical ideas about the limitation of scope of his 'political arithmetic'. It has become a commonplace of the received interpretation of Bentham's moral theory to emphasize the role of calculation within his account of moral reasoning. This idea is derived from Halévy,[70] but is found in many subsequent commentators, some of whom differ from Halévy on certain parts of his account. Bentham adds credence to this interpretation by his use of terms such as 'political arithmetic.'[71] However, it is also clear that Bentham was aware of the difficulties of founding such an exact science of human nature and also that the character of this science was rather more modest than his rhetoric has led us to believe. It is clear from some of Bentham's other writings that he did not intend his legislative

---

[67] Bowring, i. 310 and 322.   [68] BL Add. MS 33550, fo. 121.
[69] Bowring, i. 322.
[70] Halévy, *The Growth of Philosophic Radicalism*, p. 492.
[71] Bowring, iv. 540.

science to have the mathematical or formal precision of modern positive economic analysis. While the model derived from *An Introduction to the Principles of Morals and Legislation*, chapter 4 indicates the procedure of the individual agent in determining between various conceptions of individual well-being, it is not the model that is appropriate to the legislator in determining how he should secure the maximum of social well-being. The true character of Bentham's legislative science is more akin to medicine than it is to mathematics or arithmetic:[72] 'Experience, observation and experiment, these are the foundations of all well-grounded medical practice: experience, observation and experiment, such are the foundations of all well-grounded legislative practice.'[73]

In this passage Bentham reveals the empirical character of his psychological theory and legislative science. This empirical conception of the science of legislation is carried over into the procedures that the legislator adopts in order to determine the effects of particular sanctions on certain classes of actions and motives. Instead of attempting precise calculations of the value of an individual's subjective experience in order to determine how he will react to the legislator's sanctions, he adopts the procedures of an empirical science, and attempts to infer from observation-based generalizations how individuals will respond to particular policies. This empirical science yields axioms of mental pathology, and it is upon these that the legislator builds his legislative science. These axioms do not provide the legislator with deductive certainty. They are inferences from experience that do not take account of the variety of circumstances which might qualify his conclusions. However, the generalizations that underpin Bentham's axioms of mental pathology are justified while they provide for a practicable science of society. Bentham's criteria for the appropriateness of these axioms is similar to the utilitarian standards he used to judge other principles within his social theory. In the 'Principles of the Civil Code' he argued that these axioms are justified when they met the following criteria: '*1st*, If they approach more nearly to the truth than any other which can be substituted for them; and *2ndly*, If they may be employed by the legislator, as the foundation of his labours, with less inconvenience than any others';[74] and in 'Pannomial Fragments' he wrote:

By an axiom nothing more is meant than a sort of rule which by certain properties the conjunction of which is peculiar to it, the usefulness is preeminent in comparison to other rules. These properties are,
1. Incontestableness.
2. Comprehensiveness.
3. Clearness.[75]

---

[72] Harrison argues that despite Bentham's aspiration to be the Newton of parts of the science of man, the Newton Bentham had in mind was the Newton of the *Optics*, which was based on observation and experiment, rather than the *Principia*, which was deductive and mathematical (*Bentham*, p. 141).   [73] BL Add. MS 33550, fo. 114.
[74] Bowring, i. 305.   [75] BL Add. MS 33550, fo. 68.

The impression given by the above passages and by the role of axioms within Bentham's psychology is radically different from the 'political arithmetic' to which Halévy refers. These axioms do not involve the legislator in making any calculations on the effects of actions of particular individuals because he eschews any concern with individual sensibility and particular circumstances. The legislator is concerned with constructing rules which apply to all individuals with respect to certain classes of actions. They cannot be grounded in the particular experience of any one individual. Consequently, the fact that these axioms of mental pathology do not take into account the precise content of subjective experience creates no significant problems for the Benthamite legislator.

Bentham did not develop many of these axioms, but he did give examples of axioms applicable to equality, which are the rules of diminishing marginal utility. Other axioms might include the 'self-preference principle', those which refer to security as a condition of pleasure and the disappointment of expectations as a constant source of pain.

The axioms are most applicable to the principles underlying the Civil or Distributive Law, because these are concerned with the distribution of rights and titles most conducive to the maximum of social well-being, and the means by which this distribution can be realized. Given that the legislator cannot determine the particular goals and interests of his subjects, he needs to be able to determine the conditions necessary for the pursuit of that interest irrespective of its content. The axioms furnish the means by which the legislator is able to determine these necessary conditions of interest satisfaction.

Though Bentham's legislative science is not based on calculation to the extent that Halévy suggested, there are still occasions when the legislator needs to be able to determine the value of a particular interest to an agent. He cannot rely on the subjective evaluation of the agent concerned. Therefore, he needs a public criterion by which to measure the value of an object of action. The criterion Bentham identifies is money. As I have already argued Bentham's use of the concept of 'idiosyncratical value' means that the subjective value of an interest cannot be reduced to purely monetary terms. This refutes C. B. Macpherson's argument that money and pleasure become interchangeable terms.[76] Indeed the notion of 'idiosyncratical value' contradicts Macpherson's claims that the propositions 'Every individual by his very nature seeks to maximize his own pleasure without limit' and 'each seeks to maximize his own wealth without limit' are extensionally equivalent. For given 'idiosyncratical' values the prescription to maximize pleasure would involve the owner in retaining an object of property, despite its exchange value. The prescription to maximize wealth would involve the owner in the sale of the object, despite the fact that its exchange value could never compensate for its loss.

[76] C. B. Macpherson, *The Life and Times of Liberal Democracy* (Oxford, 1977), 25–7.

Bentham did not intend to make the strong claim that pleasure and money are extensionally equivalent, which Macpherson attributes to him. Instead he chose money as the public criterion for determining the value of a particular class of interests because it is an accepted medium of exchange. Individuals utilize money as a means of evaluating the objects of these interests. They buy and sell property, taking the market-price mechanism as a means of determining the value of the object. This does not imply that all objects of property, or all values can be given a market price. In the case of determining the compensation due to a functionary on the abolition of his post, remuneration is a means of removing the pain of loss, and this implies that pleasures derived from a salary can be exchanged for a fixed sum of compensation. The use of money only provides a criterion for the value of pleasure in those circumstances in which the legislator is trying to determine the exchange value of an object. It does not provide an exact measure of the value of all pleasures or interests.

The calculations that the legislator has to make in the progress of his reforms are not precise ones as to the value of particular pleasures, but are cost-benefit analyses using money as the criterion for measuring the benefits. Consequently, Bentham's legislative science does not have the mathematical certainly implied by the notion of 'political arithmetic'. This lack of mathematical precision does not appear to worry him for he wrote:

How far short soever this degree of precision may be, of the conceivable point of perfection—of that which is actually attained in some branches of art and science— how far short soever of *absolute* perfection—at any rate, in every rational and candid eye, unspeakable will be the advantage it will have, over every form of argumentation, in which every idea is afloat, no degree of precision being attained, because none is ever so much as aimed at.[77]

Bentham's psychological theory has two functions. It provides a descriptive analysis of the conditions of individual motivation and the basis of his legislative science. I have argued that while the individual agent is able to determine the precise value of pleasure in his subjective experience, the legislator is unable to do this and has to operate with axioms of 'mental pathology' which are empirically based. He is not in a position to determine the substance of an individual's interest or its subjective value. As Bentham wrote: 'happiness, to be anything, must be composed of pleasures; and, be the man who he may, or what it is that gives pleasure to him, he alone can be judge.'[78] This has important consequences for Bentham's theory of justice. Firstly, though pleasure is a single sensation, the legislator cannot assume that all individuals react in the same way to the creation of particular pleasures. Different individuals can derive different quantities of pleasure from the same end. Therefore, the legislator is unable to secure

[77] Bowring, iv. 542.
[78] *Not Paul. but Jesus* (London, 1823), p. 394.

each individual's substantive conception of interest. Secondly, the legislator cannot provide precise calculations of the value of pleasure. Thus, he is unable to found the sort of rationalistic 'political arithmetic' which Halévy attributes to Bentham. Thirdly, because the legislator is limited in his ability to form precise calculations of the value of individual subjective experience he attempts to provide public reasons for action based on observation and experience. In the theory of justice developed in the remainder of this work it will be seen how Bentham uses the concepts of expectation and disappointment as public criteria of pleasure and pain. It will also become clear that Bentham was concerned with the conditions necessary for interest satisfaction rather than the realization of substantive interests as the means of maximizing social well-being. The necessary conditions of interest satisfaction are based on the axioms of mental pathology which are inferred from experience and observation. Therefore, the most important part of Bentham's psychological theory was the empirical portion rather than the attempt to provide an objective calculus of pleasure.

Before turning to the details of Bentham's theory of justice I will discuss the function of the principle of utility. To this I now turn.

3

The Principle of Utility and the Criterion of Moral Judgement

IN addition to providing the basis of Bentham's psychological theory, the 'two sovereign masters' of pleasure and pain also provide the foundation of his moral theory. Thus he wrote: 'It is for them alone to point out what we ought to do, as well as to determine what we shall do.'[1] This chapter is concerned with Bentham's principle of utility which is built upon the concepts of pleasure and pain.

While the 'two sovereigns' passage provides some indication of the direction in which he developed his psychological theory it provides little substantial idea of the character of his moral theory. It is universally accepted that Bentham was a utilitarian, but it is not clear from this passage alone the sort of utilitarian theory that he adopted. Indeed it is an underlying premiss of my argument in this chapter and the rest of the work, that the first five chapters of *An Introduction to the Principles of Morals and Legislation* provide little indication of the true character of Bentham's utilitarian thought. This is despite the fact that they are still taken as the definitive statement of his moral theory.[2] As explained in the introductory chapter, the argument of this work advances the claim that Bentham had a utilitarian theory of distributive justice which was developed in the Civil Law writings. Furthermore, his utilitarian theory is not given a definitive statement in the first chapters of *An Introduction to the Principles of Morals and Legislation*, as many commentators have assumed,[3] rather the theory of distributive justice developed in the Civil Law writings reveals the true character of utilitarian morality of politics. In this chapter I will concentrate

---

[1] *IPML* (CW), p. 11.

[2] In his recent edition of a number of Essays by J. S. Mill, Alan Ryan introduces the collection with a selection from the first ten chapters of *IPML* as a definitive statement of Bentham's moral theory, in order to contrast it with Mill's theory of utility. See A. Ryan (ed.), *John Stuart Mill and Jeremy Bentham: Utilitarianism and other Essays* (Harmondsworth, 1987). While Ryan is a recent author who reflects the reliance on *IPML* as the definitive source of Bentham's theory of utility, he is only the most recent of a number of writers on the history of utilitarianism to make this assumption. See e.g. E. Albee, *A History of English Utilitarianism* (New York, 1902), A. Quinton, *Utilitarian Ethics* (London, 1989), and D. D. Raphael, 'Bentham and the Varieties of Utilitarianism', *Bentham Newsletter*, 7 (1983), 3–14, and id. (ed.), *British Moralists: 1650–1800* (2 vols., Oxford, 1969).

[3] Critics such as Parekh still use *IPML* as the primary source of Bentham's distinctively utilitarian thought. See Parekh 'Bentham's Justification of the Principle of Utility', in id., *Jeremy Bentham: Ten Critical Essays* (London, 1974).

largely on that portion of his utilitarian theory which is revealed in *An Introduction to the Principles of Morals and Legislation*, and other published writings such as *A Fragment on Government* and *Constitutional Code*, and show why they were not intended to express Bentham's complete utilitarian theory of morality.

The reaction of most commentators to Bentham's moral theory is generally dismissive. Thus the received interpretation[4] of Bentham's moral thought has characterized him as a crude act-utilitarian who contributed nothing to the development of utilitarian theory.[5] As J. B. Schneewind has argued, among most of his contemporaries Bentham's reputation was largely based on his advocacy of reform projects, and not on his moral theory.[6] This in part explains why Bentham's moral theory has received so little attention. Even those who were personally close to Bentham, like J. S. Mill, thought that he sacrificed any theoretical development in moral theory to his commitment to practical reform projects. Mill's interpretation has influenced the judgement of subsequent commentators who are equally dismissive of Bentham's moral theory. Thus Leslie Stephen, who was not wholly unsympathetic to Bentham's thought, could write that 'The writings in which Bentham deals explicitly with the general principles of Ethics would hardly entitle him to a higher position than that of a disciple of Hume without Hume's subtlety; or of Paley without Paley's singular gift of exposition.'[7]

He also argues that 'from Hume to J. S. Mill, the doctrine [utilitarianism] received no substantial alteration'.[8] Stephen's argument has influenced many subsequent writers on the history of utilitarianism.[9] Another historian of English utilitarianism, E. Albee, has argued that:

the one important respect in which Bentham departs from his predecessors is in his dubious attempt to reduce Ethics to 'moral arithmetic', in the grimly literal sense. This, however, cannot be regarded as a real advance in ethical theory, but quite the contrary. The inevitable conclusion, then, seems to be that Bentham contributed almost nothing of importance to Ethics, considered strictly as such, though he unquestionably did more than any of his contemporaries to bring the utilitarian theory into popular ethical discussions.[10]

---

[4] See Chap. 2 n. 2, above.

[5] Early expressions of the received interpretation are found in L. Stephen, *History of English Thought in the Eighteenth Century* (3 vols., London, 1876), and *The English Utilitarians* (3 vols., London, 1903), Albee, *A History of English Utilitarianism*, and E. Halévy, *The Growth of Philosophic Radicalism*, trans. M. Morris (London, 1972). Stephen's and Albee's interpretation is reflected in recent commentators such as J. P. Plamenatz, in *The English Utilitarians* (Oxford, 1966) and 'Bentham and his School', in *Man and Society* (2 vols., London, 1963).

[6] J. B. Schneewind, *Sidgwick's Ethics and Victorian Moral Philosophy* (Oxford, 1977), 129–30.   [7] Stephen, *The English Utilitarians*, i. 236.

[8] Id., *History of English Thought in the Eighteenth Century*, ii. 87.

[9] Plamenatz, *The English Utilitarians*, p. 22.

[10] Albee, *A History of English Utilitarianism*, p. 190.

In the last chapter it was argued that Bentham was not committed to the precise 'political arithmetic' which both Halévy and Albee accuse him of advocating.[11] Further, while Albee devotes a whole chapter to a writer like Hartley, two to Tucker and Cumberland, and three to Spencer, Bentham is dealt with in the same chapter as Paley. While Albee's work is no longer accepted as a standard history of utilitarian theory, along with those of Halévy and Stephen it remains influential among subsequent commentators. The problem is that it will not be possible to reassess Bentham's contribution to the development of utilitarian moral theory until his own theory receives a full and sympathetic interpretation which ranges beyond the first few chapters of *An Introduction to the Principles of Morals and Legislation*. The writings of Ryan[12] and Parekh[13] only serve to confirm the interpretation of Albee, Halévy, and Stephen in that they confine their attention to *An Introduction to the Principles of Morals and Legislation* as the primary source of Bentham's utilitarian theory. The further problem is that Bentham is consistently characterized as a crude act-utilitarian who thought little about the detail of his moral theory and the precise specification of the principle of utility. Unlike Mill, Bentham has not been the beneficiary of a body of revisionist scholars who have reassessed his theory in light of contemporary developments in utilitarian theory. Most works on his utilitarian theory have concentrated on the question of how he intended to reconcile an egoistic theory of motivation with a utilitarian theory of morality. The most discussed of recent works on Bentham's utilitarian theory, Lyons's *In The Interest of the Governed*, was devoted almost exclusively to this question. He argued, in contrast to the received interpretation, that individuals' self-interested motivations effected a natural harmony with the dictates of public benevolence over time, and, therefore, there was no incompatibility between self-interest and impartial benevolence in Bentham's thought. Lyons's theory has been criticized by most subsequent commentators. Unfortunately, the discussion that has centred on Lyons's theory has drawn attention away from any attempt to provide a systematic reinterpretation of Bentham's moral theory.[14] Consequently, there has been no discussion of the role of the principle of utility as a source of individual moral obligation or whether or not Bentham has a direct of indirect theory of utility.

The argument of this chapter will centre on three components of the received interpretation of Bentham's moral theory. The first section will be devoted to his use of pleasure and pain as the criteria of meaningfulness for

[11] Bentham uses the phrase 'political arithmetic' at Bowring, iv. 540.

[12] Ryan (ed.), *John Stuart Mill and Jeremy Bentham*, pp. 7–64.

[13] Parekh, 'Bentham's Justification of the Principle of Utility', pp. 96–119.

[14] Even H. L. A. Hart, who has written a number of important papers which reflect on Bentham's utilitarian moral theory, has failed to provide a systematic account of his moral theory. See Hart, *Essays on Bentham* (Oxford, 1982).

ethical terms, and will concentrate on the principle of utility as a metaethical principle. This will involve a discussion of whether he attempted to establish a strict synonymy between good and pleasure, and thus whether he committed the 'naturalistic fallacy', as G. E. Moore has suggested.[15] This section will show how the principle of utility functions as the criterion of moral judgement. The next section will deal with Bentham's justification of the principle of utility as the sole criterion of moral judgement. Here it will be argued that unlike Mill he did not attempt a formal defence of the principle of utility, but consciously rejected the possibility of providing such a defence. However, Bentham did attempt an informal defence of the principle by showing how rival metaethical principles were untenable because either they collapsed into absurdity or else they were unable to provide for the possibility of a public moral language.

The principles that will be considered are the 'principle of asceticism' and the 'principle of sympathy and antipathy'. This chapter will also briefly consider Bentham's rejection of natural-rights theories as possible candidates for the basis of morality. Though Bentham does not include natural rights theories in his discussion of the 'Principles Adverse to Utility' in *An Introduction to the Principles of Morals and Legislation*,[16] it is clear from his repeated attacks on the language of natural rights that he considered such theories as rivals to the principle of utility. In the course of outlining Bentham's rejection of natural-rights theories as morally basic, this section will explain the role of a utilitarian system of moral rights in his theory of distributive justice. The third and final section of this chapter discusses the principle of utility as an action-guiding principle and a source of individual moral obligations. This section will determine how Bentham intended the dictates of utility to be understood, and to what extent it was intended to function as a direct source of moral obligation for the legislator and individual agents.

Though H. L. A. Hart has suggested that Bentham adopts an indirect utilitarian theory of obligation[17], the conventional interpretation maintains that he was a direct act-utilitarian. A recent revisionist critic of Bentham, G. J. Postema has argued that he has an act-utilitarian theory. However, he does not discuss whether Bentham had a direct utilitarian theory which maintains that the legislator and the individual agent are under an obligation to pursue the maximum of social well-being.[18] Works within the received interpretation maintain that Bentham's act-utilitarianism was the source of direct utilitarian account of moral obligation, but this argument is rarely supported. Despite accepting that he had a direct utilitarian theory of

---

[15] Moore, *Principia Ethica*, p. 18.
[16] *IPML* (CW), pp. 17–33.
[17] Hart, 'Natural Rights: Bentham and John Stuart Mill', *Essays on Bentham*, pp. 86–7.
[18] G. J. Postema, *Bentham and the Common Law Tradition* (Oxford, 1986), 147–58, 210–17.

moral obligation these works also acknowledge the role of legal norms and rules in realizing the maximum social well-being. This results in arguments such as Lyons's claim that utilitarian theory in general and Bentham's in particular cannot account for legal rights.[19] Though Lyons's argument is unsuccessful there remains the question of how far Bentham intended legal rules and norms to function within his political theory as sources of obligation or whether they were intended to function as mere rules of thumb which are useful as a means of maximizing social well-being.

In the wider context of the present book the final section of this chapter will be the most significant. The overall object of this work is to argue that Bentham did not intend to supply a direct utilitarian theory of moral obligation, but rather that he employed a utilitarian theory of justice which provided the framework within which individuals could pursue their own conceptions of well-being. This chapter contributes to that end by showing that Bentham did not employ a direct act-utilitarian theory of moral obligation, and this is essential in order to make room for the theory of distributive justice as a component part of his political morality. It will also be argued that he did not reject a direct utilitarian theory simply because of contingent difficulties in determining the individual's subjective experience. In the last chapter it was argued that Bentham was aware of such difficulties. However, if these were the sole reason for rejecting a direct utilitarian policy then there remains the possibility that advances in technology might make it possible to pursue such a policy in the future. Therefore, if it is only contingent difficulties in constructing the utilitarian calculus that justify a reliance on liberal institutional arrangements, Bentham has not provided an adequate answer for those who argue that utilitarianism cannot accommodate individual entitlements.

In this chapter I argue that Bentham does not advocate a direct utilitarian theory of moral obligation, nor an indirect utilitarian theory of the sort attributed to J. S. Mill by Lyons or Gray.[20] However, I will not provide a detailed discussion of the reasons why Bentham forgoes an appeal to a direct utilitarian theory because these are not presented in the works considered in this chapter. They are to be found in the Civil Law writings which are discussed extensively in later chapters. The object of this chapter is a negative one as it argues that Bentham did not hold certain positions that have been traditionally attributed to him in the received interpretation of his political theory. Bentham's positive theory will be developed throughout the remainder of this work and summarized in the concluding chapter.

[19] D. Lyons, 'Utility and Rights', *Nomos*, 24 (1982), 107–38.
[20] J. Gray, *Mill On Liberty: A Defence* (London, 1983), and D. Lyons, 'Mill's Theory of Morality', *Nous*, 10 (1976), 101–20, 'Human Rights and the General Welfare', *Philosophy and Public Affairs*, 6 (1977), 113–29, 'Mill's Theory of Justice', *Values and Morality*, 1–20, and 'Benevolence and Justice in Mill', *The Limits of Utilitarianism*, pp. 42–70.

Finally, the connecting thread that runs between the three themes that are discussed in this chapter is that they are all found in the received interpretaion of Bentham's political theory. While the target of many of the arguments in this chapter will be Parekh, this is simply because he has criticized Bentham on all of these themes in one paper,[21] and is, therefore, a fair representative of that tradition of interpretation. He is not, however, alone in making such criticisms of Bentham's moral theory, and other proponents of the received interpretation will be considerered in the course of this chapter.

I

In the 'two sovereigns' passage Bentham argues that pleasure and pain 'point out what we shall do'.[22] The two concepts which are at the heart of his psychological theory also provide the basis for the principle of utility. However, the exact relationship between the concepts of pleasure and pain, and the formal concepts of moral discourse, good, right, and ought, has remained problematic. Some recent critics have argued that Bentham asserted an exact synonymy between the concept of pleasure and good. Therefore, that action which produces the greatest amount of pleasure is equivalent to that action which produces the most good. Parekh describes Bentham's position as asserting that 'pleasure and good are conceptually identical and two different ways of describing the same thing. Pleasure, in other words, is not just a good, or *the* good, but *goodness itself*.'[23] He then attempts to argue that this synonymy forms the basis of Bentham's defence of the principle of utility, despite the fact that Bentham claimed no such proof could be provided or was necessary. Plamenatz also argues that Bentham attached a descriptive meaning to moral terms so that they mean 'conducive to the greatest amount of pleasure'. He writes that Bentham 'usually defines a right action as the action which under the circumstances is conducive to the greatest amount of pleasure, or to the greatest excess of pleasure over pain.'[24] On the basis of this descriptive definition of these terms Plamenatz argues that Bentham attempted to infer the principle of utility from statements concerning what one ought to do or what it is right to do. If the meaning of the terms right and ought is given by the greatest amount of pleasure, then it is possible to infer one's obligations simply from the meaning of the terms. Thus the statement; 'x is the right action' means that the action x is that which results in the greatest amount of pleasure. Consequently, Plamenatz argues that Bentham thought a person's obligations could be inferred from the meaning of the term ought. If this was Bentham's position then it is seriously weakened by the fact that the

---

[21] Parekh, 'Bentham's Justification of the Principle of Utility', pp. 96–119.
[22] *IPML* (CW), p. 11.
[23] Parekh, *Ten Critical Essays*, p. 103.
[24] Plamenatz, *Man and Society*, ii. 2.

definitions render statements that one ought to do that which results in the greatest amount of pleasure tautologous. They would end up simply asserting that to do that which results in the greatest amount of pleasure would result in the greatest amount of pleasure.

The arguments of Parekh and Plamenatz all draw on G. E. Moore's concept of the 'naturalistic fallacy'. Moore's thesis is one of the most notorious in the discussion of the logic of moral language in this century, and has consequently influenced the interpretation of the history of Ethics.[25] His thesis concerns the meaning of the term good in the context of moral discourse. In *Principia Ethica* he argued that the term good in the context of moral discourse is a simple indefinable term, and he compared it to the colour concept yellow which he argued is equally simple and indefinable. He wrote:

Consider yellow, for example. We may try to define it, by describing its physical equivalent; we may state what kind of light-vibrations must stimulate the normal eye, in order that we may perceive it. But a moment's reflection is sufficient to shew that those light-vibrations are not themselves what we mean by yellow . . . Yet a mistake of this simple kind has commonly been made about 'good'. It may be true that all things which are good are *also* something else, just as it is true that all things which are yellow produce a certain kind of vibration in the light. And it is a fact, that Ethics aims at discovering what are those other properties belonging to all things which are good. But far too many philosophers have thought that when they named those other properties they were actually defining good; that these properties, in fact, were simply not 'other', but absolutely and entirely the same with goodness. This view I propose to call the 'naturalistic fallacy'.[26]

In order to defend the claim that good is indefinable Moore drew on a chemical model of analysis, where a word is defined by breaking it down into its component parts in the same way that a chemical compound is analysed by resolving it into its constituent elements. Good, however, cannot be analysed and is, therefore indefinable in the same way as yellow is simple and indefinable. An 'open question' argument is used to show that good cannot be analysed into any natural property. This implies that the term good does not stand for any natural property such as pleasure or desire because it is always reasonable to raise the meaningful question: *Is pleasure good?* Thus Moore wrote:

it is very easy to conclude that what seems to be a universal ethical principle is in fact an identical proposition; that if, for example, whatever is called 'good' seems to be pleasant, the proposition 'Pleasure is the good' does not assert a connection between

[25] The 'naturalistic fallacy' is introduced in Moore, *Principia Ethica*, p. 10. The literature on Moore's thesis is extensive and includes important discussions by W. K. Frankena, 'The Naturalistic Fallacy', *Mind*, 48 (1939), 464–77, R. M. Hare, *The Language of Morals* (Oxford, 1952), J. L. Mackie, *Ethics: Inventing Right and Wrong* (Harmondsworth, 1977), and A. N. Prior, *Logic and the Basis of Ethics* (Oxford, 1949).

[26] Moore, *Principia Ethica*, p. 10.

two different notions, but involves only one, that of pleasure, which is easily recognised as a distinct entity. But whoever will attentively consider with himself what is actually before his mind when he asks the question 'Is pleasure (or whatever it may be) after all good?' can easily satisfy himself that he is not merely wondering whether pleasure is pleasant.[27]

If pleasure is given as the meaning of good, as Bentham argues according to Parekh,[28] then the question *Is pleasure good?* would be equivalent to the question *Is pleasure pleasant?* and the claim that *Pleasure is good* would collapse into the tautologous claim that *Pleasure is pleasurable*.

There has been much discussion of Moore's claim, and whether it constitutes a fallacy. In one famous discussion, W. K. Frankena argues that at the most Moore's argument supports a 'definist fallacy' where the mistake consists in defining the word good in terms of another entity.[29] Even the effectiveness of this version of the thesis depends upon showing that good really is indefinable, and Frankena acknowledges that this is the true point of controversy. Therefore, for Parekh and Plamenatz to criticize Bentham in terms of Moore's 'naturalistic fallacy' raises more questions than it answers. Does Bentham acknowledge the indefinability of good and did he attempt to connect good and pleasure as synonyms as Parekh implies? Also, does Bentham attempt to infer the principle of utility from a descriptive definition of certain basic moral concepts in terms of that which results in the greatest quantity of pleasure, as both Parekh and Plamenatz argue?

Moore certainly thought that Bentham committed the 'naturalistic fallacy'[30] because he defined right and good interchangeably rather than regarding the right as those actions which are a means to what is good. As both Parekh and Plamenatz offer no textual evidence for their claims, it suggests that they have relied on Moore's argument and subsequent reinterpretations of the 'naturalistic fallacy' instead of any detailed discussion of what Bentham actually said. Moore's argument is not concerned with the detailed interpretation of Bentham's moral theory so it is not surprising that he offers little evidence for his contention. This suggests that this element of the received interpretation of Bentham's moral theory rests on nothing stronger than the testimony of G. E. Moore. Following Hume, Bentham was always conscious of the requirement not to conflate descriptive and normative statements. However, the claim advanced by Parekh and Plamenatz, that Bentham defined right in terms of utility suggests they thought Bentham committed the 'naturalistic fallacy' in the more precise formulation offered by Moore.

The first chapters of *An Introduction to the Principles of Morals and*

---

[27] Moore, *Principia Ethica*, p. 16.
[28] Parekh, *Ten Critical Essays* p. 103.
[29] Frankena, 'The Naturalistic Fallacy', pp. 464–77.
[30] Moore, *Principia Ethica*, pp. 18–19.

Legislation offer no substantial corroboration of the claim of those commentators who have relied on Moore's argument. The closest that Bentham comes to defining good in terms of the general happiness can be seen in two passages in the first chapter. In the first he wrote: 'By utility is meant that property in any object, whereby it tends to produce benefit, advantage, pleasure, good, or happiness, (all this in the present case comes to the same thing).'[31] Here Bentham claims that good and pleasure are extensionally equivalent, and this can be interpreted to mean that they are synonyms. However, from the context of the passage it is clear that Bentham was not trying to establish an identity of meaning between these terms. Instead he used them all in an informal manner to refer to the ultimate object of value without implying any ontological identity between them. This passage certainly offers no evidence for Parekh's claim that Bentham intended good and pleasure to function as synonyms. In the second passage Bentham wrote:

Of an action that is comformable to the principle of utility, one may always say either that it is one that ought to be done, or at least that it is not one that ought not to be done. One may say also, that it is right it should be done; at least that it is not wrong it should be done: that it is a right action; at least that it is not a wrong action. When thus interpreted, the words *ought*, and *right* and *wrong*, and others of that stamp, have a meaning: when otherwise they have none.[32]

Again this passage asserts that the terms right and ought only have meaning when used in the context of the principle of utility. It does not claim that pleasure and right are synonyms. In fact good does not appear among the list of fifty-four 'Synonyms to the word "pleasure" ' which Bentham gives in the *Table of the Springs of Action*.[33] It must necessarily follow that if good is not a synonym for pleasure then pleasure cannot function as a synonym for good. This lends support to Amnon Goldworth's claim that 'There is no passage in Bentham's writings where he expresses the view that pleasure is good or good is pleasure, in the sense of defining the terms "pleasure" and "good".'[34]

What is clear from the two passages above is that Bentham is not attempting to establish an identity between good and pleasure. Instead his argument is rather more subtle. These two passages show that he is giving a philosophical explanation of the meaning of these moral terms, and this involves establishing the framework for their effective employment. The principle of utility is used by Bentham as a metaethical principle which provides the criterion of meaningfulness for moral judgements, and for the terms of moral discourse. The criterion he adopts for the meaningfulness of

---

[31] *IPML* (CW), p. 12. [32] Ibid., p. 13.

[33] Deontology (CW), p. 87.

[34] A. Goldworth, 'Bentham's Concept of Pleasure and its Relation to Fictitious Terms', *Ethics*, 82 (1972), 335.

such terms are derived from reflection on the point of moral discourse. In another passage from *An Introduction to the Principles of Morals and Legislation* Bentham wrote:

By the principle of utility is meant that principle which approves or disapproves of every action whatsoever, according to the tendency which it appears to have to augment or diminish the happiness of the party whose interest is in question: or, what is the same thing in other words, to promote or to oppose that happiness.[35]

In this passage it is clear that the principle of utility is supposed to function as the criterion of moral judgement. It also shows that Bentham was aware that moral judgements reflect approval and disapproval, they commend and condemn actions. Therefore, they are not merely descriptive judgements as the 'naturalistic fallacy' suggests. Consequently, the terms of moral discourse reflect the function of moral judgements, and are not merely descriptive terms as Plamenatz suggests.[36] Bentham's agument is that these expressions of approval or disapproval must be governed by the principle of utility because this alone provides an objective criterion for determining between such judgements. Therefore, when moral discourse is used it is either concerned with the effects of certain conduct on the community as a whole or else it is meaningless. This is what Bentham meant when he wrote: 'When thus interpreted, the words *ought*, and *right* and *wrong*, and others of that stamp, have a meaning: when otherwise, they have none.'[37] The principle of utility which links moral judgements with the effect of conduct on the well-being of the community is a metaethical principle because it provides the criterion of meaningfulness of moral terms. This is not the same as providing analytical definitions of the terms of moral discourse. Therefore, there is no ground for arguing that Bentham commits the 'naturalistic fallacy' by attempting to establish an identity of meaning between good and pleasure. The identification of the criterion of meaning for moral discourse does not involve any simple process of definition as G. E. Moore suggests in his thesis of the 'naturalistic fallacy'.

There remains one apparent difficulty that the metaethical principle which determines the meaningfulness of moral discourse is the principle of utility, and is, therefore, a normative principle or principle of moral judgement. This leaves the question whether Bentham does not try and derive the normative principle from the metaethical principle, and thus derive an ought from an is. If this is so then Bentham could still be described as committing a version of the 'naturalistic fallacy', as it has sometimes been interpreted in this manner, and he would be subject to Plamenatz's criticism that he tried to derive the principle of utility from his definition of moral terms. However, there is sufficient textual evidence to refute this claim.

[35] *IPML* (CW), pp. 11–12.
[36] Plamenatz, *Man and Society*, pp. 1–6.
[37] *IPML* (CW), p. 13.

Bentham was unequivocal in claiming that the normative principle of utility could not be proved. He wrote:

Has the rectitude of this principle been ever formally contested? It would seem that it had, by those who have not known what they have been meaning. Is it susceptible of any direct proof? it should seem not: for that which is used to prove every thing else, cannot itself be proved: a chain of proofs must have their commencement somewhere. To give such proofs is as impossible as it is needless.[38]

This passage confirms that Bentham did not claim that the principle of utility is true by definition as Plamenatz has argued, and that he does not try to derive a normative proposition from a descriptive one.[39] The object of this section is not to defend Bentham's argument as conclusive for this depends on his ability to demonstrate that only the principle of utility can provide the conditions of meaningfulness for moral discourse. The history of Ethics demonstrates that the principle of utility is not universally regarded as the only possible criterion of meaningfulness in moral discourse. The aim of this section is simply to argue that Bentham did not commit a crude 'definist fallacy' in establishing the principle of utility, nor did he commit the 'naturalistic fallacy' if this is interpreted as deriving an ought from an is statement. However, though Bentham did not attempt to prove the principle of utility as the sole criterion of meaningfulness in moral discourse, and as the criterion of moral judgement, he did provide some indirect support for this claim. The next section will consider Bentham's strategy to support the principle of utility without providing a formal proof of that principle.

The claim that the principle of utility is the criterion of moral judgement is reflected in two of Bentham's most famous published works. The passages from *An Introduction to the Principles of Morals and Legislation* illustrate the role of the principle of utility as a standard of judgement. He wrote that the principle of utility is 'that principle which approves or disapproves of every action whatsoever, according to the tendency which it appears to have augment or diminish the happiness of the party whose interest is in question.'[40] He also argued that while men may not use the principle as a means of 'ordering of their own actions', as an action-guiding principle, they use it as a means 'for the trying of their own actions, as well as of those of other men' or as a standard of moral judgement.[41] Even in the most famous statement of the principle of utility in *A Fragment on Government*, Bentham wrote that: '*it is the greatest happiness of the greatest number that*

---

[38] Ibid.

[39] This interpretation of the meaning of Bentham's principle of utility was influenced by discussion in the following: A. Goldworth, 'Bentham's Concept of Pleasure and its Relation to Fictitious Terms', R. Harrison, *Bentham* (London, 1983), and 'The Only Possible Morality', *Proceedings of the Aristotelian Society* (suppl., 50 (1976), 21–42, H. L. A. Hart, 'Introduction', *IPML*, and R. D. Milo, 'Bentham's Principle', *Ethics*, 84 (1974), 128–39.

[40] *IPML* (CW), p. 12.   [41] Ibid.

is the measure of right and wrong',[42] implying that the principle of utility is the criterion by which the legislator and the individual citizen is supposed to judge all actions. This is also reflected in the motto of the good citizen, '*To obey punctually; to censure freely*'. The principle of utility functions as the standard by which the individual citizen and the legislator is to censure or judge the existing laws and institutions. However, at least in this context the principle of utility is not specified as an action-guiding principle in the sense that it does not specify individuals' obligations. If the principle of utility were an action-guiding principle in this context it would undermine the injunction to '*obey punctually*'.[43] This is because Bentham does not specify that the good citizen is to '*obey punctually*' only in those contexts where the greatest happiness of the greatest number will result.

In the third section of this chapter I will consider the principle of utility as an action-guiding principle given its role as the criterion of moral judgement in his published writings. Before turning to this problem I shall discuss Bentham's informal defence of the principle of utility.

II

In the last section it was argued that Bentham did not commit the 'naturalistic fallacy', and that contrary to Parekh's claim he did not attempt to prove the principle of utility on the basis of his theory of the meaning of the terms of moral discourse. This has only lent support to Bentham's own claim that the principle of utility cannot and need not be proved, as it is that on which any chain of moral reasoning must rest. However, when Bentham argues that the principle of utility cannot be proved he merely intends that no formal proof of the truth of the principle can be provided. This does not mean that there are no reasons which count in favour of the principle of utility as the basis of morality. In *An Introduction to the Principles of Morals and Legislation*, chapter 2, Bentham discusses two principles which he regards as possible rivals to the principle of utility: the principles 'of asceticism' and 'of sympathy and antipathy'. At this point Bentham is at his weakest, for most commentators suggest that he succeeded in merely caricaturing all rival conceptions of morality.[44] In this section I will discuss the defects of these two rival theories, along with the natural-rights arguments as a possible basis of morality.

Bentham did not attempt to define the basic concepts of moral discourse in terms of the principle of utility, but he did argue that it alone enabled moral discourse to function. If moral debate is to be effective, and Bentham was always concerned with the effectiveness of an institution or practice as the justification of its existence, then moral discourse must provide an

---

[42] *Fragment* (CW), p. 393.   [43] Ibid., p. 399.

[44] D. D. Raphael, 'Bentham and the Varieties of Utilitarianism', *Bentham Newsletter*, 7 (1983), 3–14.

objective criterion of moral judgement such that disputes can come to a rational settlement. He argument that only the principle of utility provided such an objective criterion. However, in order to establish this claim he had to show that no other metaethical principle could provide for the resolution of moral conflicts. This argument is reflected in a series of questions Bentham posed at the end of *An Introduction to the Principles of Morals and Legislation*, chapter 1. Firstly, however, he disposes of one easy objection to the principle of utility as the foundation of morality. He wrote:

When a man attempts to combat the principle of utility, it is with reasons drawn, without his being aware of it, from that principle itself. His arguments, if they prove any thing, prove not that the principle is *wrong*, but that, according to the application he supposes to be made of it, it is *misapplied*. Is it possible for a man to move the earth? Yes; but he must first find out another earth to stand upon.[45]

This passage was concerned with arguments that referred to the counter-intuitive consequences of the applications of the principle of utility as a ground for rejecting it as the basis of morality. In a footnote Bentham refers to Alexander Wedderburn who is reported to have described the principle of utility as expressed by Bentham as a 'dangerous one'.[46] Bentham was dismissive of Wedderburn's criticism on the grounds that the danger was merely that of a reduction in Wedderburn's power and wealth as the beneficiary of a number of superfluous offices. However, if this sort of criticism has any persuasiveness this is because it has been misapplied, and that standard which the critic uses in order to illustrate the counter-intuitive consequences is really the principle of utility. According to Bentham, in order for these criticisms to have any meaning they must be based on the principle of utility.

However, for those who still wish to contest the role of the principle of utility, he redirects attention from the shortcomings of particular utilitarian calculations to the fundamental objective of any political morality. Underlying Bentham's adoption of the principle of utility as the basic standard of morality is the view that it is concerned with the well-being of the community. If anyone rejects this claim then he asks what do they conceive the point of morality to be. In the following chapter, 'Of Principles Adverse to that of Utility', he applies this question to those moral principles which are not concerned with the communal well-being in order to argue that this alone militates against their acceptability. Bentham also questions whether a person who rejects the principle of utility is prepared to adopt any other principle, and if so whether this amounts to more then his own subjective preference. If the person accepts his own considered judgement as the sole criterion of morality, then it is legitimate to ask whether he accepts this for himself alone or does he either legislate for others by subjecting them to his own judgement or does he accept the anarchical conclusion of

[45] *IPML* (CW), p. 14.   [46] Ibid.

allowing them the equal right to apply their own judgement as the standard? In *An Introduction to the Principles of Morals and Legislations*, chapter 2 he applies this question to a class of principles he discusses under the heading of 'The Principle of Sympathy and Antipathy'.

The first of the 'Principles Averse to Utility' is the 'Principle of Asceticism'. According to Bentham this principle:

> approves or disapproves of any action, according to the tendency which it appears to have to augment or diminish the happiness of the party whose interest is in question; but in an inverse manner: approving of actions in as far as they tend to diminish his happiness; disapproving of them in as far as they tend to augment it.[47]

Bentham has been accused of caricaturing his opponents on the grounds that none of them held principles which approved of actions in so far as they diminished happiness, and disapproved of actions when they augment it. He does make a serious point in attacking this principle which applies to certain kinds of religious morality as well as Stoic ethics. Bentham admits that the Stoics did not raise pain and unhappiness to the level of the good, rather they only claimed that it is not an evil. The theological version of the principle has taught that the pursuit of pleasure is a self-indulgence, and that the pursuit of abstinence is a virtue.

In its weaker version, Bentham argued that the case for abstaining from certain pleasures is itself derived from a utilitarian judgement 'that certain pleasures, when reaped in certain circumstances, have, at the long run, been attended with pains more than equivalent to them.'[48] However, as Bentham has already stated, the misapplication of the principle is not sufficient to disprove it, nor does it provide grounds for a contrary principle. The stronger case, that pain is raised to the level of the good, is contested on the grounds that it is untenable as a principle of morality. He argued that even those who are partisans of this principle have not been able to apply it consistently as the sole principle of morality. For while on one level an individual can accept that pain is not an evil, if this is extended to the level of a political morality then society itself would collapse. Bentham wrote: 'The principle of asceticism never was, nor ever can be, consistently pursued by any living creature. Let but one tenth part of the inhabitants of this earth pursue it consistently, and in a day's time they will have turned it into a hell.'[49] To argue that pain is not an evil would allow all sorts of crimes to be tolerated along with institutions which serve the sinister interests of the minority at the expense of the majority. A morality which did not acknowledge its fundamental point as the well-being of the community would result in anarchy. Underlying Bentham's position is the claim that social interaction and a stable social order are premised on the universal

---

[47] *IPML* (CW), pp. 17–18.
[48] Ibid., p. 21.
[49] Ibid.

acceptance of communal well-being as the object of morality. He saw political society as an enterprise[50] which is directed at the well-being of the whole community. While those within the practice of morality might dispute what constitutes communal well-being, they have to accept this as the point of morality in order to be engaging in a dialogue which can terminate in an objective solution to practical problems. This is because the objective resolution of moral arguments is presupposed by the very practice of morality. Therefore, a principle which does not enable such objective resolutions is automatically disqualified as the basis of morality.

The importance of morality, and the need to solve practical problems and resolve disputes is based on Bentham's conception of the social enterprise. Therefore, the basic principle of morality must also be one that is consistent with this enterprise, and this implies that it premisses communal well-being as the object of morality. For Bentham, a shared moral language alone does not render social and political interaction possible. It is a shared conception of the point of social life and political morality which makes possible such a shared language.

It might be argued that Bentham spoils his case by caricaturing his opponents, as most commentators agree that none of them ever held the strong view that pain and evil are not bad, and therefore, ought to be tolerated or promoted within society. However, there is a substantial point underlying Bentham's deliberate overstatement of his opponents' case. If the claim that pain is not an evil is raised to the status of the foundation of morality then it follows that any action which causes pain is not necessarily wrong, and there is a good case for tolerating it. This, as Bentham has argued, would mean the destruction of society. If, on the other hand, it is argued that certain painful actions are not to be tolerated or are to be considered evil, then he asks what criterion is used to make such distinctions? His point is that it cannot be the principle of utility, as that has been forgone, so the follower of the 'principle of asceticism' cannot argue that those actions which are most destructive to the communal good should be condemned. Yet if it is not the principle of utililty, what grounds can be applied? The 'principle of asceticism', and those who argue that pain is not an evil have no objective criterion for rejecting actions which are destructive to the community. It is this absence of criteria for the limitation of the application of the principle which is the main target of Bentham's criticism, and is why he caricatures the position in order to show the consequences of its unlimited application.

The same argument about the absence of objective criteria for the application of the principle is raised in the case of the second principle, that

---

[50] The idea that social life is premissed by any one rationally determinable enterprise is criticized in M. Oakshott, *Rationalism in Politics* (London, 1962) and *On Human Conduct* (Oxford, 1975), and in F. A. Hayek, *The Constitution of Liberty* (London, 1960).

of 'sympathy and antipathy'. This principle includes all moral principles which rely on an internally perceived criterion for their application. He wrote:

By the principle of sympathy and antipathy, I mean that principle which approves or disapproves of certain actions, not on account of their tending to augment the happiness, nor yet on account of their tending to diminish the happiness of the party whose interest is in question, but merely because a man finds himself disposed to approve or disapprove of them: holding up that approbation or disapprobation as a sufficient reason for itself, and disclaiming the necessity of looking out for any extrinsic ground.[51]

Bentham's target in this passage is a simplistic emotivism which maintains that all moral principles are simply expressions of a particular individual's approval and disapproval. Under this heading Bentham includes the theories of Shaftesbury, Hutcheson, Hume, Beattie, Price, Clarke, and Wollaston. Bentham, again lapses into caricature, for none of the authors argues that whatever a particular individual disapproves of is wrong and whatever he approves is right. What does unite them, and what is the real target of Bentham's criticism is that all of these writers rely on a subjective criterion in order to distinguish between right and wrong. Thus he is attacking the possibility of moral sense theories and all other theories which rely on similar notions, such as 'common sense', 'understanding', 'rule of right', 'right reason', and 'doctrines of election'. None of these theories makes appeal to an external or objective criterion to distinguish between right and wrong. The ultimate criterion is internal, and the problem with a reliance on this is brought out by consideration of 'doctrines of election' which are the purest form of the thesis. In the absence of an external criterion the individual can only rely on his own persuasion that he is one of the elect. Consequently, there is no effective difference between being one of the elect and merely being of the persuasion that one belongs to the elect. Similarly, with any subjective criterion, there is nothing to distinguish between the dictates of a 'moral sense' and what the individual thinks are the dictates of his 'moral sense'. For Bentham these theories collapse into mere subjective persuasion. Therefore, they have the anarchical consequence that good or right are whatever the individual says they are, for there is no way of providing an objective determination between the dictates of 'moral sense' and a mistaken belief about the dictates of 'moral sense'. Thus Bentham argued:

It is manifest, that this is rather a principle in name than in reality: it is not a positive principle of itself, so much as a term employed to signify the negation of all principle. What one expects to find in a principle is something that points out some external consideration, as a means of warranting and guiding the internal sentiments of approbation and disapprobation: this expectation is but ill fulfilled by a proposition,

[51] *IPML* (CW), p. 25.

which does neither more nor less than hold up each of those sentiments as a ground and standard for itself.[52]

The anarchical consequences of the 'principle of sympathy and antipathy' differ depending upon whether the proponent of the theory accepts his own judgements as binding upon all others or if he allows the same right to all others to judge according to their own perceptions of right and wrong. In the former case the problem is the lack of a criterion of consistency. Without such a criterion, moral judgements become effectively meaningless, and this undermines the practice of morality. In the second case if everyone is free to judge right and wrong as they see fit, then again there is no consistency and the possibility of morality collapses. Bentham saw morality as an enterprise directed to achieving the well-being of the community. However, if each person is free to make the terms of moral discourse conform to his own particular usage and judgements, then there is no way of arbitrating between the ends of different individuals. Morality is concerned with the rules of effective social interaction, but these depend on a shared conception of the enterprise of social interaction. A system of moral judgement that lacks any public criterion of consistency cannot embody this shared conception of the enterprise of social activity. Thus the 'principle of sympathy and antipathy' is anarchical precisely because it is contrary to the enterprise of effective social interaction, and resolves the social world into conflicting individuals who are incomprehensible to each other, and therefore, antagonistic.

The third rival conception of morality is posed by natural-rights theory. Bentham does not discuss these theories separately in *An Introduction to the Principles of Morals and Legislation*, but he does devote much attention elsewhere to refuting the claims of declarations of rights.[53] While it is common to see Bentham's criticism of natural rights as a criticism of moral-rights theories I will concentrate on this criticism as distinct from all moral-right theories. Although Bentham was consistently opposed to natural rights, much of the thrust of his criticism was directed against declarations of rights, and the assumptions implicit in such declarations that rights play a foundational role in political morality. This in part explains the ridicule that Bentham heaps on the construction of the articles of the French Declaration of 1789 in 'Anarchical Fallacies'.[54] Despite his obvious hostility to the

---

[52] Ibid.

[53] Bentham's most famous criticism of the doctrine of natural rights is his detailed refutation of the Declaration of Rights of the French National Assembly contained in his 'Anarchical Fallacies' (Bowring, ii. 496–529). He also discusses natural rights in 'Pannomial Fragments' (Bowring, iii. 218–21, 'Of the Levelling System', Bowring, i. 358–64, and *Supply without Burthen*, Stark, i. 309–10, and 332–7.

[54] The best discussions of Bentham's attack on natural rights are: Hart, 'Natural Rights: Bentham and John Stuart Mill', *Essays on Bentham*, pp. 79–104, L. W. Summer, 'Rights Denaturalised' in R. G. Frey (ed.), *Utility and Rights* (Oxford, 1985), 20–41, and W. L. Twining, 'The Contemporary Significance of Bentham's Anarchical Fallacies', *Archiv für*

language of rights and his reliance on a sanction theory of duty for his analysis of this concept, it would be wrong to view him as necessarily hostile to the substantive claims of all contemporary moral-rights theories. Indeed, one of the aims of this work is to demonstrate that Bentham developed a utilitarian theory of entitlements which he could have described in terms of the language of rights. That Bentham chose consistently to avoid using the language of rights, and employ in its place the language of securities and securities against misrule[55] is traceable to his horror at the progress of the French Revolution and the Terror which he saw as following from the methodology of the declaration. One recent commentator[56] has even suggested that proximity to the events of the French Revolution is what explains the difference in attitude between Bentham and J. S. Mill to the language of rights. Mill argues from substantially the same position as Bentham, yet never saw any difficulty in reconciling the language of moral rights with a utilitarian theory. The principle of utility could provide precisely those existence conditions and criteria for the application of rights which, according to Bentham is lacking in the case of natural rights.

It will be seen that while Bentham's argument is effective against natural-rights theories it is not necessarily so against all moral-rights theories. However, given that the target was natural-rights theories it is disingenuous to criticize Bentham for not providing an argument that is effective against a wider range of targets.[57] In 'Anarchical Fallacies' Bentham wrote: '*Natural rights* is simple nonsense: natural and imprescriptible rights, rhetorical nonsense—nonsense upon stilts.'[58] This passage clearly shows his intention was to criticize natural-rights theories, and this contention is further supported by a passage from 'Pannomial Fragments', where he wrote: 'There are no other than legal rights—no natural rights—no rights of man, anterior or superior to those created by the laws. The assertion of such rights, absurd in logic is pernicious in morals.'[59]

The argument that natural rights are 'absurd in logic', rests on the claim that in order to be effective a right requires the imposition of duties on all those who are not the beneficiaries of the right. A duty in turn requires a normative force, or that which creates obligations as conclusive reasons for action. On Bentham's analysis of law the normative force of a duty is

---

Rechts- und Sozialphilosophie, 61 (1975), 325–56. Neither Hart nor Twining stress any possible distinction between natural rights theories and moral rights theories. Sumner alone concentrates on Bentham's arguments against natural rights as opposed to all types of rights theory.

[55] 'Securities Against Misrule', in Jeremy Bentham, *Securities Against Misrule and other Constitutional Writings for Tripoli and Greece*, ed. P. Schofield (CW) (forthcoming).
[56] Sumner, *The Moral Foundation of Rights* (Oxford, 1987), p. 140.
[57] Twining, 'The Contemporary Significance of Bentham's Anarchical Fallacies'; see also the final essay in J. Waldron, *Nonsense upon Stilts: Bentham, Burke and Marx on the Rights of Man* (London, 1987).   [58] Bowring, ii. 501.   [59] Ibid., iii. 221.

provided by the sovereign, and the recognition of the sovereign as a legitimate authority and a valid source of rules. Modern positivist theories of law no longer make specific reference to a legislator, but still locate the normative force of a duty within a system of rules, which are accepted as being authoritative by those to whom they apply. The important point is that the normative force of the duty is located within an authoritative system of rules, whether that authority originates with a sovereign legislator's coercive power, or in conventional habits of obedience. In the case of a natural right there is no such authoritative system of rules which provides the normative force of a natural duty. This is because a natural right must itself be morally basic in order to provide the basis of morality. Once it ceases to be a morally basic criterion on which subordinate moral principles are based, the necessary incompatibility between natural rights and utilitarianism disappears, and with it part of the intuitive appeal of natural-rights theory. It might be argued that the normative force of a natural duty is located within it's relations to a system of natural laws. This simply relocates the problem, for while Bentham recognized the existence of natural causal laws or those on which science is based, he did not recognize the existence of natural normative laws. Unlike Locke, Bentham did not construct his moral theory within a Christian moral framework which is governed by moral laws.[60] In order for there to be natural normative laws, nature herself would have to be a legislator. This would involve the location of a criterion of authenticity by means of which those natural laws and the duties derived from them could be identified. The problem is that nature either offers no criterion of authenticity or else it offers an almost unlimited supply of criteria for identifying natural laws.

Thus Bentham wrote in *Supply without Burthen* that 'the language of natural rights require[s] nothing but a hard front, a hard heart and an unblushing countenance. It is from the beginning to the end so much flat assertion.'[61] By this Bentham meant that appeals to natural rights never solve any practical moral disputes. As has already been argued, Bentham took the solution of practical disputes as the purpose of the practice of morals. Therefore, if he showed that a rival principle could not provide a consistent criterion for determining moral judgements then he had placed

---

[60] The importance of the Christian framework of Locke's moral theory is emphasized in J. Colman, *John Locke's Moral Philosophy* (Edinburgh, 1983), and J. Dunn, *The Political Thought of John Locke* (Cambridge, 1969), and *Rethinking Modern Political Theory* (Cambridge, 1985), 13–67. Rosen has recently argued that Bentham's Moral and Political philosophy can be interpreted as a sustained attack on the received Lockeian doctrine of Liberalism. Part of this rejection of Locke's theory can be traced to Bentham's abandonment of a theological framework within which moral rights theories can function. Given this abandonment of Locke's theological framework Bentham saw the necessity to reject rights theories altogether and this explains his hostility to secularized versions of the Lockeian rights theory such as the French Declaration of Rights. See F. Rosen, 'Jeremy Bentham', in D. Miller, J. Coleman, W. Connolly, and A. Ryan (eds.), *The Blackwell Encyclopaedia of Political Thought* (Oxford, 1987), 37–40. [61] Stark, i. 335.

the burden of proof on the rival principle to provide an account of the practice of morals within which it functioned. Bentham did not mean to imply that in a particular case of practical decision-making an argument from the principle of utility will provide a criterion by which to resolve the dispute, whereas an appeal to natural rights will not. For given a natural law is it possible to derive subordinate principles which can be applied in order to provide determinate results. The difficulty with natural rights is in providing the criterion by which to identify a substantive rights claim. A further problem with rights theories is that given a case of conflict between two rights claims, the only criterion the natural-rights theorist can have for arbitrating between them is an internal one. This creates difficulties because an internal criterion only provides a rule for the application of a particular right, and it does not provide a priority principle which arbitrates between different rights claims. An appeal to an external criterion such as utility would provide a priority principle, but such an appeal would mean that the natural-right principle is no longer morally basic. The only possible alternative for the natural-rights theory is an appeal to an external criterion that is non-moral, for this would retain the status of the principle as morally basic. However, this raises again the problem that nature provides no such criterion for determining the application and priority of natural-rights principles, because virtually any natural characteristic could be appealed to as the criterion for determining moral priority. In 'Of the Levelling System'[62] Bentham illustrates how the lack of a priority principle which limits the application of a natural-rights principle results in absurd consequences. Having shown how the unrestricted extension of an equal right to substantive equality will undermine all social benefits, he responds to the charge that he is combating shadows because the principle was not meant to be applied in this way. He wrote:

It is for equality so far and so far only as it is practicable, and practicable to advantage shall we content? for the lopping off of superfluities of over grown and excessive opulence: for alleviating the sufferings of excessive misery: for planting and maintaining the virtuous rise of industrious proprietors for planting and maintaining plenty without luxury and independence without insolence. To push any system to an absurd excess, and then give the abuse as the system itself, what can be more uncandid or inconclusive?[63]

Bentham recognized that attempts could be made to limit the scope of application of the principle in the light of some of the consequences he referred to earlier in the work. However, the proponents of natural-rights theories have no right to make such modifications of the scope of the principle. If they make a tacit appeal to utilitarianism then they have abandoned the claim that the right is morally basic. If they did not make

---

[62] Bowring, i. 358–64.
[63] UC lxxxviii, 72.

such an appeal, then what was the criterion by which the application of the right should be governed? Bentham argued that there cannot be any such criterion consistent with a natural-rights claim. He wrote:

It is—not that you will find it difficult to stop at a proper place, but that you ought not to stop any where: . . . it is not that you may be led by the heat of temper to untoward accidents beyond the bounds which the principle you set out upon has prescribed to you, but that you can not stop anywhere short of ruin without dereliction of your principle.[64]

Bentham's fundamental criticism of natural-rights theories was that they lacked a criterion of authenticity just as the principles of 'asceticism' and 'sympathy and antipathy'. The absence of an identifying criterion and priority rules means they are unable to resolve practical moral questions. This automatically disqualifies them as the basis of morality. However, as with the other two principles considered, the most important ground for rejecting them is that they are anarchical. They fail to provide a rational objective structure for moral judgement, and thus undermine the conditions of social interaction. For without public and objective criteria of moral judgement, and a public framework for the resolution of disputes, the enterprise of society cannot continue, and the result is anarchy.

   Bentham's criticisms of rival moral principles are not comprehensive in the sense that he has not undermined all possible alternative bases of morality. However, his discussion is not as worthless as some have argued, for underlying the caricature is a series of important conditions which a rival moral principle would have to meet. Therefore, the principle of utility will only be disproved as the basis of morality if another principle can better satisfy these conditions.

III

The principle of utility has traditionally been interpreted as a principle of moral obligation and a source of authoritative reasons for action. Not only are individual agents supposed to determine right from wrong by appeal to the principle of utility, but they are also supposed to determine how to act. The principle of utility is on this interpretation a principle of practical reason. While much has been written about the justification of the principle of utility or its importance within Bentham's political thought, very little has been written about how it was supposed to function as the basis of practical reasoning. In this final section I will consider the relationship between the criterion of moral judgement and the basis of moral obligation.

   It is generally accepted by most commentators that Bentham had an act-utilitarian theory of morality. This interpretation is shared by those who subscribe to the received interpretation as well as revisionists like

---

[64] Ibid., 77.

Postema.[65] However, it is unclear what is implied by the claim that Bentham was an act-utilitarian. It could mean that the standard for judging actions and institutions is the principle of utility, but that these judgements are not the direct source of obligations or authoritative reasons for action. Or it could mean that an individual ought to do what in each case results in the greatest happiness. In the latter case the result is a direct utilitarian theory of moral obligation, and in the former an indirect theory. Postema does not make clear which interpretation is appropriate. In each case there are theoretical difficulties. In the former the problem is that of the relationship between the principle of utility as a directly applicable principle of judgement, but not as source of obligations. In the latter case the problem is that of the effects of a direct act-utilitarian policy.

The standard criticism of a direct act-utilitarian theory is that it places unrealistic demands on individual agents, and that it results in moral catastrophe.[66] If the individual is required to act according to the principle of utility, then it is quite possible that he could be obliged to act in a way that overrides individual rights and entitlements. In most cases this may not pose such a serious problem. However, it is argued that there is no reason why in certain circumstances this could not require the overriding of important rights, such as those to personal liberty or the right to life. Similarly, in the case of the legislator, if he is required to act on all occasions to maximize utility then there is the possibility that this might entail sacrificing the rights of minorities and punishing the innocent. While such questions have constituted the contemporary discussion of utilitarian moral theory, it would be wrong to think that these are simply modern problems which were not raised at the time Bentham was writing. One of the main criticisms raised against the radical act-utilitarian theory of Bentham's contemporary William Godwin was that if prevented the formation of expectations, and therefore undermined some of the most basic institutions of society. Honesty and promise-keeping are only two of the many social institutions that would have been destroyed by an unrestricted act-utilitarianism. J. B. Schneewind[67] paraphrases the argument of Thomas Green,[68] a critic of Godwin, when he writes: 'A good man of this kind

---

[65] Postema, *Bentham and the Common Law Tradition*, pp. 155–9.

[66] The problems of act-utilitarian theories are discussed in D. H. Hodgson, *The Consequences of Utilitarianism* (Oxford, 1967), D. Lyons, *Forms and Limits of Utilitarianism* (Oxford, 1965), J. L. Mackie, *Ethics: Inventing Right and Wrong* (Harmondsworth, 1977), and 'The Disutility of Act-Utilitarianism', *Philosophical Quarterly*, 23 (1973), 289–300, P. Singer, 'Is Act-Utilitarianism Self-Defeating', *Philosophical Review*, 81 (1972), 94–104, and G. J. Warnock, *The Object of Morality* (London, 1971). Rawls and Nozick interpret the problems of act-utilitarianism as a problem of providing an adequate account of distributive justice. See J. Rawls, *A Theory of Justice* (Oxford, 1972), and R. Nozick, *Anarchy, State, and Utopia* (Oxford, 1974).

[67] Schneewind, *Sidgwick's Ethics and Victorian Moral Philosophy*, p. 146.

[68] T. Green, *An Examination of the Leading Principle of the New System of Morals in Mr Godwin* (London, 1798).

would be worse than an ordinary villain, who, evil though he may be in some ways is at least predictable. A Godwinian would be totally unrealiable.' Godwin was not, however, the only object of such criticism. A similar argument is advanced against Bentham by Sir James Mackintosh in his *Dissertations on the Progress of Ethical Philosophy* (1830).[69] He argues that an act-utilitarian morality would undermine expectations by destroying social institutions such as promise-keeping, which are so vital to morality and ordered social interaction. Over one hundred and thirty years later the very same argument is used by G. J. Warnock in *The Object of Morality* (1971) and D. H. Hodgson in *The Consequences of Utilitarianism* (1967). Given that these arguments were current at the time Bentham was writing, it is possible that when Alexander Wedderburn is reported as describing Bentham's principle of utility as 'a dangerous one'[70] it is the consequences of an unrestricted principle to which he refers, and not to its implications for his own position and wealth, as Bentham suggests.

Though Rawls's criticism of utilitarianism is based on an attack on utilitarian practical reasoning, it also reflects a criticism of the consequences of act-utilitarian theories. Indeed, Rawls's argument that utilitarianism cannot account for individual entitlements depends on the premiss that the legislator and the individual are under an obligation to act in such a way as to maximize social well-being. This is implicit in his claim that teleological theories, of which utilitarianism is the most important example, define the good independently of the right.[71] He continues:

the theory accounts for our considered judgements as to which things are good (our judgements of value) as a separate class of judgements intuitively distinguishable by common sense, and then proposes the hypothesis that the right is maximizing the good as already specified.[72]

This argument entails that distributive considerations involving individual entitlements are independent of the specification of the good, and can at best be means to that end. Although rights and liberties may serve as contingent conditions for the maximization of the good, when they conflict with a more direct means to a greater quantity of the good they ought to give way. To override rights in this way is, according to Rawls, contrary to our understanding of their function, for it results in the claim that 'there is no reason in principle why the . . . violation of the liberty of a few might not be made right by the greater good shared by the many.'[73] There are two aspects to Rawls's argument. Firstly, he maintains that utilitarianism cannot provide for individual rights and titles, because any utilitarian justifiation of these practices is contingent upon their maximizing happiness. Secondly, he

---

[69] Sir J. Mackintosh, *Dissertations on the Progress of Ethical Philosophy* (Edinburgh, 1830).   [70] *IPML* (CW), p. 14.

[71] Rawls, *A Theory of Justice*, p. 25.   [72] Ibid.

[73] Rawls, *A Theory of Justice*, p. 26.

argues that even when a utilitarian theory does attempt to justify individual entitlements, it does so for inadequate reasons. This is because utilitarian thought is premissed on a model of rational decision-making which is only appropriate for an individual agent and not for a society. While an individual can discount present satisfactions against future satisfactions a utilitarian legislator cannot discount the satisfactions of some against those of others without failing to accord them full and equal moral respect as persons. The concept of right, which includes distributive justice, places specific requirements on an acceptable account of social and moral reasoning. Thus, the concept of right rules out the acceptability of principles which do not respect the rights and titles of individual agents.

One possible response to the Rawlsian challenge would be to accept the radical consequences of utilitarian morality even when this conflicts with accepted liberal values.[74] However, utilitarian theorists such as Bentham and Mill have accepted liberal values and individual entitlements. Therefore, any adequate account of Bentham's utilitarian theory must be able to supply a justification of such entitlements. If these individual entitlements are to have more than a contingent status within his political morality, then it must be shown that the specification of the principle of utility entails individual entitlements and a distributive principle. However, in order to show that the principle of utility can function as a principle of right, it is necessary to demonstrate that it is not a direct source of moral obligation, with the legislator and the individual agent being required to maximize social well-being in all circumstances.

The remainder of this work will provide the grounds for the claim that Bentham had a utilitarian theory of distributive justice which justifies individual rights and entitlements. In the remainder of this chapter I shall discuss the status of his principle of utility as an action-guiding principle.

Postema has recently argued that Bentham has a direct act-utilitarian theory of practical reason.[75] This entails that all actions and institutions must be justifiable in terms of the maximum of social well-being. He does not directly consider whether Bentham intended individual agents to be under a direct obligation to pursue the dictates of utility. However, he does suggest that the principle of utility is a direct action-guiding principle, writing that: 'It is not only the ultimate evaluative principle, it is the sole sovereign *decision principle*.'[76] Postema's argument is based on the

---

[74] One recent philosopher who has been prepared to accept the radical implications of an unrestricted act-utilitarianism is J. J. C. Smart ('An Outline of a System of Utilitarian Ethics', in J. J. C. Smart and B. Williams (ed.), *Utilitarianism For and Against* (Cambridge, 1973)). Historically, only W. Godwin appears to have accepted the full anarchical implications of an unrestricted act-utilitarianism. See Godwin, *Enquiry Concerning Political Justice*, ed. F. E. L. Priestley (Toronto, 1946).

[75] Postema, *Bentham and the Common Law Tradition*, pp. 147–90.

[76] Ibid., p. 159.

utilitarian justification of Bentham's legal theory. This shows that Postema does not think Bentham had a simple act-utilitarian theory which entails the legislator acting in all circumstances in order to maximize social well-being. In pursuit of the maximum of social well-being the utilitarian legislator relies on legal rights and norms as a means of providing the co-ordinating conditions of social interaction. Therefore, the legislator does not achieve the maximum of social well-being by distributing some positive good. Rather, he creates the conditions within which each individual is able to pursue his own end without conflicting with others. It is by providing the co-ordinating conditions of social interaction that the legislator creates a framework within which the maximum social well-being results. Postema also argues that Bentham relies on expectation utilities to justify these rules and practices within an act-utilitarian system. But as Postema makes clear, Bentham is referring to a species of utilities derived from adherence to a set of rules or norms. When and only when these rules give rise to significant utilities can they override direct utility calculations. They do not entail any principled restriction of the agents attention, and they do not provide authoritative reasons for action unless adherence to them will be maximally beneficial. While I accept much of Postema's argument it faces one important difficulty.

In discussing Lyons's argument that Bentham cannot account for the normative force of legal rights, Postema argues that Bentham simply rejects the claim that rights can function as authoritative reasons when they conflict with the conclusion of a utility calculation.[77] Therefore, an individual is free to assess the consequences of respecting a legal property right, and if he can increase social well-being while increasing his own well-being and not harming that of another, by ignoring the right he is free, indeed duty-bound, to do so. If the individual is under an obligation to maximize social well-being, then he must be under an obligation to ignore the right in such circumstances. This does not capture Bentham's intention. Bentham's discussion of security of property suggests that he was not prepared to sacrifice property rights to individual utility calculations.[78] Instead he argues the property is important as a source of well-being, and that it must be secured against interference. In *A Fragment on Government*, Bentham wrote that the motto of the good citizen was '*To obey punctually; to censure freely*'.[79] This suggests that while the individual citizen is free to judge the system of laws according to the principle of utility, he is, nevertheless, required to conform his actions to the requirements of the law. Finally, in the later writings on Civil Law, Bentham used the 'disappoint-ment-preventing principle' as the sole means of justifying interference with property rights. While Postema is right to argue that the justification of the

---

[77] Ibid., pp. 321–4.
[78] Bowring, i. 307–12.
[79] *Fragment* (CW), p. 399.

practice of rights within a utilitarian system must be reducible to utilitarian considerations, Bentham did not accept that individual utility calculations provided the grounds for moral obligation. Thus, Bentham did not have a direct act-utilitarian theory, as Postema suggests, for the principle of utility is not an authoritative source of reasons for action.

There are further problems for the interpretation of the principle of utility as a direct source of moral obligation. A direct utilitarian theory must be self-defeating if it implies that individual agents are obliged to act according to the dictates of the principle of utility. Bentham does not expressly develop this argument, but it can be derived from the importance he attaches to expectation as a condition of social well-being, and his interpretation of the practice of morality as an enterprise aimed at the communal good. The individual pursuit of utility must be self-defeating because the individual agent is unable to provide the conditions which co-ordinate his actions with others. He is unable to establish regular patterns of behaviour which give rise to expectations and expectation utilities. Therefore, his actions will not form part of a co-ordinated pattern of action from which the communal good arises. This argument does not rest on the claim that the individual agent cannot determine the balance of pleasure and pain. It is based on the more complex claim that morality is a collective enterprise, and is, therefore, concerned with the conditions of social interaction. According to Bentham, social well-being cannot arise out of uncoordinated individual action; otherwise his criticism of the 'principle of sympathy and antipathy' would collapse. Social interaction, and therefore social well-being, depends upon the existence of rules and norms which give rise to expectations and expectation utilities. If the individual agent is obliged to do that which maximizes social well-being then he will always have to calculate whether to act in accordance with these social rules, and this would undermine the development of expectations. If an individual will only respect a right when a utility calculation justifies his doing so, that right will not serve as a condition of expectations, because it remains an open question whether it functions as an authoritative reason for action. Unless legal norms and rights function as authoritative reasons they cannot function as a source of expectation. Expectations result from regularities of behaviour, which rights and legal norms can provide but which individual utility calculations cannot. The effectiveness of this argument depends on the claim that the most important source of utilities are those which are derived from or dependent upon the conditions of social interaction.

A similar argument applies in the case of the legislator. Bentham wrote:

It is plain, that of individuals the legislator can know nothing: concerning those points of conduct which depend upon the particular circumstances of each individual, it is plain, therefore, that he can determine nothing to advantage. It is only with respect to those broad lines of conduct in which all persons, or very large and permanent descriptions of persons, may be in a way to engage, that he can have any pretence for interfering; and even here the propriety of his interference will, in most instances, lie very open to dispute.[80]

This passage does not imply that the legislator cannot directly pursue the maximum of social well-being because he is unable to determine the content of subjective experience. Both Rawls and Hart argue that Bentham cannot be interpreted as asserting the radical inaccessibility of subjective experience for this would undermine the possibility of any form of interpersonal comparisons.[81] While Bentham was certainly aware of the difficulties involved in making interpersonal comparisons of interests, it would be implausible to argue that he thought no such comparisons could be made.

If the legislator were under the direct obligation of an act-utilitarian theory, he would face the same problems as the individual agent. While he would have a reason to conform his actions to rules in order to establish a regular pattern of behaviour, he would also have a reason to override those rights and laws he has created when the maximum of social well-being could be achieved. The creation of a stable pattern of expectations requires a level of consistency in the legislator's actions that would preclude his acting on the results of a direct utility calculation, if this interfered with them. An obligation to do that in each circumstance which maximizes social well-being would always leave open the possibility of the legislator having to override fixed patterns of expectations, and this would undermine the regularity of the legislator's behaviour on which the stability of expectation depends. While all authoritative reasons for action must be reducible to act-utilitarian ones, this does not imply that the individual or the legislator is under a direct obligation to pursue the maximum social well-being in all circumstances.

In contrast to Postema's direct act-utilitarian interpretation of Bentham's principle as an action-guiding principle, H. L. A. Hart has recently suggested that Bentham had an indirect utilitarian theory. He writes:

Bentham's statement that this principle is the standard of right and wrong 'in the field of morality in general' and of government in particular must be taken to mean that it is a standard of morality not for the *guidance* of individual conduct but only for the critical *evaluation* of it, determining what may be properly demanded by way of action from individuals and when moral sanctions may be used to obtain it. This is consistent with remarks made by Bentham such as his statement that 'men in general embrace this principle . . . if not for the ordering of their own actions, yet for the trying of their own actions, as well as those of other men.'[82]

In a discussion of Bentham and Mill on the subject of natural rights, Hart argues that Bentham 'roughly sketched . . . an indirect variant of utilitarian

[80] *IPML* (CW), p. 290.
[81] See Rawls, *A Theory of Justice*, p. 91, and Hart, 'Bentham: Lecture on a Master Mind', *Proceedings of the British Academy*, 48 (1962), 304.
[82] Hart, 'Introduction', *IPML* (CW), p. xlviii.

theory'.[83] Hart's argument is that Bentham cannot have had a direct utilitarian theory of moral obligation because he had a sanction theory of duties. He writes:

Though Bentham calls the principle of utility 'the measure of right and wrong' and regards it as constituting the standard by which both the law and the conventional morality of any society should be judged, he plainly does not think that obligations or duties (which he treated, as Mill also did, as equivalent) are generated by the principle of utility. For him, a necessary condition of a man having an obligation to act in a certain way is the likelihood of suffering in the event of failure so to act.[84]

Hart argues that the principle of utility does not give rise to obligations because these are dependent upon the imposition of sanctions. Therefore, it is these sanctions which are the direct reasons for action, and utility is only indirectly a source of obligation, in so far as these obligations can be given a utilitarian justification. Bentham provides for the possibility of moral obligations within his theory, by relying on the moral sanction as a means of giving effect to these obligations. However, there is no necessary connection between the requirements of the moral sanction and the requirements of utility unless the conventional morality is also an explicitly utilitarian morality, whereby the moral and social pressures which create moral obligations are informed by the principle of utility. The principle of utility does not directly give rise to obligations because these are dependent upon the imposition of sanctions. Therefore, it is these sanctions which are the direct reasons for actions, and utility is only indirectly a source of obligations, in so far as these obligations can be given a utilitarian justification. Consequently, while Lyons is correct to point out in his discussion of Mill's moral theory, that Bentham's sanction theory of duties does not give rise to an account of moral obligations, he is wrong to attempt to draw a substantial contrast between Bentham's and Mill's theory of obligation.[85] For both thinkers, to be under an obligation one must be liable to suffer punishment for non-compliance with one's duty, but just as Mill introduces the notion of justifiable constraints, in order to give an account of *moral* obligation, so it can be argued that Bentham was only required to accept an obligation as *moral* when it was justifiable in terms of the principle of utility.

Bentham's discussion of the moral sanction as a source of obligations can be a diversion here, for he merely intended to identify a possible source of sanctions, namely those derived from the opinion of others, and not to endorse the opinions embodied in conventional morality as giving rise to genuine *moral* obligations. However, any system of obligations will give rise

---

[83] Id., *Essays On Bentham*, pp. 86–7.
[84] Ibid.
[85] Lyons, 'Mill's Theory of Morality', p. 111.

to expectation utilities, and therefore will have a presumptive justification. But that does not mean that some other configuration of obligations and morally justifiable rules could not give rise to a greater overall sum of utility. Indeed the function of the 'security providing-principle',[86] within Bentham's Civil Law writings, was to identify a distribution of rights and titles which could form the basis of a utilitarian code of law.

In order for Hart's argument to be successful, it would have to be the case that Bentham did not intend the principle of utility to be a direct source of reason for action independently of the existence of conventional moral sanctions. However, Bentham did acknowledge the principle of utility as a reason for action when he wrote: 'Every act which promises to be beneficial upon the whole to the community (himself included) each individual ought to perform of himself.'[87] He clearly thought the direct appeal to the principle of utility could be a source of reasons to act. Therefore, Hart cannot be right to argue that Bentham had an indirect theory of obligation, as this is usually understood to imply that the principle of utility functions as a criterion for determining rules which are the source of moral obligation.[88] However, the possibility of the direct appeal to the principle of utility as a source of authoritative reasons for action raises again the problems discussed in relation to Postema's interpretation. How is a sanction theory of duties to be reconciled with the principle of utility as a source of authoritative reasons for action? The solution is to be found in Bentham's use of the term ought. It has become an unquestioned convention of contemporary Ethical theory to regard the statement *I ought to do x* as equivalent to the statement *I am under an obligation to do x*.[89] This convention is partly the consequence of Kantian Ethics although it is also traceable to the Christian Natural Law tradition. However, given Bentham's sanction theory of duties it is unlikely that he intended his use of the term ought to imply the presence of an obligation or duty. Thus, conventional moral obligations are indirectly related to the principle of utility via the mediation of institutions and practices which confer rights and duties. To this extent Bentham employs indirect utilitarian strategies, and this supports Hart's theory. Yet, when Bentham wrote: 'Every act which promises to be beneficial upon the whole to the community (himself included) each individual ought to perform of himself', he is not arguing that every individual is under a duty so to act, rather he is arguing that he has a reason though not necessarily a conclusive reason, so to act. His use of the term

---

[86] UC lxi, 47, and BL Add. MS 33550, fo. 55.

[87] *IPML* (CW), p. 285.

[88] Unlike rule-utilitarian theory, the act-utilitarian principle at the source of indirect theories of obligation remains a source of appeal for modifying the rules and institutions which give rise to moral obligation. The problems of rule-utilitarianism are discussed in Lyons, *Forms and Limits of Utilitarianism* (Oxford, 1965).

[89] This convention is questioned in C. H. Whiteley, 'On Duties', *Proceedings of the Aristotelian Society*, 53 (1953), 97–104.

ought in this context signifies reasons for action, unlike the stronger Kantian sense which implies the presence of duties and obligations. These utilitarian reasons are not necessarily conclusive, whereas an obligation derived from an institution with a utilitarian justification is intended to be conclusive.

Bentham does not have a direct act-utilitarian theory of moral obligation, nor does he have a strictly indirect theory. The interpretations of both Postema and Hart capture aspects of Bentham's theory. Hart is right to maintain that obligations are dependent on the existence of coercive sanctions. Therefore, the principle of utility cannot be a direct source of obligations. However, Bentham maintains that even in the absence of sanctions an individual has a reason to act in accordance with the principle of utility, though not a conclusive reason. Postema is also right to argue that all authoritative reasons for action must be justifiable in terms of the principle of utility. However, he overstates his case by arguing that the individual's obligations are simply determined to appeal to utility calculations. The principle of utility as a practical principle is not concerned with the balance of pleasure over pain. Instead, it requires individuals to act in accordance with rights and legal norms which direct action toward the end of the maximum of social well-being. The co-ordination of social interaction requires a respect for fixed patterns of behaviour. Because the communal good depends on the co-ordination of social interaction the principle of utility as an action-guiding principle necessarily reflects the rights and norms which constitute those conditions. While moral judgement is concerned with quantities of pleasure and pain considered in the abstract, these are necessarily dependent upon rights, duties, and rules. An individual agent determines what he ought to do by consideration of the rights and duties which constitute the social world. He does not have to abstract from these practices the quantity of pleasure over pain. The effectiveness of this argument depends on Bentham's claim that the conditions of social interaction facilitate the most significant class of pleasures. Those natural pleasures which are independent of the conditions of social organization are insufficient to account for the variety of interests that individuals have in modern societies.

These conditions of social interaction provide the foundation of obligations because of the significant utilities that are derived from them. However, it is not the greater utility which transforms them into conclusive reasons for action. They become conclusive reasons for action because the legislator imposes coercive sanctions on non-compliance with them. Therefore, while the greater utility derived from these practices accounts for their utilitarian justification, their effectiveness as conclusive reasons for action does not depend on a utility calculation, but on the threat of sanctions. This is why I have argued that the individual agent is not under a direct obligation to do that which maximizes social well-being, for this would involve the rejection of the claim of rights in determining how to act. Instead, the individual agent is required to act in accordance with rights and duties because of the imposition of sanctions, irrespective of his judgement of the utility of such obedience. Only by foregoing the individual's direct obligation to pursue utility can those patterns of expectation necessary for the maximum of social well-being be maintained. This also explains how Bentham was able to reconcile the motto of the good citizen '*To obey punctually; to censure freely*'[90] with the requirements of a utilitarian morality.

Within this framework of obligations which provide the co-ordinating conditions of social interaction, the individual is free to pursue directly the dictates of utility. To what extent an agent will do this depends on how far he sees the general interest and his own particular interest converging. The object of private Deontology is to point out the ways in which the private and public interest converge. The more successful this educative task, the greater the tendency for individuals to pursue the dictates of utility within the context of a utilitarian system of obligations. However, this system of obligations provides a framework within which individual agents can act on direct utilitarian reasons, without their actions undermining the conditions of social interaction on which the most important sources of utility depend. In this way Bentham combines aspects of a direct and indirect utilitarian theory.

In the same way that the utilitarian obligations provide a framework within which the individual agent can act on direct utilitarian reasons, they also provide a framework within which the legislator can act. As the source of all legal coercive sanctions the legislator cannot be obliged to act in accordance with the principle of utility. However, in his later Democratic writings, Bentham uses the formal sanction of Public Opinion, and its institutionalized form, the Public Opinion Tribunal, as a sanction to be employed against legislative deviations from the requirements of general welfare.[91] Nevertheless, as long as the legislator accepts that the principle of utility is the only possible basis of a morality of politics, and the conception of the enterprise of social interaction that underlies the principle, then he has a reason to conform his actions to the principle of utility. In order to achieve the maximum social well-being, it has been argued that he must employ indirect utilitarian strategies, and this entails that he act in accordance with rules and respect the pattern of expectations that arise from regularities in his own actions. Therefore, the principle of utility implies a principle of right in the hands of the legislator just as much as in the hands of the individual agent. The legislator is only able to act on direct

---

[90] *Fragment* (CW), p. 399.

[91] The best extended discussion of the public opinion tribunal and its importance within Bentham's Constitutional theory is to be found in Rosen, *Jeremy Bentham and Representative Democracy* (Oxford, 1983).

utilitarian reasons within the framework of utilitarian obligations if he is to accept utility as the basis of his actions. He can only apply direct utilitarian reasons within the context of the framework rather than across it. This means he cannot decide whether to punish the innocent in order to maximize social well-being, but he can determine the level of punishment appropriate to a particular offender by means of a utility calculation.

There remains one possible source of difficulty for this interpretation. If the legislator is not obliged to act in accordance with the dictates of direct utility calculations, how is he able to reform existing institutions when it is clear that an alternative distribution of rights would result in a higher degree of social well-being? It is clear that Bentham did not adhere to a rigid rule-utilitarianism like that of Hume.[92] However, if the legislator is restricted to acting on direct utilitarian reasons within the context of the utilitarian system of obligations, how can he reform the structure of that system? In a later chapter I will argue that Bentham solved this problem within his theory of distributive justice by appeal to a principle which is sensitive to the considerations which underlie the utilitarian system of obligation and which enables the modification of that system without undermining the stability of expectations which are derived from it.

The next four chapters will deal with the substance of Bentham's theory of distributive justice, and the sources of utility upon which the utilitarian system of obligations is grounded.

[92] The interpretation of Hume as a rule-utilitarian is discussed in J. Harrison, *Hume's Theory of Justice* (Oxford, 1981), 27–33.

4

Security, Expectation, and Liberty

THE fundamental difference between the interpretation offered in this work, and that of its most important rival concerns the role of justice within Bentham's moral theory. In his book *Bentham and the Common Law Tradition*, G. J. Postema writes:

No moral concept suffers more at Bentham's hand than the concept of justice. There is no sustained, mature analysis of this notion to match that of Mill's discussion in *Utilitarianism*. Seldom willing to take the notion seriously, he was most inclined to respond to talk of justice in an entirely polemical fashion, dismissing it summarily as, at best, innocently vague and potentially obscurantist, but more often a mask for social antipathy and malevolence.[1]

In this passage Postema draws a contrast in the treatment of the concept of justice between Bentham and J. S. Mill, based on recent revisionist interpretations of Mill's theory of justice.[2] While Lyons has argued that for Mill justice and moral obligation are analytically connected to the liability of sanctions, and consequently only indirectly connected to considerations of utility, Postema argues that in Bentham's case the concept of justice simply refers to a particular species of utility. He also maintains that, for Bentham, the popular contrast between justice and utility in so far as it has any justification refers to the utility of adhering to fixed general rules. These rules give rise to expectation utilities, and where these rules are sufficiently important the requirement of obedience can conceivably outweigh any particular direct appeal to the principle of utility. However, Postema makes clear that despite their potential importance, expectation utilities are, nevertheless, only one species of utilities and do not involve any principled limitation on the direct application of the principle of utility.[3]

Clearly Postema's overall interpretation of the role of justice within Bentham's utilitarian science of legislation differs from that presented in this book, where it is argued that Bentham developed and employed a theory of distributive justice in his Civil Law writings. Despite posing this contrast between Mill and Bentham on justice, it is interesting that Postema also identifies a number of passages where Bentham clearly ties justice to justified rules in the same way as Mill's rule- or sanction-based theory.[4] In his Commonplace book Bentham wrote: 'Justice is beneficence: in the cases

---

[1] Postema, *Bentham and the Common Law Tradition* (Oxford, 1986), 148–9.
[2] See D. Lyons, 'Mill's Theory of Morality', *Nous*, 10 (1976), 101–20.
[3] Postema, *Bentham and the Common Law Tradition*, p. 154.
[4] Ibid., pp. 156–8.

in which the non-performance of it is considered as punished or punishable by the force of one or other of the several sanctions: principally the political, including the legal, and the moral or popular.'[5] Here Bentham explicitly connects justice with those aspects of benevolence which can be required as duties and for which sanctions can be imposed for non-compliance. In further passages from an 'Article on Utilitarianism',[6] Bentham comes even closer to the Millian version, analysing justice in the following way:

In and by the employment given to the word 'justice', two assumptions are implicitly contained: assumption 1. that by competent authority the general rule of action has been laid down: assumption 2. that whatsoever be meant by rectitude and propriety, this rule is itself, reference had to the situation in which it is thus placed, a right and proper one.

and later Bentham continues:

If then so it be that the rule thus exhibited in the character of a maxim or dictate of justice is the same which on this same occasion would be found to be a dictate, or say precept, emanating from the greatest happiness principle, then thus far are the notions of the author of the rule in a state of conformity and due subordination with reference to the greatest happiness principle: and the dictate, or say precept, thus deduced on the greatest happiness principle may be said to be a dictate of justice in consideration of the determinateness of the form of words by which it stands expressed.

However, having located these passages, Postema argues that they do not affect his overall act-utilitarian interpretation of Bentham's position, because such an analysis played no role in his legal or political theory, and therefore it was not an argument that Bentham thought very important. In one sense Postema is quite right in his claim, for there is no sustained treatment of justice similar to that of chapter 5 of Mill's *Utilitarianism*, nevertheless, he is wrong in his assertion that no such analysis was employed by Bentham in his writings. It can be argued that Bentham did address the problem of distributive justice in terms of such an analysis in his Civil or Distributive Law writings, where he was concerned with what configuration of rights a utilitarian legislator would want to distribute in the interests of maximizing social welfare.

In so far as there has been any scholarly attention given to Bentham's Civil Law writings, this has tended to concentrate on the analysis of Civil Law found in *Of Laws in General*.[7] However, what is of more interest from the perspective of defending the claim that Bentham had a theory of distributive justice are those principles of Civil Law which would underlie

    [5] Bowring, x. 511.
    [6] *Deontology* (CW), p. 308. For the significance of these passages in Bentham's theory see F. Rosen, 'Utilitarianism and Justice: A Note on Bentham and Godwin', *Enlightenment and Dissent*, 4 (1985), 47–52.
    [7] *OLG* (CW), pp. 209–19 and 247–50.

the distribution of rights and titles which are presupposed in the specification of a utilitarian account of harms or offences. The character of these principles is discussed in a series of manuscripts written at a number of times throughout Bentham's career.[8] None of the manuscripts or the works constructed from them[9] contains a sustained treatment of the principles of distributive justice within Bentham's work, but they do provide enough material to indicate the character of those principles. At the beginning of the 'Principles of the Civil Code', Bentham wrote:

In his distribution of rights and obligations, the legislator, we have already said, should have for his object the happiness of the body politic. In inquiring more particularly in what this happiness consists, we find four subordinate objects—
Subsistence.
Abundance.
Equality.
Security.
. . . The more perfect the enjoyment of all these particulars, the greater the sum of social happiness, and especially of that happiness which depends upon the laws.[10]

These four objects of legislative action remain Bentham's principle concern throughout his Civil Law writings.[11] In this way the Civil Law manuscripts provide an account of the basic sources of utility which concern the legislator in constructing a utilitarian principle of right. The next four chapters, which concentrate on the substance of Bentham's theory of distributive justice, will explore the conditions for the principle of right which underlies a utilitarian system of obligations. The discussion in these chapters is based on material from Bentham's Civil Law writings. The aim of this portion of the argument is to reconstruct the form of Bentham's theory of distributive justice from the fragmentary character of these diverse writings and to reconcile this with the interpretation of Bentham's utilitarian theory given in the previous chapter. The rest of this chapter will concentrate on the importance of security within the theory of distributive justice, and will argue that security is the most important source of utility because it is a necessary condition of personal continuity and of interest formation. The next chapter will be concerned with the other main source of utility, namely subsistence. Subsistence refers to the primary material condition of individual well-being. The next chapter will also discuss the role of abundance and equality as objects of legislative action and show how these are modifications of security and subsistence.

The later Civil Law writings consider the nature of the principles that

---

[8] UC c, 96–186, UC lxi, 9–10, 19–21, 26–66, 83–97, and BL Add. MS 33550, fos. 48–144.

[9] See 'Pannomial Fragments', Bowring, iii. 21–30, BL Add. MS 33550, fos. 48–144.

[10] Bowring, i. 302.

[11] See UC xxx, 26–32 and 41–59, UC xxxi, 260–85, UC xxxvii, 18–23, 50–68 and BL Add. MS 33550, fos. 48–144.

determine the distribution of rights and obligations which in turn provide the formal conditions of security and subsistence. Therefore, the next two chapters will be concerned with the 'security-providing principle' and the 'disappointment-preventing principle'. The first principle identifies the realm in which security is to be maintained and the distribution of rights and obligation which constitute that end. The second principle is concerned with reconciling the principle of right based on the 'security-providing principle' with the pattern of expectations which already obtains within any given social order and the utilities that are derived from it. Together they determine both the formal structure and the substantive character of Bentham's theory of distributive justice. This second part of the argument provides the substance of Bentham's answer to the form of anti-utilitarian argument advanced by modern critics such as Rawls.

The argument of the next four chapters assumes that Bentham did not have a direct act-utilitarian theory of moral obligation and provides the substantive justification for the interpretation of Bentham's utilitarianism advanced in the last section of the previous chapter. However, the discussion in this section also provides the grounds or defending Bentham as a liberal. It will be argued that given Bentham's characterization of human nature as purposive, the configuration of rights and titles prescribed by the principle of right will be one that maximizes social well-being by extending to each agent as wide a sphere of personal inviolability as possible. This will provide the secured framework within which the agent can form and pursue his interest without interference from others. Because the utilitarian system of obligation provides the framework within which interests are formed the legislator can maximize social well-being by providing the conditions of interest formation and realization. The concluding chapter will concentrate on how far Bentham incorporated a liberal principle of right within his theory of justice, and the role of equality as a component of that distributive principle.

The first task involved in reconstructing Bentham's theory of distributive justice from the fragmentary Civil Law manuscripts is to explain why security is the most important of the objects of legislative policy and the primary source of utility.

I

Critical discussion of Bentham's utilitarianism has traditionally emphasized his inability to derive a distributive principle from the principle of utility.[12]

---

[12] See P. Burne, 'Bentham and the Utilitarian Principle', *Mind*, 58 (1949), 367–8, A. Goldworth, 'The Meaning of Bentham's Greatest Happiness Principle', *Journal of the History of Philosophy*, 7 (1969), 315–21, and L. Werner, 'A Note about Bentham on Equality and about the Greatest Happiness Principle', *Journal of the History of Philosophy*, 11 (1973), 237–51.

Most commentators have concentrated on whether the principle of utility is a distributive or an aggregative principle. In their respective discussions of utility both Goldworth[13] and Werner[14] argue that Bentham's adoption of different versions of the principle does not affect the argument that he had an aggregative theory. Werner argues that although Bentham appears to have adopted two different formulations of the principle in his career, his subsequent abandonment of the dual-standard interpretation, 'the greatest happiness of the greatest number',[15] only confirms that the principle of utility was an aggregative principle.[16] However, given that the principle of utility is the criterion of moral judgement, the discussion of whether it contains a distributive principle is irrelevant. Apart from the historical interest of Bentham's final formulation of the principle, the question of whether he had a dual-standard or a single-standard principle is not significant for a discussion of the principle of utility as an action-guiding principle. The principle as the criterion of moral judgement determines the respective value of various objects or actions in terms of the quantity of pleasure or utility they give rise to. The problem with attempting to derive a principle of right from a direct appeal to this conception of the criterion of value is that is impossible. The greatest quantity of the standard of value is the greatest good whether that is concentrated in one object or distributed among many. Thus Goldworth and Werner come to the same conclusion as Rawls; that the principle of utility is unable to give weight to distributive principles because these must always be overridden if the quantity of the good is so maximized.

The Rawlsian argument is that utilitarianism begins with a concept of the good and the injunction to maximize it. This, he argues, is antithetical to any conception of right which is sensitive to individual entitlements and the differences between persons. Defending Bentham against Rawls involves showing that maximizing the good necessarily has distributive implications, but it does not entail that the principle of utility is a straightforward distributive principle, for Goldworth and Werner have argued conclusively that this is not the case. Rather it involves arguing that the practical pursuit of the maximum of social well-being entails a principle of right. Such an argument can be based on the view that while pleasure or utility is the standard of value it does not exist in abstraction, but is a function of certain objective states of affairs. In the previous chapter it was argued that the conditions of social interaction provide the most significant source of pleasures. Therefore, the maximum of social well-being is a function of the

[13] Goldworth, The Meaning of Bentham's Greatest Happiness Principle', p. 321.
[14] Werner, 'A Note about Bentham on Equality and about the Greatest Happiness Principle', pp. 238–42.   [15] *Fragment* (CW), p. 393.
[16] The Dual-standard interpretation of Bentham's principle of utility is discussed in R. Shackleton, 'The Greatest Happiness of the Greatest Number: The History of Bentham's Phrase', *Studies in Voltaire and the Eighteenth Century*, 90 (1972), 1461–81.

conditions of social interaction which serve as a condition of this class of pleasures. To support this claim it must be possible to establish a distinction between those utilities derived from nature and which are independent of any social arrangements, and those utilities which are a function of the conditions of social interaction. It is also necessary to show that this category of utilities is necessarily of greater weight than that derived from nature, if it is to be the justification of a principle of right. Once it can be shown that the conditions of social interaction are necessarily the source of the most significant category of utilities, then discussion of how to maximize social well-being becomes a question of which form of social organization provides the maximum social well-being. In this section it is argued that Bentham defends the claim that the most significant category of utilities is derived from the conditions of social interaction. It is also argued that this category of utilities provides the justification for security as the chief benefit of his theory of distributive justice.

Bentham introduces an important distinction between types of utility or the sources of pleasure and pain in one of his earliest works. Although this distinction is hardly developed throughout the rest of his work, it underlies, and helps to explain many of the positions he adoped in his later works, particularly those on Civil Law. In *A Comment on the Commentaries*, written between 1774 and 1776, Bentham distinguishes between original and expectation utilities, or utilities grounded in nature and those grounded on expectation. He wrote:

Interested in every act of public power there are at least two parties. The one party at whose expence it is passed, or as he may be termed in other words the party suffering, the party bound by it: the other party favoured by it. The foundation, the end, the motive, the reason (all these terms on some occasion or other we see employed) is when justified, some utility real or supposed. This utility may be either original, or derived from expectation.[17]

He did not fully explain the nature of this distinction in any of his works, but two important components of it can be identified. Firstly, the notion of expectation utilities depends on the projection of the individual self into the future. Expectation utilities are also connected with the concept of disappointment, which is integral to Bentham's theory of distributive justice, and was premissed upon the role of expectation utilities within that theory. Expectation utilities are derived from the prospect of being able to achieve a future benefit such as the satisfaction of a complex interest. Pains of expectation or disappointments arise from failure to receive an expected benefit in the future. Bentham developed this future regarding dimension of expectation utilities in a later passage from the *Comment*:

an act the nature of which is to produce a pain of disappointment, punishing for instance the usurpation of a thing which another has been led to expect the use of,

---

[17] *Comment* (CW), pp. 230–1.

the ground is, utility resulting from expectation. For disappointment to take place, and consequently for the pain which it is of the nature of disappointment to produce, it must have been preceded by expectation.[18]

The future-regarding aspect of expectation utilities provides a connection with the good of security, and the legal rights which are derived from it. In the 'Principles of the Civil Code',[19] Bentham used the future-regarding aspect of security to distinguish it from the three other objects of legislative policy, and to explain the priority given to security:

> Among these objects of the law, security is the only one which necessarily embraces the future: subsistence, abundance, equality, may be regarded for a moment only; but security implies extension in point of time, with respect to all the benefits to which it is applied. Security is therefore the principle object.

This is a misleading claim, for it is clear from Bentham's early and late Civil Law writings that both abundance and equality are future-regarding objects of policy. However, the substantive point, that security is necessarily future-regarding is re-emphasized in a late manuscript where Bentham wrote: 'security turns its eye exclusively to the future.'[20]

Security is future-regarding because it is concerned with establishing and maintaining stable patterns of behaviour on which expectation utilities are premissed. This interdependence of the good of security and expectation utilities was established early in Bentham's career, when he maintained in an undated manuscript composed in the 1780s that: 'security depends on the care taken to save from disturbance the current of expectation.'[21] This position was restated in later writings dating from the 1820s.[22]

Drawing on this integral relationship between security and expectation it is possible to distinguish between original and expectation utilities. Unlike utilities derived from expectation, original utilities are not essentially future-regarding. This is because they are sources of pleasure or pain which are independent of any beliefs, desires, or interests of an agent. Bentham uses the concept of original utilities to acknowledge that given the physical constitution of human beings, certain actions and objects will function as sources of pleasure or pain irrespective of any cognitive attitude a person may adopt towards them. Bentham illustrates this argument with an example:

---

[18] Ibid., p. 231.   [19] Bowring, i. 302.
[20] UC lxi, 47.   [21] UC xxxii, 1.
[22] UC c, 167. Rosen discusses Bentham's use of security in his paper 'Bentham and Mill on Liberty and Justice', in G. Feaver and F. Rosen (eds.), *Lives, Liberties and the Public Good* (London, 1987). The significance of expectation is derived from the use of security. However, while security functions as an important concept within the works of Hobbes, Locke, De Lolme, and Montesquieu, only Bentham provides a detailed explanation of its importance in terms of expectation. The notion of expectation has since become an important one in the field of economic theory although it is used in a different sense to refer to expected utility. Bentham uses the term to refer to beliefs that are based on a system of public rules, and expectation utilities to refer to those utilities that are derived from such rule systems.

Of an act of power punishing a crime that is of such a nature to produce pain of sufferance in the object of it, beating for example, the ground is *utility original*. For whether a man expects to be safe from beating or does not, beating is at all events a pain to him.[23]

In this passage Bentham introduced a distinction between those sources of pleasure which are derived from our physical constitution as human beings, and those sources of pleasure which are a function of our interests, beliefs, and desires. Because original and natural utilities are sources of pleasure or pain irrespective of interests, beliefs, and desires, they are not dependent on the provision of security or the conditions of social interaction. Therefore, they are of little concern to Bentham in the development of his theory of distributive justice, although they form an essential part of the subject-matter of the Penal Law. The important sources of pleasure and pain within Bentham's theory of justice and political morality are those which are a function of complex interests in modern societies, and these are necessarily dependent on the formal conditions of social interaction.

The second characteristic difference between original and expectation utilities concerns the way in which beliefs feature in the formation of the latter. In the case of original utilities the sensation of pleasure is the immediate causal outcome of a particular action. Thus in Bentham's example of being beaten,[24] the sensation of pain that results from the beating necessarily follows irrespective of the agent's beliefs or conscious interest. Indeed it is possible for someone to experience the sensation of pain derived from the beating without them understanding what is happening to them.

With utilities derived from expectation the epistemic grounds for the beliefs upon which they depend play a constitutive role in the specification of those utilities. The higher the degree of certainty, or the greater probability that the object of the action will be obtained, the greater the expectation, and consequently the greater the utility derived from it. The utility of expectation is related to the minimization of chance and contingency within the realm in which an agent determines his conception of well-being. The higher the degree of certainty that no intervening circumstances will upset the realization of a particular project the higher the expectation utility which is causally related to the realization of that interest. Furthermore, given that the objects of action include not only particular desires and preferences, but within an individual's own plan of life, a preference or desire for a particular way of life, then the utility derived from the secured expectation will in some cases be immeasurably valuable. What underlies Bentham's argument is the view that most of the significant sources of interest, particularly those which give rise to the complex patterns of social interaction which characterize modern societies, are

---

[23] *Comment* (CW), p. 231.   [24] Ibid.

developed within the context of elaborate patterns of belief about how other individuals will act. The beliefs which are most important in the formation of complex interests are derived from formal regularities in behaviour. Beliefs about how others will act are indispensable in the formation of particular conceptions of well-being which depend on how an action will affect others' behaviour. To a certain degree all interests require a degree of social co-operation in the form of non-interference. Without the ability to premiss action and interest formation on such beliefs, rational action would be impossible.

In order to minimize contingency which is essential in order for expectations to arise, there must be some public framework which provides the justification for those beliefs which underlie individual decision-making in the context of social interaction. These decisions can only be made on a rational basis within the context of a pattern of secured expectations. Stable patterns of expectation can only arise within the context of an authoritative system of rules. The most important difference between an original utility and a utility derived from expectation is that the former is a natural pleasure or pain which could theoretically obtain within a state of nature, whereas expectation utilities are a function of authoritative systems of rules. This implies that utilities derived from expectation are a function of the conditions of social interaction. A utility derived from expectation can only be enjoyed because of the institutions of law and morality which embody the essential conditions of social interaction. These and other basic institutions of political society impose a minimal degree of regularity on human behaviour, and remove an important source of contingency.

The importance Bentham attached to the institution of law and political society, as the source of all utilities derived from expectation, is expressed in the following passage from a manuscript written during the 1780s:

The case is that in a society in any degree civilized, all the rights a man can have, all the expectation he can entertain of enjoying anything that is said to be his is derived solely from the law. Even the expectation which a thief may entertain of enjoying the thing which he had stolen forms no exception.[25]

Bentham made the radical claim that not only was the law the basis of all legitimate expectations and rights, but also that it was the source of all illegitimate expectations as well, such as those of the thief. His argument is in two parts. Firstly, in some natural state where there are no laws, there is no theft, and there cannot be any violation of property. Secondly, and more importantly, the motive for theft is in part parasitic upon the security that law gives to private property. The thief chooses to steal an object only because he expects to derive some utility from the object, whether direct enjoyment or through money derived from the sale of the object. However,

---

[25] UC xxxii, 157.

his choice is only credible against the background of a general prohibition on violation of property rights embodied in the legal system, so that until such a time as his crime is discovered his possession enjoys the same protection as that of the original owner. Thus until such a time the only threats to his expectation of enjoying the property arise from the small number of other thieves. The law sees to it that the majority of other people will respect this apparent property right as if it were genuine. The thief is a 'free-rider' upon the law-abidingness of the majority of other people. Once thieves become the majority, then their own expectation of deriving benefit from theft dissolves as the pattern of expectations on which property rights are based collapses.

On the more general question of the importance of law and political institutions as the source of all utilities based on expectation, Bentham's argument was similar to that of Hume in the *Treatise*.[26] For Hume, one of the primary justifications of the institutions of justice and property within political society was the security they afford individuals in view of the scarcity afforded by nature and the partiality of human nature. Later, in a discussion of the sources of allegiance to government, Hume re-emphasized the utility of political society and government:

I seek, therefore, some such interest more immediately connected with government, and which may be at once the original motive to its institution, and the source of our obedience to it. This interest I find to consist in the security and protection, which we enjoy in political society, and which we never attain, when perfectly free and independent.[27]

Hume's argument is similar to Bentham's in recognizing the dependency of theft on the expectations derived from a system of laws and consequently property rights:

tho' I assert, that in the *state of nature*, or that imaginary state, which preceded society, there be neither justice nor injustice, yet I assert not, that it was allowable, in such a state, to violate the property of others. I only maintain that there was no such thing as property.[28]

For Hume and Bentham, the utility of political society, and the institution of law was to be found in the minimization of the influence of contingency. Their recognition of the possible partiality and selfishness of human nature suggests that contingency could not be totally eliminated from social life. However, both saw the minimization of contingency by the institution of law as one of the chief grounds of political obligation, and this also explains their hostility to arbitrary government. Tyranny and arbitrary government reintroduce the effects of contingency into social and political life, and so

---

[26] Hume, *Treatise*, III. 2. ii. 485.
[27] Ibid., III. 2. ix. 550–1.
[28] Ibid., III. 2. iii. 501.

collapse civil society into a state no better than the pre-social state where contingency reigned.

Expectations are derived from habits, customs, promises, and from any regularity of behaviour that is a consequence of social interaction. As has been argued, the chief source of these expectations is the law which provides the highest degree of certainty. However, not all of these patterns of behaviour need to be based directly on the law. Some conventions can enjoy the protection of the law without themselves being directly embodied within it. Promise-keeping can have the full sanction of the law in a wide variety of cases, such as in all binding contracts. However, the obligation to uphold many interpersonal promises makes no reference to the law, it simply relies on an informal social convention that has no physical coercive sanctions. Yet it would be wrong to think that because these informal social conventions can subsist without making reference to the wide system of law, that some of the conventions which provide for regularity and the minimization of contingency between separate individual's actions, could exist independently of political society.

Bentham's most important concern in the Civil Law writings was with expectations that were derived from law. However, this does not imply that he was unaware of the significance of conventions that do not make direct reference to law. Instead it implies that the law is the most important source of these expectations,[29] and that conventions that do not refer directly to law are, nevertheless, parasitic upon it. Law provides the basic framework of social interaction by delimiting spheres of personal inviolability within which individuals can form and pursue their own conceptions of well-being. However, although law draws the boundaries of social interaction by distributing rights and duties, and imposing sanctions, it cannot account for the dispositions necessary to acknowledge the importance of these rules within individual practical reasoning. These dispositions are derived from other practices which also constitute the conditions of social interaction. After the law, the most important of these practices is morality, which includes institutions like promise-keeping. In the case of promises, the transfer of rights, whether to person or property, that takes place in promising presupposes certain antecedent rights which ultimately, for Bentham as for Hume, had their origin in the law. In a pre-social condition where there were no antecedent rights or a system of laws it is not clear how such conventions could arise.

Hume and Bentham unequivocally abandoned the natural law framework of their predecessors Grotius, Pufendorf, Hobbes, and Locke, so that in so far as they are concerned with a pre-social state, or state of nature, it is one very different from that envisaged by Locke. In Locke's theory, government is created in order to secure already existing social institutions such as

[29] UC xxxii, 157.

private property. For Bentham as for Hume, political society and government do not originate in a self-conscious rational choice undertaken by all those who accept its authority in the original position in order to protect some pre-existing rights and entitlements to private property. Political society and government evolved together. The question for Hume and Bentham, is to show how far we are obligated to them and why. Similarly, the institutions Locke grounds in the state of nature, are for Bentham and Hume the outcome of the development of conventions within civil society in response to certain features of the human condition.

Bentham had little time for theorizing about the state of nature, and, again, in this as in much else, his position mirrored that of Hume. In a body of manuscripts[30] that were incorporated into the 'Principles of the Civil Code',[31] Bentham answered the rhetorical question that in deciding which articles the law should take for the objects of its protection, must the law at some point have relied on natural expectations? That is, expectations which were derived from sources anterior to the law.[32] His answer was negative. If the answer had been affirmative then the distinction between original and expectation utilities would have collapsed. Nevertheless, Bentham acknowledged that there is some intuitive appeal to the view that expectations could arise in a pre-social state, and were thus not a function of normative bodies of rules: 'Certainly occasions there must have originally been, and will have been still in which one man must have found a greater facility in securing to himself the enjoyment of certain things than any other man.'[33] This intuitive appeal does not substantiate the claim, and Bentham went on to deny that expectations could originate in a pre-social state without the benefit of law and the conventions and practices that surround it. His argument was that, although a savage might store some of the fruits that he gathers or the animals that he has killed, this does not constitute the origin of secured expectations to the enjoyment of property. If the savage enjoys only a very limited degree of intercourse with his fellow men, then the greater is the chance of being able to enjoy his produce at a future date. However, not all men in a primitive state can have enjoyed the circumstances of Robinson Crusoe. On the other hand, if his intercourse with his fellow men is greater than that of Robinson Crusoe, then his expectations will only last until such a time as he is overcome with sleep. If it is still argued that the natural expectations that originate in a pre-social state are actually stronger than anything considered so far, then Bentham argued this fails to prove that there are strong natural patterns of expectation, and on the contrary only provides evidence for a primitive system of political society and law:

In the rudest and earliest state therefore of society whatever property a man possesses, whatever articles of property he expects to have the enjoyment of his

---

[30] UC xxxii, 157.   [31] Bowring, i. 308.

[32] UC xxxii, 157.   [33] Ibid.

possession, his expectation if derived from any thing more permanent than the casual forbearance of those in whose presence he has occasion to find himself must be derived from something (a principle) which can be called by no other name than *law*.[34]

Natural expectations only appear a plausible source of real expectations and the rights and entitlements derived from them because they involve applying features of political society to a pre-social state. However, once the expectations are disentangled from the legal systems and conventional practices on which they depend, they actually disappear. Bentham's argument was premised on the notion that expectations are the consequence of the conditions of social interaction. These conditions give rise to mutual regularities in behaviour because they are a source of authoritative reasons for action. To assume that such behavioural regularities could arise in a pre-social state is to assume that nature provides such reasons, and this is precisely what was denied by Bentham's psychological theory and his criticism of natural-rights theories.[35] The presupposition of harmonious interaction in the absence of a source of authority is one of the major premisses of anarchist theory. Bentham clearly rejected the possibility of such harmonious interaction in the absence of authoritative reasons by arguing that the appearance of such behavioural regularities would be a purely contingent matter, and something on which the individual agent could not rely. Thus while the savage may well find that others do not interfere in his enjoyment of his store of food, he cannot count on this non-interference as the basis of more complex interests. The fact that others do not interfere with the savage's enjoyment of his goods is a matter which could change at any moment. Therefore, the savage cannot have natural expectations because expectations are premised on non-contingent regu-larities in social interaction. Once the savage has authoritative reasons as the basis for his expectation, then he ceases to be a savage, and resides in a form of social organization which acknowledges the existence of primitive laws. Bentham's attitude to theories of the state of nature was dismissive, precisely because nothing could be gained from them unless they import features of civil society.

Another argument which Bentham did not develop, but which was certainly implicit in his position, was the view that expectations and the practices and regularities on which they are based, play such an important constitutive role in the projects, plans, and goals of individuals, that an individual in the state of nature, without the benefits of political society, would be virtually unrecognizable. This position is rather crudely brought to the surface in the case of the thief. Without the laws, conventions, and practices which characterize political life, certain options, desires, and projects would not be possible, just as it would be impossible to be a thief in

[34] Ibid.   [35] See Chap. 3, above.

a society without a system of law that embodies property rights. It can, however, be inferred from Bentham's position, that the character of the interests pursued by individuals in modern societies is a product of the form of social organization. This is not to assert the strong Marxist claim that the social structure plays a causal role in determining a particular individual's interests. However, it is clear that the majority of interests and activities which become the objects of individual action could not arise outside of the conditions of social interaction embodied in the law and the practice of morality. For Bentham economic activity is an important example of this, in that it is premissed on stable patterns of social interaction which give rise to expectations, and requires the existence of private property and enforceable contracts, all of which could not exist in the state of nature.[36] Again it is possible that Bentham's hostility to state of nature theories is based on the rejection of a Christian natural-law framework, which would provide authoritative reasons for action and a series of sanctions to support these reasons in the absence of formally constituted political society and sovereign legislator.[37]

Expectations and· the utilities derived from them are of supreme importance within the legislative project, for it is these which underlie the whole notion of security and its role in the realization conditions of individual well-being. Security is at the same time the product of the conventions and practices that constitute legal systems, as well as those which are parasitic upon them. It is the high value attached to these expectations which in turn translates into the high acceptance utility of the pattern of rights and titles derived from Bentham's theory of distributive justice. He conveyed the importance he attached to expectations in the Civil Law, when he wrote:

Expectation: this is the grand word that ought to be perpetually sounding in the ears of whoever undertakes to compose or modify a code of Civil Law. Expectation is the basis of every proprietory right: it is this affords whatever reason there can be for giving a thing to one man rather than another.

Keep the current of expectation inviolate, in these words are contained the quintessence of everything which utility can dictate on this extensive ground.[38]

It may still be unclear why expectation utilities are the most significant class within a utilitarian system. In one important sense it appears that they are not the most significant class of utilities. After all, under the category of original utilities must be placed all pleasures and pains applying directly to a person's body. Assaults on the person, murder, and other such acts of

---

[36] For Bentham's theory of justice as the framework for his economic theory, see P. J. Kelly, 'Utilitarianism and Distributive Justice: The Civil Law and the Foundations of Bentham's Economic Thought', *Utilitas*, 1 (1989), 62–81.

[37] I have discussed this in relation to Bentham's rejection of Lockean natural rights theory, at Chap. 3 n. 60, above.   [38] UC xxix, 6.

violence come under the category of physical pains. Surely, therefore, it is the prevention of physical pain that must be the most important concern of the legislator in a utilitarian system. Even those critics who are most conservative on questions of the rights of property are unlikely to rank them higher than the prevention of physical pain and suffering. If security of expectation is a necessary condition of the realization of an individual's ultimate project or goal, then surely security of person must be a prior condition of security of expectation.

It is certainly the case that security of person, or freedom from violence and physical injury is a necessary condition for the possibility of purposive actions. The category of pain most obviously suggests physical suffering, violence, or injury. Equally it can be argued that of the harms that are the object of criminal law, only a small portion actually concern violation of the person. So while it is the case that freedom from physical violation is a necessary component of a person's real interest, it is only a small portion of that real or permanent interest. Accordingly, security of person only attracts a small portion of the legislator's concern.

The reason why security of person occupies only a small portion of an individual's real interest while so much importance is attached to expectation utilities, is a function of the constitutive role they play in the formation of an individual's projects and goals. The expectations that are produced by law, convention, and habit, account for more of the legislator's attention because it is within the boundaries provided by these practices that individuals develop and pursue their own conceptions of well-being. There is also a good case for arguing that violation of the person is often causally connected to prior conflicts between individuals over their particular interests. Just as the institution of law creates certain categories of offences, and thus makes certain acts wrong,[39] so law at the same time as creating entitlements could be described as creating the conditions in which disputes over titles occur, and in which some make recourse to violence. The more important a particular project is to an individual, the more its frustration by another individual provides the conditions in which some turn to violence. Given the purposive character of human action, in Bentham's view gratuitous violence will form only a small part of the legislator's concern. This is because the legislator is concerned with the conditions of social interaction, and no distribution of rights can prevent or accommodate all irrational actions.

One of the most important conclusions of the discussion of Bentham's psychological theory was that there is no good evidence to suggest that his conception of human nature is simply concerned with desire satisfaction at the crudest level. There is no suggestion that Bentham simply thought all desires and preferences operated on the same level, and that all men were

---

[39] J. Rawls, 'Two Concepts of Rules', *Philosophical Review*, 64 (1955), 3–32.

simply 'wantons,'[40] the victims of whatever present desires they happen to have. Similarly, Bentham's employment of the notion of 'idiosyncratical' values, or 'values in affection', suggests that he did not accept a crude version of value commensurability. The use of this notion also provides some scope for arguing against Rawls that the simple commensurability thesis found in prudential reasoning in Bentham's hedonistic psychology does not entail a simple commensurability of values in moral and political decision-making.[41]

Expectations are important within the context of Bentham's moral and psychological theory because of the dimension they add to the choices individuals are able to make among goals and projects. It has been suggested that expectation plays a constitutive role in the formation of desires, interests, and the goals and projects which depend on them. There are two arguments underlying this claim. Firstly, patterns of expectation render possible certain forms of choice, which in turn facilitate the formation of certain classes of desire or preferences. Earlier in this chapter it was suggested that part of Bentham's hostility to state of nature theories might be explained by the fact that without security of expectation certain types of activity and goal would be impossible. This argument only works if expectation makes possible most of those choices which characterize civilized life in a modern society. His argument is that expectation is necessary if individuals are to choose and pursue their own ends. The reason that such weight is placed on expectation is that it provides the dimension within which an individual can make strategic choices about goals and projects which in turn determine individuals' conceptions of well-being. Expectation is that dimension within Bentham's moral psychology by means of which he can incorporate hierarchies of ends within individual decision-making. It is able to play this crucial role because it involves beliefs about the future which are themselves dependent on the predictability of the behaviour of other individuals, particularly public functionaries,[42] as a result of social institutions, practices, and habits. These beliefs enable the

---

[40] For the notion of a 'Wanton' see H. G. Frankfurt, 'Freedom of the Will and the Concept of a Person', *Journal of Philosophy*, 68 (1971), 5–20, and the discussion of C. Taylor, 'What is Human Agency?', *Philosophical Papers* (2 vols., Cambridge, 1985), ii. 15–44.

[41] See the discussion in J. Griffin, *Well-Being* (Oxford, 1987), pp. 75–83.

[42] Public functionaries are the most important concern of the individual agent because their actions have the greatest effects on overall patterns of expectation. The fact that public functionaries are able to exercise the greatest influence on security of expectation in part explains why Bentham devoted so much time to constructing a form of constitutional arrangement which provides stability of expectation while allowing the legislator to act in pursuit of the maximum social well-being.

The best discussion of the form of Bentham's constitutional theory and its place within his utilitarian philosophy is F. Rosen, *Jeremy Bentham and Representative Democracy* (Oxford, 1983). See also R. Harrison, *Bentham* (London, 1983), 195–224, L. J. Hume, *Bentham and Bureaucracy* (Cambridge, 1981), and M. H. James, 'Bentham's Democratic Theory at the Time of the French Revolution', *Bentham Newsletter*, 10 (1986), 5–16.

individual to form projects and goals in the future, with a degree of certainty that whether or not they are realized, the pursuit of these goals will be co-ordinated with the actions of others so that there is a greater likelihood of their being realized. The individual is, therefore, able to build up a conception of how he wishes his life to progress, that is, he can adopt a hierarchy of values or desires which provide a coherence within his life. He is able to subordinate transient present desires for future ends, while at the same time the supreme end or desire of his life will play a causal role in the origination of intermediate desires, interest, and subordinate projects.

All this is not to suppose that these future goals cannot or will not change quite radically over time. It is quite clear that this possibility is not precluded by Bentham's psychology; indeed, it is likely that as subordinate projects and desires originate in the pursuit of a primary goal, they will actually modify or even displace that primary goal. Human life is often a continuous progress through various conceptions of how the individual sees himself in the future, each conception being modified in the light of new circumstances, with only the most indeterminate connections between these various projects and goals. The individual's choice of goals and projects, or of second-order desires about future desires, involves the projection of a conception of the self into the future. The ability to make this projection is a necessary condition of personal continuity and coherence. Expectation, therefore, provides a framework within which an individual builds up a sense of personality within the context of social action, for it connects us with other people, particularly those closely connected to us, and to future generations. Knowledge and belief about the regularities of behaviour are essential for shaping one's own projects, and in this way expectation becomes the primary condition of preference formation. In this sense secured expectation is not dissimilar to one of the 'primary-goods' Rawls identifies in his theory of distributive justice.[43] These 'primary-goods' are supposed to be the necessary conditions of preference formation and realization, whatever one's conception of the good. Bentham suggests that the framework provided by patterns of expectation is the essential background for a recognizably human or civilized life. He made these weighty claims in a passage from the 'Principles of the Civil Code', where he wrote:

This disposition to look forward, which has so marked an influence upon the condition of man, may be called expectation—expectation of the future. It is by means of this we are enabled to form a general plan of conduct; it is by means of this, that the successive moments which compose the duration of life are not like insulated and independent points, but become parts of a continuous whole. Expectation is a chain which unites our present and our future existence, and passes

---

[43] J. Rawls, *A Theory of Justice* (Oxford, 1972), pp. 90–5.

beyond ourselves to the generations which follow us. The sensibility of the individual is prolonged through all the links of this chain.[44]

It is not clear whether Bentham saw an individual's conception of the self as an outcome of identifying with certain roles and interests that he assumes and pursues. If he did make such an identification between an individual's sense of self and his goals and projects, it would add further support to Bentham's commitment to a strong conception of private property rights and the view that some subjective valuations, particularly 'values in affection',[45] can be given no objective measure.

Bentham made some attempt to contrast human nature with animal natures in terms of the significance of expectation, which again emphasizes the importance of expectation in the formation of human personality. He wrote:

In order to form a clear idea of the whole extent which ought to be given to the principle of security, it is necessary to consider, that man is not like the brutes, limited to the present time, either in enjoyment or suffering, but that he is susceptible of pleasure and pain by anticipation, and that it is not enough to guard him against an actual loss, but also to guarantee to him as much as possible, his possessions against future losses. The idea of his security must be prolonged to him throughout the whole vista that his imagination can measure.[46]

While it has been customary and largely correct to see the scope of Bentham's conception of well-being as including the pleasure and pains of all sentient creatures, it should be clear that this does not create the problems suggested by Parekh.[47] Bentham is not committed to placing human pleasures on the same level as those of sheep. Although it is true that the suffering of animals is just as worthy of concern as that of a man in any utilitarian calculation, this does not entail that Bentham ought to make a place for animals to protect their expectations from the depredations of sinister interests by giving them a vote in a representative democracy. His reason for excluding animals from the democratic process is that while animals are pleasure-seeking on a simple level, they do not have a conception of themselves which can be projected through time in order to give coherence to their respective projects. Therefore, animals do not experience utilities derived from expectation, and neither do they suffer disappointment.

The second reason why expectations play a constitutive role in the formation of desires and interests is that they provide the framework for prudential rationality, and consequently individual choice. Prudential

---

[44] Bowring, i. 308.

[45] For reference to 'values in affection' see Bowring, i. 310 and 322, BL Add. MS 33550, fo. 121.   [46] Bowring, i. 308.

[47] Parekh, 'Bentham's Justification of the Principle of Utility', in id. (ed.), *Jeremy Bentham: Ten Critical Essays* (London, 1974), p. 96.

rationality requires the ability of an individual agent to project himself into the future through his desires and projects. This involves the ability to take a longer-term perspective, and to make decisions between present and future satisfactions. The connection between stable patterns of expectation and the conditions of prudential rationality is not simply that prudence requires the ability to project a coherent and persisting conception of the self into the future. Expectation does provide the conditions for a persisting conception of the self, and it is also a structural precondition for the formation of interests and desires. However, prudential rationality is primarily concerned with ordering interests and desires into a coherent conception of well-being. This is why prudence is characterized as the ability to discount among various interests and desires. For this ordering of interests to qualify as rational and not arbitrary it must be subject to an external criterion. This external criterion is provided by the existence of fixed patterns of expectation, and it is in this sense that expectation provides the framework for rational choice.

On the basis of knowledge and belief about stable patterns of behaviour the individual is able to distinguish between his various desires and interests in order to form a coherent structure of interest that will maximize his well-being. If the individual were to attempt to rely on a private-ordering criterion there would be no way to distinguish his choices from arbitrary choices. Either his discrimination is based on knowledge and beliefs about behavioural regularities in the social realm or they are arbitrary and irrational. Bentham implies that the only reasonable grounds one has for ordering and discriminating between various conceptions of individual well-being are the beliefs and expectations about the behaviour of others. It is only by ordering his interest in the context of expectations about others actions, that the individual agent can hope to maximize his own well-being. For Bentham the measure of individual rationality was the measure of an individual's effectiveness in maximizing his own well-being or satisfying as many of his interests as possible. Therefore, prudential reason is premissed on the existence of stable patterns of expectation. This ability to discount between present and future interests is partly the reason why Rawls argues that the model of individual prudential rationality is an inappropriate model for social and political decision-making.[48]

Expectation and the projection of the self into the future through one's projects and desires is not only a necessary precondition of prudential thinking, it is also what makes prudential rationality important. In the pre-social state there is almost no good reason to sacrifice what one has today for what one might need tomorrow, because there is no good ground for expecting that one will be able to enjoy what one has accumulated. The rational option would always be to satisfy as far as possible present desire,

[48] Rawls, *A Theory of Justice*, pp. 22–4.

with very little consideration about the status of that desire. Man in the pre-social state is more likely to be a 'wanton'[49] than a prudential agent. However, in political society, where there are patterns of behaviour from which expectation can be derived, the question of how far to sacrifice a present interest for a future interest becomes very important, particularly in determining which future projects one ought to adopt, or how far one ought to modify a future project in the light of its cost or intermediate consequences. This further supports the claim that a man in a state of nature would in important respects be unrecognizable because he would not be able to construct the complex patterns of interest which characterize human nature in modern societies.

Bentham did not make the moral claim that a recognizably human life must involve the making of important strategic choices over the question of ultimate ends. He relied totally on an empirical conception of the person, so that it was always possible that some men would choose to act as 'wantons'. By having no conception of themselves persisting over time, some men will have no more important desires than those for food, warmth, or sexual gratification which are dictated by their physical constitutions, and which arise independently of any ordered conception of interest. However, it would be implausible to suggest that, given the possibility of such individuals, secured expectations is not the most important source of utility. It is more likely that the whole weight of experience supports the view that most individuals make some sort of ordering decisions in their lives, or at least have a conception of themselves which orders their desires and choices. Bentham made no attempt to prove this empirically, but the lack of evidence he presented for this claim does not render it implausible. It is clear that Bentham assumed that the majority of individual agents made the sort of choices among interests that depend on expectations because of the weight he attaches to this notion within his moral psychology.

It remains a matter of degree how far an individual is solely responsible for the interests and desires that he might adopt and pursue within his life. Bentham was certainly aware of the role of religion, education, and social position in the formation of particular ends and projects within an individual's life. He was also critical of the consequences of these institutions on the formation of individual character. Therefore, while Bentham may have approved of an ideal of self creation which freed the individual from the influences of the church and other sources of sinister interest he did not presuppose this in identifying the conditions of interest formation and realization.[50]

---

[49] See n. 40, above.

[50] Bentham regarded the Church, Parliament, and the Legal Profession as the main sources of sinister interests. These institutions had a direct influence on the forms of particular interest that individuals could develop and pursue because they are the sources of the religious, political, and legal sanctions. These sanctions provided the conditions within which customary

The existence of secured patterns of expectation must underlie any conception of autonomous agency because it forms the context of prudential rationality within which that conception must function. Nevertheless, security of expectation has an equally important role in the adoption of choices and projects within a non-autonomous life. It is the non-autonomous life that Bentham was primarily concerned with because the majority of men, while able to make rational choices between a variety of ends and goals, did not approach the more stringent requirements of an ideal of personal autonomy. The conception of human nature that Bentham must incorporate within his utilitarian theory is similar to that described by S. I. Benn as 'autarchic'.[51] Here the individual is seen as self-governing, in the sense of not being subject to the will of another in the determination of his interests and desires. However, this concept of personality falls short of an ideal of autonomy in that while the individual is able to make rational choices among the options available to him, he might still be subject to direction by uncritically accepting the choices and options that society presents to him. The autonomous agent not only makes strategic choices between complex interests and projects, but is also able to establish a critical distance between himself and the choices that society makes possible. By distancing himself from the society which is largely responsible for the forms of life most individuals adopt, the autonomous agent is able to adopt a critical attitude to those choice options, so that in making a particular choice he is legislating for himself and is not the victim of social influence.

An ideal of autonomy is especially important in J. S. Mill's political morality, particularly in his essay *On Liberty*,[52] for it is this which provides

moral education took place. Therefore, the Church, Parliament, and the Law would aim to discourage the formation of dispositions and interests which would contradict the authority of these institutions.

In view of the effect these institutions have on the formation of interests, some recent commentators have interpreted Bentham's later constitutional theory as an attempt to 'individualize' all social forces. See M. P. Mack, *Jeremy Bentham: An Odyssey of Ideas. 1748–1792* (London, 1962), p. 10.

L. J. Hume argues that Bentham 'attacked the sources of influence in Parliament, in the Courts, in the Church, in social and economic relations, in spoken and written communications. In so doing he was attempting to extirpate all the instruments by which will might act on will, or in more positive terms to provide for the emancipation of all individual wills, and for their free exercise throughout the political system. By this time he had seen that a radical reform of the parliamentary and electoral system was not sufficient to achieve such an emancipation; political reform in the narrow sense would have to be supplemented by reforms extending to every aspect of society which might create 'a state of habitual dependence' by one will on another. At that point, as Mack saw, his individualism became prescriptive; he was aiming at the thoroughgoing individualization of society, the destruction of its distinctively social forces and characteristics', *Bentham Newsletter*, 1 (1978), 15, see also L. J. Hume, *Bentham and Bureaucracy* (Cambridge, 1981).

[51] S. I. Benn, 'Freedom, Autonomy and the Concept of a Person', *Aristotelian Society Proceedings*, 76 (1976), 109–30.

[52] J. S. Mill, *On Liberty*, in *Essays on Politics and Society*, ed. John M. Robson, 2 vols. (The Collected Work of John Stuart Mill, xviii and xix), xviii. 213–310. See the discussion in

the basis of his strong commitment to liberty within his utilitarian theory. It is the role and emphasis given to the ideal of personal autonomy more than anything else which is responsible for the customary distinction between the theories of Bentham and J. S. Mill.[53] Mill based his ideal of autonomy on a conception of human flourishing which according to a recent commentator has Aristotelian overtones.[54] On this view an active autonomous life, in which the individual agent creates his own social world by questioning every item of traditional and received wisdom, is the ideal towards which mankind is advancing. Mill acknowledged that this ideal was only beginning to be realized in modern liberal democratic states, and that in some less culturally advanced society the formal or political requirements of this ideal ought not obtain. Bentham does not presuppose a progressive conception of human personality in the same way as J. S. Mill, but neither does he presuppose a static conception of personality that is unaffected by cultural change. Therefore, while rationality is a necessary condition of an ideal of autonomy, it is the form that rationality takes which determines the nature of that ideal. Bentham implied a degree of rationality as a condition of human agency, but this form of rationality does not depend on an expressly developed conception of progressive human nature.

Bentham acknowledged the influence of certain social determinants which he described as sinister interests in the formation of projects and desires, and the ability to descriminate between them in order to develop a conception of individual well-being. This is very close to Mill's conception of individual agency. Yet it differs from a strong conception of autonomy because the individual is not required to reconstruct the conditions of interest formation and realization in terms which he can accept as rationally acceptable reasons. Mill implies that the fully rational and autonomous agent will be able to justify to himself the reason for all social institutions and practices which he takes as binding. For Bentham it is simply necessary that such reasons are publicly available to each agent. Therefore, an agent who does not adopt a critical stance to all of the social conditions which

---

J. Gray, *Mill On Liberty: A Defence* (London, 1983), 73–86, and F. R. Berger, *Happiness, Justice and Freedom: The Moral and Political Philosophy of John Stuart Mill* (Berkeley, Calif., 1984), 232–53. The implication of these arguments is that Mill did not attempt to force his commitment to liberty into a utilitarian framework, as B. Semmel has argued (*John Stuart Mill and the Pursuit of Virtue* (New Haven, Cann., 1984), 154–85). Rather, Gray and Berger argue that Mill thought that his conception of liberty was an implication of his utilitarian theory of justice. Whether Mill had good reason for thinking that his commitment to liberty followed from his utilitarian theory has been the source of much recent debate within Mill scholarship.

[53] Gray, Berger, and Semmel all argue that there is a significant gulf separating the theories of Mill and Bentham. It has become customary to argue that Mill is an interesting thinker only to the extent that he can be distinguished from his Benthamite heritage. However, some recent Mill scholars have argued that there is a greater degree of continuity between Bentham and J. S. Mill. See S. Hollander, *The Economics of Stuart Mill* (2 vols., Oxford, 1985), ii. 602–76, and J. C. Rees, *John Stuart Mill's On Liberty* (Oxford, 1985), 9–77.

[54] Gray, *Mill on Liberty*, pp. 80–1.

affect his choice of interests, is, according to Bentham, still rational in so far as he is responsible for that choice. Bentham and Mill differ in their characterizations of the nature of human agency which is to be reflected in the principle of right underlying their respective theories of distributive justice. Nevertheless, it is clear that there is a significant degree of similarity in the substance of their theories of justice.[55]

Security of expectation is the most important of the basic sources of utility because it provides the conditions for the development of a concept of personal identity and the coherence of that conception of the self through time, and thus facilitates the complex patterns of expectation which characterize modern societies. In this way it is a necessary condition of the formation and realization of the most important category of interests which are premissed upon the conditions of social interaction. However, a number of problems remain. The provision of security implies the distribution of a pattern of rights and titles which form the conditions within which expectations develop. Therefore, the main task facing Bentham is to provide a distributive principle which determines the pattern of rights which the legislator is to institute. In the next section it will be argued that security provides the conditions for the exercise of freedom, and that Bentham's intention of replacing liberty with security does not entail the abandonment of liberty, but a reconstruction of the concept within the context of a utilitarian theory. However, if security and liberty are to be effectively connected within Bentham's theory of justice, then it is necessary to provide a utilitarian principle of right which determines a realm of security in which an agent is able to exercise the widest possible freedom that is compatible with the same security for others. How Bentham solves this distributive question determines whether he can be regarded as a liberal. A recent commentator on Bentham's Poor Law writings has argued that his reliance on security as a means of removing contingency from the social realm has the effect of eradicating the public space within which individuals can exercise their liberty.[56] Contingency can only be overcome by constructing a system of security that provides individual agents with no effective choice. Bahmueller suggests that contingency and liberty are necessarily related, and one can only be reduced by diminishing the other. However, Bahmueller neither attempts to determine the character of the distribution of rights that Bentham intended, nor the areas of the social realm which are ordered by this distribution. Bahmueller's position fails to acknowledge that expectations are dependent upon the minimization of contingency, and that

---

[55] The similarity between their theories can be explained in terms of the reconciliation between Mill and Benthamite ideas during the late 1850s and early 1860s. Hollander, *The Economics of Stuart Mill*, ii. 602–76. This does not, however imply a complete similarity in their theories. Mill has a much stronger commitment to an ideal of liberty based on a progressive conception of human personality. Nevertheless, the conditions necessary for the exercise of that liberty are described in Benthamite terms such as security.

[56] C. F. Bahmueller, *The National Charity Company* (Berkeley, Calif., 1981), 1–11.

these are a necessary condition of interest formation and realization. The minimization of contingency must, therefore, be a necessary component of the realization conditions of liberty. The remaining problem is to determine that area of the social realm in which contingency must be minimized. This will involve identifying the form of basic expectations upon which interest formation and personal continuity depend. Once the character of these spheres of personal inviolability has been identified, it is possible to determine an arrangement of rights and titles which provides both the conditions of interest formation and personal continuity, but which leaves a sufficient degree of public space to enable individual agents to pursue their conceptions of interest. The answer to this first problem will be provided in Chapter 6, which develops the 'security-providing principle' as a formal distributive principle which determines the character of the Bentham's principle of right.

The second problem concerns the fact that expectations arise from any form of social organization, including those forms which do not conform to the utilitarian principle of right. However, given that expectations are the most significant source of utility, the utilitarian legislator cannot simply override the existing distribution of rights in favour of the utilitarian theory of right. This would not only create a massive disutility arising from the violation of existing expectations, but it would also undermine those dispositions which are essential in order for expectations to develop and function. Chapter 7 will show how Bentham reconciles the claims of the existing pattern of expectations with his utilitarian principle of right by appealing to the 'disappointment-preventing principle', and show how his awareness of this problem, and his attempt to resolve it in his theory of distributive justice, remains an advance over J. S. Mill's theory of justice.

However, before discussing the other major source of utility which underlies his theory of distributive justice, I will consider some of the arguments that have been advanced against the view that Bentham valued freedom within his moral theory, and suggest that Bentham's position is best interpreted as embodying the rejection of a presumptive defence of liberty in favour of a utilitarian justification of the value of liberty. The aim of this section is to show that despite Bentham's abandonment of the language of liberty it is still possible for him to maintain the same substantively liberal commitment to the value of freedom within a utilitarian theory.

II

One of the main revisionist aims of this work is to defend Bentham's theory of distributive justice as a version of liberalism which remains neutral between individual conceptions of the good. This neutralist[57] interpretation

---

[57] A neutral theory of liberalism is one which defines the right independently of substantive conceptions of the good. This means that it attempts to provide the ordering conditions of

of Bentham's theory of distributive justice is expressed in the following passage from the 'Principles of the Civil Code':

The Legislator is not the master of the dispositions of the human heart: he is only their interpreter and their servant. The goodness of his laws depends upon their conformity to the general *expectation*. It is highly necessary, therefore, for him rightly to understand the direction of this expectation, for the purpose of acting in concert with it.[58]

Despite this clear statement of a neutralist liberal position in Bentham's theory, there has still been substantial criticism of his theory on the grounds that he neglects the value of liberty. This criticism takes a number of different forms, but all centre on two arguments. The first is that he begins his early writings with a negative concept of liberty, as freedom from constraint, but then abandons this negative conception in favour of security. The second point of criticism is that Bentham places great emphasis on control and constraint by adopting this concept of security, and that this strongly contrasts with the traditional liberal emphasis on liberation, spontaneity, and self-creation. It is thought that Bentham's concentration on legal concepts like security reflect his concern with control at the expense of an ideal of freedom.

Bentham is consistently criticized by many recent commentators for subordinating liberty to security, and for emphasizing the illiberal notions of control and constraint. This criticism has its recent origin in D. G. Long's important study *Bentham on Liberty*, (1977), in which he emphasizes the role of control and constraint within Bentham's discussion of liberty, which he sees at the heart of his legal theory. Long concentrates his study on a series of early manuscripts and published works, which, he argues, show the development of the groundwork of Bentham's later legislative project. These early manuscripts, written in the 1770s and 1780s, are concerned with the definition of basic political concepts. Long argues that Bentham's intention was the development of a new political vocabulary

---

social interaction without making reference to the aims that individuals have in acting. The most famous neutral theories of justice are the deontological theories of justice defended by Ackerman, Dworkin, and Rawls. See B. Ackerman, *Social Justice in the Liberal State* (New Haven, Conn., 1980), R. Dworkin, *Taking Rights Seriously* (London, 1977), and Rawls, *A Theory of Justice*. These neutral theories have recently come under attack from J. Raz, in 'Liberalism, Autonomy, and the Politics of Neutral Concern', in P. A. French, T. E. Uehling, Jr., and H. K. Wettstein (eds.), *Midwest Studies in Philosophy*, 7, *Social and Political Philosophy* (Minnesota, 1982) and *The Morality of Freedom* (Oxford, 1986), 110–62; see also the discussion in S. Mendus, *Toleration and the Limits of Liberty* (London, 1989), 110–45.

Utilitarianism is not usually considered a neutralist theory because it is argued that the good is pleasure or welfare and that this determines the form of the principle of right. However, I have argued that while pleasure or welfare is the criterion of value within a utilitarian theory, it still provides a principle of right which is neutral between individuals' conceptions of happiness, pleasure, or welfare.

[58] Bowring, i. 322.

which was to be free from mystification and confusion of the language of law and politics as Bentham found it. His dissatisfaction with the contemporary vocabulary of politics, particularly in the case of liberty, was expressed in a manuscript written between 1770 and 1780:

Liberty therefore not being more fit than other words in some of the instances in which it has been used, and not so fit in others, the less the use that is made of it the better. I would no more use the word liberty in my conversation when I could get another that would answer the purpose, than I would brandy in my diet, if my physician did not order me: both cloud the understanding and inflame the passions.[59]

The solution to these inadequacies of language was a form of linguistic analysis, in which fictitious terms that only served to confuse political and moral debate, and perpetuate weak arguments for indefensible institutions, were replaced by new terms. These new terms would expose the interest-serving character of the arguments which underpinned the old concepts of political and moral discourse. One of the fictitious terms that needed to be replaced was liberty. While Bentham had provided an analysis of liberty in terms of the absence of coercion,[60] he proceeded in the same body of manuscripts to abandon altogether the concept of liberty, subordinating it to that of security. Thus he wrote: 'In whichever of the three last senses *liberty* be understood it is either a branch of security, it is either comprised under the head of security, or it is of no value.'[61] It is this replacement of liberty with security which, for Long, confirms Bentham's abandonment of the terms of liberal argument because security is inextricably connected to the concept of law which on Bentham's view was necessarily coercive.[62] The whole of Long's argument is based on this view of Bentham's legislative project, as an attempt to mould the individual personality by means of law. He argues that Bentham's conception of motivation is a stimulus response theory,[63] which in certain respects is a predecessor of B. F. Skinner's behaviouralism, and that the legislator uses this in order to create stable patterns of behaviour by imposing sanctions to discourage antisocial actions. According to Bentham freedom and law are antithetical terms, and Long argues that Bentham favoured law as opposed to liberty.

Another author who suggests that Bentham adopts an illiberal position is

---

[59] UC c, 170.   [60] Ibid., 167.   [61] Ibid., 156.

[62] See the discussion of Long in M. D. A. Freeman, 'Jeremy Bentham: Contemporary Interpretations', in R. Faucci (ed.), *Gli italiani e Bentham dalla 'felicità pubblica' all'economia del benessere*, i (Milan, 1982), 33–6. Freeman contrasts Long's interpretation of Bentham's emphasis on coercion and security with the classical liberal notion of law as a means of facilitating social interaction in order for individuals to lead a more full life. Following Postema, I have argued that the emphasis on coercion is not incompatible with the notion of law as the conditions of social interaction within which individuals can pursue their interests (*Bentham and the Common Law Tradition*, pp. 147–90).

[63] Long, *Bentham on Liberty*, p. 25.

J. R. Dinwiddy.[64] He also argues that Bentham subordinates liberty to security, and believes that the pursuit of utility and respect for liberty are incompatible. Dinwiddy takes literally Bentham's motto for the inmates of his Panopticon school: 'Call them soldiers, call them monks, call them machines, so they are but happy ones, I should not care'[65] and uses this as the basis of his argument that:

Bentham made it clear that he did not value liberty for its own sake . . . To him liberty was an emotive term, the use of which in politics distracted attention from the fact that it was essentially by restricitons on freedom that happiness was made possible.[66]

Dinwiddy, like Long, concentrates on liberty as the absence of coercion, and security as the product of law. Law is seen as an instrument of social control, emphasis is placed on the unlimited sovereign and the characterization of law as commands. Thus he provides a familiar picture of Bentham's utilitarian legislator as a manipulator of individual characters in order to form a harmonious social order. Dinwiddy particularly emphasizes the incompatibility of liberty and happiness. Bentham's monistic-value theory establishes the priority of happiness over all other sources of value including liberty and individuality. Dinwiddy does not attempt to argue that these concepts can be interconnected within a utilitarian theory of distributive justice, despite the fact that much recent Mill scholarship has been concerned with establishing the compatibility of these two concepts within Mill's theory of justice.[67]

The third recent work which sets out to deny Bentham's liberal credentials is C. F. Bahmueller's *The National Charity Company* (1981). Bahmueller concentrates on Bentham's Poor Law proposals as a paradigm for his utilitarian political morality. From his study of the Poor Law proposals he develops the following scathing indictment of Bentham's political and moral theory:

Bentham's poor law reform was replete with a repressiveness so pervasive, so soul-destroying, and with so little regard for either the civil liberties or the emotional sensitivities of those whose health (moral as well as physical) and happiness it sets out to promote and protect, that its administrative progressiveness pales in the comparison. Left in Bentham's hands, the poor would in respects essential to those who refuse to travel 'beyond freedom and dignity', be worse off than in fact they were.[68]

---

[64] J. R. Dinwiddy, 'The Classical Economists and the Utilitarians', in E. K. Bramsted and K. J. Melhuish (eds.), *Western Liberalism: A History in Documents from Locke to Croce* (London, 1978), 12–25.   [65] Bowring, iv. 64.

[66] Dinwiddy, 'The Classical Economists and the Utilitarians', p. 21.

[67] See Lyons, 'Benevolence and Justice in Mill', pp. 42–70.

[68] Bahmueller, *The National Charity Company*, p. 2.

In this passage, Bahmueller puts the greatest emphasis of all Bentham's recent critics, on the use of the law as a means of controlling and reconstructing human personality. Consequently, Bahmueller argues that Bentham had no commitment to liberty, but a totalitarian desire for control, order, and certainty.

All of the criticisms advanced by the three authors concentrate on the role of law within Bentham's utilitarian theory. They rely on an interpretation of Bentham's utilitarianism which leaves no room for the value of freedom or liberty within his thought. They also argue that because he attached no value to liberty he had no difficulty in banishing it from his system. Underlying these criticisms is the view that a negative theory of liberty as the absence of constraint is a paradigmatic liberal argument. The abandonment of a negative conception of liberty in favour of a concept based on a coercive theory of law is, according to this argument, sufficient to show that Bentham had no substantial commitment to the value of liberty.

However the claim that the pursuit of utility and a commitment to liberty are incompatible is a relatively recent one[69] that has arisen out of attempts to provide a formal defence of a liberal political theory. One of the main sources for these recent arguments against Bentham's utilitarian theory of liberty is to be found in Isiah Berlin's famous paper 'Two Concepts of Liberty'.[70] Berlin derives his distinction between the two concepts of liberty from a review of the arguments for freedom presented throughout the history of political philosophy. The distinction draws on a Hobbesian conception as the model of negative liberty and a Rousseauan model for positive liberty. Unlike some recent commentators[71] Berlin does not attempt a formal analysis of the concept of freedom. However, underlying Berlin's distinction there are two basic forms of argument. Firstly, he is committed to a pluralist conception of value which distinguishes questions of liberty from those of justice or security, and he rejects any monistic conception of value which connects liberty with other values. Secondly, Berlin suggests that positive conceptions of liberty tend towards totalitarianism because they distinguish between a 'noumenal' self and an empirical self. This 'noumenal' self embodies an individual's real interests, and knowledge of this 'noumenal' self enables the legislator to force an individual to be free, by forcing him to act on his real as opposed to empirical preferences. This latter strand of argument is only relevant to the discussion of Bentham, to the extent that it is used to support the view that only the negative theory of

---

[69] Mill appears to have seen no fundamental incompatibility between utility and liberty, whatever formal difficulties he may have had in combining the two within his utilitarian theory of justice.

[70] I. Berlin, 'Two Concepts of Liberty', in *Four Essays on Liberty* (Oxford, 1969), 118–72.

[71] See J. P. Day, 'Individual Liberty', in A. Phillips-Griffiths (ed.), *Of Liberty, Royal Institute of Philosophy Lecture Series*, 15, 1983), 17–29, G. C. MacCallum, 'Negative and Positive Freedom', *Philosophical Review*, 76 (1967, 312–34, and F. Oppenheim, *Political Concepts* (Oxford, 1981).

liberty embodies a conception of liberal value. Although Berlin's argument has attracted much controversy[72] it has had a significant influence among political theorists concerned with the concept of liberty. It has also had an influence on the history of political thought in so far as it has provided a standard by which to judge the liberal credentials of many modern political theorists.

In the case of Bentham the influence of the debate begun by Berlin is to be found in the difficulty many commentators have with reconciling a monistic conception of value with a liberal commitment to liberty. What is perhaps worse in Bentham's case, as Long has argued,[73] is that Bentham began with an analysis of liberty as a negative concept, and then abandoned it in favour of security. This suggests the complete abandonment of any commitment to liberty as such, a point Long goes on to argue. Long[74] misapprehends the character of Bentham's theory because he concentrates his discussion of Bentham's theory of liberty on the attempt to reform the language of political thought as a necessary preliminary to developing the legislative project. While Bentham undoubtedly was concerned with the reform of the language of politics, this was subordinate to his utilitarian concern with the reform of political institutions. It is not that Bentham wanted to abandon the use of certain concepts because non-utilitarian theories could be derived from them. Rather it is that Bentham's definitional concerns actually disguise his real concern, which was the criticism of rival theories of political morality which were in competition with utilitarianism. G. J. Postema has recently argued that Bentham's definitional projects are not preliminaries to the utilitarian project, but are a subordinate means of pursuing that project.[75] Postema argues, in particular, that some of the analyses given to fundamental legal concepts in *Of Laws in General*, are dictated by Bentham's utilitarian concerns.[76] It is clear that Bentham need not have provided the purely negative concept of liberty. Such analysis is not directly prescribed by utility. Bentham could have given an account of liberty in terms of security of expectation as liberty under the law and contrasted this with licence, which implies the total absence of all constraint, in a way similar to Locke and more recently Ronald Dworkin.[77]

Underlying Bentham's negative analysis of liberty, there is a utilitarian enterprise that is more substantial than that of clearing away the

---

[72] For the controversy that has arisen around Berlin's argument see T. Baldwin, 'MacCallum and the Two Concepts of Freedom', *Ratio*, 26 (1984), 124–42, C. Taylor, 'What's Wrong with Negative Liberty', in A. Ryan (ed.), *The Idea of Freedom* (Oxford, 1979), 175–93, and W. L. Weinstein, 'The Concept of Liberty in Nineteenth Century English Political Thought', *Political Studies*, 13 (1965), 145–62.

[73] Long, *Bentham on Liberty*, pp. 73–5.   [74] Ibid., pp. 65–83.

[75] Postema, 'The Expositor, the Censor, and the Common Law', *Canadian Journal of Philosophy*, 9 (1979), 643–70.   [76] Ibid., p. 645.

[77] J. Locke, *Second Treatise*, Chap. 2, sect. 6 (*Two Treaties of Government*), R. Dworkin, 'What Rights Do We Have', *Taking Rights Seriously* (London, 1977), 267.

ambiguities of language as a preliminary to the legislative project. Bentham alluded to the character of this enterprise in a manuscript from the same group of early manuscripts that Long uses in his account of Bentham's theory of liberty. He wrote: 'In whichever of the three last senses *liberty* be understood it is either a branch of security, it is either comprised under the head of security, or it has no value.'[78] Bentham's point is that unless the concept of liberty can be brought under the principle of utility it cannot function as a moral value and loses much of its intuitive appeal. Bentham's treatment of liberty in these early definitional writings[79] is aimed at providing a non-utilitarian analysis of the concept and drawing the implications, in order to undermine anti-utilitarian arguments based on the priority of liberty. His argument in the case of liberty is similar to his treatment of the concept of equality.[80]

Bentham's position in these early manuscripts is best interpreted as an attack on arguments which rely on a presumption in favour of liberty as an unargued first premiss. Because it is considered the chief liberal value, the burden of proof lies on those who want to deny its value to justify their case.[81] The presumptive argument in favour of liberty is based on the fact that it is liberty-limiting strategies and practices which require justification. And given that the requirement of justification is always directed at interferences with liberty it must follow that there is a prima facie or presumptive case in favour of liberty. Bentham's rejection of such a position is two-fold: firstly, while he recognizes that all limitations on liberty are an evil, some interference with liberty is essential in order to maintain and protect liberty, and secondly, the presumptive argument leaves open the question of what criteria should be used in order to distinguish those areas of liberty which must be protected and those which may be sacrificed in order to protect liberty.

The presumptive argument diverts attention from the real issues arising from the problem of liberty by obscuring the need to distinguish categories of value within the realm of liberty. While Bentham is committed to the value of freedom in his acceptance of security of expectation as the primary object of his utilitarian principle of right, he rejects the use of such presumptive arguments. Indeed, it is possible to view much of his hostility to declarations of rights and the many appeals to liberty or freedom among radical pamphleteers in light of his rejection of presumptive arguments for liberty. Bentham shared a commitment to the substance of some appeals to liberty, but he rejected the use of uncritical appeals to liberty as a means of advancing political argument. The point of his negative concept of liberty is

---

[78] UC c, 156.   [79] Ibid., 96–186 and lxix. 1–42 and 57–68.

[80] Ibid., lxxxviii, 52–81, clx. 155–76 and 197–204. This connects with Bentham's critique of the criterionlessness of rival moral theories discussed in Chap. 3, above.

[81] For a discussion of presumptive arguments for liberty see J. Feinberg, *Social Philosophy* (Englewood Cliffs, NJ, 1973), 20–2, also Hart, 'Are There any Natural Rights', *Philosophical Review*, 64 (1955), 175–91.

to show that outside of a normative framework the concept of liberty collapses into a purely descriptive term referring to the absence of constraint. An absolute commitment to liberty above all other values would be 'directly repugnant to the existence of every kind of government',[82] and would remove much of the normative force attached to the concept. Such an absolute appeal to liberty would also be an anarchical principle because of the absence of a public criterion for its application and a priority rule which facilitates arbitration between conflicts of liberty. Without a public criterion for the extension of liberty, an absolute principle of liberty collapses into an anarchical principle, because it undermines the conditions of social interaction. This is what is implied by Bentham's claim that an unrestricted liberty principle would be antithetical to any government.[83] According to Bentham, the appeal of liberty lies in its relation with other normative concepts within his moral theory. This, I believe is the main point of Bentham's rejection of liberty in favour of security. Therefore, while it is right for Dinwiddy to argue that Bentham 'did not value liberty for its own sake',[84] few political theorists have argued that liberty is good in itself, and have not introduced some instrumentalist considerations which necessarily refer the concept to a normative framework. Most classical liberals who attach supreme value to liberty nevertheless attempt some justification of the normative force of that concept. For example, J. S. Mill[85] and F. A. Hayek[86] base their commitment to liberty on its being a necessary condition of progress and the advancement of civilization.

A purely descriptive account of liberty, of the sort Bentham provides in the early manuscripts, and then rejects, enables no substantive distinctions to be drawn between types of coercion or restraint. A public health ordinance requiring the clear labelling of poisons is as much an infringement of a person's liberty as the denial of freedom of religious expression or the censorship of ideas the legislator regards as contrary to social harmony. Recent criticisms of a presumption in favour of liberty, advanced by Joseph Raz[87] and Charles Taylor,[88] reflect a similar position to that which I attribute to Bentham. Both Raz and Taylor argue that attempts to provide a completely negative account of liberty are unable to make important qualitative distinctions of the sort that are customarily made in the case of liberty. Raz says of the presumption in favour of liberty:

It does not assign any greater weight to our concern for religious freedom or for freedom of expression or for the freedom to have a family than to the freedom to kill

---

[82] UC lxxxviii, 69.

[83] For Bentham's critique of anarchical principles see Chap. 3, above.

[84] Dinwiddy, 'The Classical Economists and the Utilitarians', p. 21.

[85] Mill, *On Liberty*, in *Essays on Politics and Society* (The Collected Works of John Stuart Mill, xviii and xix).

[86] Hayek, *The Constitution of Liberty* (London, 1960), and *Law, Legislation and Liberty*, i, *Rules and Order* (London, 1973).   [87] Raz, *The Morality of Freedom*, p. 11.

[88] Taylor, 'What's Wrong with Negative Liberty', p. 183.

people we dislike, or be cruel to animals, or spend a fortnight on the summit of Ben Nevis.[89]

In the absence of some criteria by which one can identify those spheres of liberty that matter, the presumptive argument does little interesting philosophical work.[90]

When his rejection of the descriptive account of liberty is coupled with the two following arguments a good case is made for the incorporation of the value of liberty within the framework of utility as happens with the substitution of security for the concept of liberty. The first argument against the possibility of liberty acting as a self-sufficient value is that it is too indeterminate. Liberty cannot be a natural right if it is meant to imply the absence of constraint, because it would conflict with many other values which have an equal intuitive appeal. Many restrictions on freedom of action, which have the effect of protecting person and property would, nevertheless, be inconsistent with a natural right to liberty. Such a natural right, as Dworkin has recently argued[91] would be absurd because it would conflict with other practices that liberals also consider valuable. One of the strengths of utilitarianism is its ability to provide criteria for arbitrating between rival value claims. Therefore, it is precisely in such difficult circumstances that utilitarianism appears an attractive alternative to absolute moral principles. The second argument against liberty acting as a self-sufficient value takes as its target an attempt to get around the conclusion of the previous argument. If there can be no general right to liberty, it is argued there can be moral rights to specified liberties. Thus, it would be possible to argue that the most free society is one in which there is respect for the greatest number of these liberties. Bentham's criticism of the possibility of specifying such a list of liberties is that it is impossible to make such an identification of liberties outside of a normative framework which determines the qualitative distinctions among them.[92] It is impossible to identify such a class of liberties because to do so would depend on the prior existence of a system of value which gives substance to a distinction between liberty and licence. The freedom to choose and pursue one's own life plan is more important than the freedom to drive on the right-hand side of the road in the United Kingdom. However, according to Bentham, it is only possible to justify these claims against the background of a normative system which gives substance to the most important spheres of personal freedom, and which arbitrates in cases of conflict between rival values. The ability to

[89] Raz, The Morality of Freedom, p. 11.

[90] For an illustration of how Hart has moved away from the argument of 'Are There any Natural Rights', see his 'Between Utility and Rights', in A. Ryan (ed.), The Idea of Freedom (Oxford, 1979), 77–98; see also the discussion in J. Waldron, The Right to Private Property (Oxford, 1988), 100–1.

[91] Dworkin, Taking Rights Seriously, p. 267.

[92] A similar line of argument is advanced by O. O'Neill, 'The Most Extensive Liberty', Proceedings of the Aristotelian Society, 80 (1980), 45–59.

detemine a body of the most important liberties presupposes a criterion by which such an evaluation can be made. It was consistently Bentham's position that utility provided the only defensible criterion by means of which such value distinctions could be made.[93]

Given that Bentham rejected the possibility of providing a criterion for determining claims about liberty other than that provided by utility, it is not surprising that he subordinated liberty to the principle of utility. Nevertheless, the subordination of liberty within a utilitarian framework by rendering an account of freedom in terms of security, does not preclude a defence of Bentham's utilitarian political morality as substantively liberal. He rejects the presumptive argument for liberty, and it is this which is responsible for the view that he cannot have been a liberal. The spheres of security and liberty are extensionally equivalent to Bentham's theory because the former embodies the formal conditions within which an individual can pursue his interest and which are neutral among the various particular conceptions of individual well-being. The substance of any commitment to liberty is a pattern of rights which provides the framework of personal inviolability within which freedom obtains. This suggests that the provision of security is a necessary condition of liberty and that the two concepts are connected. Although I have argued that Bentham's commitment to security of expectation is partly co-extensive with a commitment to liberty, the degree of that commitment is to be measured not by securing expectations, but by how widely the realms of personal inviolability protected by security are defined. This distributive question will be discussed in a later chapter.

[93] See Chap. 3, above.

5

Subsistence, Abundance, and Equality and the Conditions of Stability

ALTHOUGH security enjoys a primary role within Bentham's theory of justice, he also acknowledged three other sources of utility which ought to concern the legislator in his construction of a utilitarian principle of right. The last chapter explained the importance of security of expectation within Bentham's political morality, this chapter, by concentrating on the objects of subsistence, abundance, and equality, will show that Bentham's conception of security of expectation does not entail only negative rights, that is, rights not to be interfered with in certain crucial respects. It will be argued that subsistence and equality incorporate positive rights or rights to certain specific benefits into Bentham's distributive principle by connecting these rights with the essential conditions for a stable social order, and thus security of expectation. This is consistent with an interpretation of Bentham's benefit theory as a version of an interest theory of rights. It will become clear that Bentham's theory of rights, where the benefits are specified in terms of the protection of the conditions of personal continuity and coherence and interest formation, is closer to contemporary interest-based theories than is recognized by most commentators.[1] Given the utilitarian principle underlying Bentham's principle of justice, there are no a priori reasons why he should be concerned solely with negative rights which protect the individual from interference.

The distinction between positive and negative rights is usually defended on the grounds that negative rights involve the agent in forbearing from some action whereas positive rights involve the agent in some action or contribution to another's good. However, while this distinction has been favoured by many thinkers who defend a negative concept of liberty,[2] it is not one that Bentham accepted. Underlying this distinction between positive and negative rights is a notion of scarcity. Scarcity of material resources is advanced as the reason why positive rights should be subordinated to

---

[1] See L. W. Sumner, *The Moral Foundation of Rights* (Oxford, 1987), 44–53, also J. Raz, *The Morality of Freedom* (Oxford, 1986), 180–3, and J. Waldron, *The Right to Private Property* (Oxford, 1988), 87–94.

[2] The distinction between positive and negative rights is reflected in Cranston's rejection of welfare rights in favour of a traditional conception of rights as protections against interference by others. See M. Cranston, *What are Human Rights?* (London, 1973).

negative rights. Yet scarcity of motivation also underlies the concept of negative rights. Rights against interference with liberty are required because there is a natural scarcity of benevolent motivations. If there was sufficient benevolence there would be no need for rights and sanctions to prevent interference. While these negative rights require forbearances from those who are not the beneficiary of the right they also require a contribution to those institutions which enforce these rights. The institutions of law enforcement, the judiciary and national defence are all required at the very minimum as the material conditions for the maintenance of a system of negative rights. Bentham acknowledged in the 'Principles of the Civil Code' that the maintenance of security was not without its costs.[3] Given that the maintenance of a system of negative rights requires a positive contribution from the beneficiaries of that system there is no ground for ruling out the provision of positive rights simply on the grounds that they require a contribution of the material conditions necessary to sustain such a system. This means that the limitation on the extension of a range of positive rights that is to be found in Bentham's theory of justice is based on practical considerations. Therefore, while the legislator cannot be expected to provide as a matter of right all those things which contribute to individual utility and interest satisfaction, he equally cannot rule out the provision, as a matter of right, of certain positive benefits which contribute to each individual's conception of well-being irrespective of its content. Bentham's conception of social happiness or well-being based on the four ends of legislative policy outlined in the 'Principles of the Civil Code' entails both negative and positive legal rights.[4]

The reason that the legislator cannot be under an obligation to provide all the positive benefits necessary to maximize an individual's utility is because he is not in a position to know the specific content of each individual's conception of interest. However, even if the legislator was in a position to determine within broad limits the substance of each person's conception of well-being he would still have the problem of co-ordinating his actions with the pattern of expectations which gave rise to the interests in the first instance. By concentrating on the provision of benefits to particular individuals the legislator will undermine the stable pattern of expectations upon which these interests are premissed because the provision of positive benefits will vary from case to case depending upon the substantial content of those interests. When the legislator's actions vary from case to case they cannot give rise to regularities upon which expectations are based, and this undermines the conditions of interest formation and realization and diminishes social well-being. Therefore, any positive rights which are incorporated within Bentham's theory of justice have to be consistent with the stability of expectations. This chapter will contend that the conception

---

[3] Bowring, i. 313–15.
[4] Ibid., 302.

of positive rights incorporated into the principle of justice indirectly contributes to the goal of securing a stable pattern of expectations.

The second section concentrates on Bentham's conception of the economy and its relation to the legislative project, and his intentions in pursuing particular policies. This section will address the question of how far Bentham was in favour of a *laissez-faire* policy as A. V. Dicey,[5] Leslie Stephen,[6] and W. H. Hutt,[7] have argued, or whether, as J. B. Brebner argues, Bentham is 'the formulator of state intervention for collectivist ends.'[8] In the course of examining these criticisms I shall argue that little is to be gained by trying to fit Bentham's theories either into the *laissez-faire* or the collectivist camp and that an attempt to defend Bentham as a neutralist liberal[9] is best achieved by exploring the role of economic freedom within his theory of justice.

I

In the last chapter it was argued that security is the primary component of the realization conditions of interest because it is both a necessary condition of an ordered social world, and of personal coherence and continuity over time. However, despite the great emphasis that is attached to security within Bentham's political morality—and the important role it plays in the explanation of his theory of justice—security is, nevertheless, only one of four components of happiness that are identified in the 'Principles of the Civil Code'.[10] The more perfectly that these four components of happiness are enjoyed—'the greater the sum of social happiness.'[11] Subsistence, abundance, equality, and security together form the four main components of social happiness. In a late manuscript from 1828, Bentham described the four objects of legislative policy as:

Maximizing universal security—securing the existence of and sufficiency of the matter of adequate subsistence of all the members of the community, maximizing the quantity of the matter of abundance in all its shapes, securing the nearest approximation to absolute equality in the distribution of the matter of abundance and the other modifications of the matter of property.[12]

In another early manuscript Bentham describes the legislator's task in relation to these four ends:

---

[5] Dicey, *Lectures on the Relation between Law and Public Opinion in England during the Nineteenth Century* (London, 1905), 44.

[6] Stephen, *The English Utilitarians* (3 vols., London, 1900), i. 310.

[7] Hutt, *Economists and the Public: A Study of Competition and Opinion* (London, 1936), 137.

[8] Brebner, 'Laissez-faire and State Intervention in Nineteenth Century Britain', *Journal of Economic History* (suppl.), 8 (1948), 59–73.

[9] See Chap. 4 n. 57, above.   [10] Bowring, i. 302.

[11] Ibid.   [12] BL Add. MS 33550, fo. 52.

the object of the legislator, we may say ought to be so to order matters as that all the several members of the community taken together may possess and enjoy the matter of subsistence and opulence in as high a degree of security as possible, and distributed amongst them with as much equality as is compatible with the superior interests of security.[13]

The four objects of legislation are constitutive of social happiness and are not simply four objects that have the highest acceptance utility. Whatever other objects one can identify as having the highest socially accepted utility, the four main objects are alone implied by the principle of utility as it is used in Bentham's political morality. Subsistence, abundance, equality, and security are the principles used in practical decision-making by the legislator, and are, therefore, intricately connected. It is for this reason that the boundaries which separate these ends cannot be easily drawn. Bentham wrote:

The boundaries which separate these objects are not always easily determined; they approach at different points, and are confounded one with the other. But it is enough to justify this division, that it is the most complete, and that we shall be called in many circumstances to consider each of the objects it contains, separately and distinct from each of the others.[14]

It is also for this reason that there can be no ultimate conflicts between these ends, though on the surface security and equality may appear to involve contrary prescriptions. The rest of this section will therefore be concerned with explaining how subsistence, abundance, and equality form the realization conditions of individual well-being, and how they indirectly contribute to security of expectation and the maintenance of a stable social order.

Of the four distinct ends of legislative policy Bentham distinguishes two classes: the first contains security and subsistence; the second contains the two remaining ends, abundance and equality. In the 'Principles of the Civil Code', he wrote:

At the first glance it is perceived, that subsistence and security rise together to the same height; abundance and equality are manifestly of a different order. Indeed, without security, equality could not endure a single day. Without subsistence, abundance cannot exist. The two first ends are like life itself: the two last are the ornaments of life.[15]

This division of the four ends of legislative policy into two classes, and the attaching of more value to the former rather than the latter, is another indication that security and subsistence are the main sources of utility upon which the legislator premisses his principle of right. In the course of this

---

[13] UC c, 171.
[14] Bowring, i. 302.
[15] Ibid., 303.

chapter it will be argued that abundance and equality is entailed by the provision of subsistence and the maintenance of security.

In terms of their priority as necessary conditions of free purposive action, it is not clear whether it is subsistence or security of expectation which should be given pride of place. Security of expectation enjoys some claim to priority, in that without security of expectation there can be no personal continuity over time, because there will be no possibility of building up long-term projects. Without these much of the value that liberal theorists have placed on the concept of freedom, however understood, disappears. Nevertheless, while security of expectation is a necessary condition of agency, and thus essential in explaining the value attached to freedom and self-direction, subsistence in so far as it is a necessary condition of existence enjoys a priority even over the value of secured expectations. While without security of expectation one cannot form any but the most basic desires, without subsistence one cannot do anything at all. In this way security can be seen as providing the formal conditions of free purposive action. The reason why Bentham concentrates on the provision of the minimum material conditions of action is because the means of subsistence are the basic conditions of any action whatever. A more substantial conception of the material means of action would depend on an account of the interest or project upon which it is premissed. It is only at the minumum level that the notion of the material conditions of action can be separated from any particular conception of individual well-being. In this way security and subsistence can be distinguished as components of an individual's good irrespective of his substantial conception of well-being. This is particularly important given that Bentham's aim was to construct a principle of right which is independent of any substantive conception of the good.

The apparent priority of subsistence over security of expectation does explain further why Bentham gave a higher priority to security and subsistence than to abundance and equality. However, this priority of subsistence is only an appearance, for in a manuscript dated 1819 Bentham quite clearly subordinates subsistence to security.[16] This leaves a rather confusing picture of the role and importance of subsistence. The incorporation of subsistence into Bentham's conception of well-being involves two strands of thought. In the first, the provision of subsistence entails the positive provision of the minimum material conditions of purposive action to those who are unable to secure it for themselves. In this case the means of subsistence are a distinct benefit, and the rights to subsistence are positive rights to the provision of this benefit. The second strand of thought involving subsistence connects it much more closely with the negative rights entailed by the provision of security of expectation. Bentham recognized that the provision of subsistence depends for the majority of people on a stable framework within which they can engage in productive activity.

---

[16] UC xxxvii, 8.

Therefore, guaranteeing subsistence also involves the legislator in maintaining the stable pattern of negative rights upon which economic relationships are premissed. Consequently, the provision of subsistence entails the security of expectation, just as securing expectation entails the positive provision of subsistence. In this way it becomes clear how the separate objects of legislation cannot always be clearly distinguished, and how they are ultimately only aspects of the primary goal of maximizing social well-being.

The inclusion of subsistence as a component of individual and social well-being turns attention from a purely negative conception of freedom to one which includes positive titles to the material conditions necessary for free purposive action.[17] The reason for this change in emphasis which is to be found in Bentham's work is that subsistence is intended not merely as a condition of interest formation, but it is also the primary material condition of interest satisfaction. Throughout Bentham's writings the one unchanging component is that the ultimate object of any legislator ought to be the pursuit of the maximum social well-being. It has been consistently maintained throughout this work that Bentham intended this to be achieved by creating the conditions in which each person is able to realize his own conception of the good. In practice the goals of some have to be subordinated to the general good because they interfere in the pursuit of another individual's end or violate his property: this minority whose conception of the good necessarily involves conflict with others are defined

---

[17] While J. S. Mill claimed in his 'Obituary of Bentham' in the *Examiner* that Bentham made no contribution to Civil Law, (10 June 1832, pp. 370–2, repr. in *Essays on Ethics, Religion and Society* (ed. John M. Robson (The Collected Works of John Stuart Mill, x), 495–8) it is nevertheless clear that Mill's utilitarian theory mirrored that of Bentham's Civil Law writings, particularly in the importance he attached to security and subsistence. Mill suggests in *Utilitarianism* (*Essays on Ethics, Religion and Society*, ibid., 250–1) that security and subsistence are the most important components of an individual's interest. He even argues that subsistence is prior in importance to security: 'The interest involved is that of security, to everyone's feelings the most vital of all interests. Nearly all earthly benefits are needed by one person, not needed by another and many of them can, if necessary, be cheerfully foregone, or replaced by something else; but security no human being can possibly do without; on it we depend for all our immunity from evil, and for the whole value of all and every good, beyond the passing moment; since nothing but the gratification of the instant could be of any worth to us, if we could be deprived of everything the next instant by whoever, was momentarily stronger than ourselves. Now this most indispensable of all necessaries, after physical nutriment, cannot be had, unless the machinery for providing it is kept unintermittedly in active play.' In this passage Mill establishes the priority of security after subsistence. It is also clear just how close Mill's position is to that of Bentham, for security and subsistence are the two main components of interest which underlie Bentham's theory of distributive justice.

Mill's use of the concepts of security and subsistence in the development of his own account of a utilitarian theory of justice has led some Mill scholars to argue that there was a substantial reconciliation between Mill and Bentham by the time the former came to develop his own utilitarian theory in the 1850s and 1860s. See S. Hollander, *The Economics of John Stuart Mill* (2 vols., Oxford, 1985), 602–76, F. Rosen, 'Bentham and Mill on Liberty and Justice', in F. Rosen and G. Feaver (eds.), *Lives, Liberties and the Public Good* (London, 1987), 121–38, and J. Viner, 'Bentham and J. S. Mill the Utilitarian Background', in *The Long View and the Short* (Glencoe, 1958), 306.

as criminals. When Bentham limits the legislator's task to the pursuit of the greatest happiness of the greatest number, all he intends to imply is that when certain people continue to act in violation of certain necessary institutions and social practices then the satisfaction of their desires must be sacrificed to those who manage to order their conceptions of well-being, and live harmoniously.

The conditions necessary for each person to be able to realize his own conception of the good are security of expectation within which that conception can be worked out, and subsistence or the physical conditions enabling that person actively to pursue his own conception of the good. The maximum social well-being is achieved by securing as wide a distribution of these realization conditions as possible by means of the utilitarian principle of right underlying Bentham's theory of justice. There does arise a slightly peculiar problem on any account of utility, and this concerns the well-being of future generations: given that the greatest happiness is achieved by securing the satisfaction of as many as possible of the interests of those individuals, there remains the question could the greatest happiness by further increased by the increase of the population, and the satisfaction of the projects and goals of these future people? The problem of the increase in population is considered by Bentham, and will be addressed later in this section in connection with a different issue. However, the particular strain of argument that is found in the above question is one that Bentham can avoid addressing head on. It is clear at least from the account of Bentham's utilitarianism which I am defending that the legislator does not play a creative role in determining the substance of each individual's particular conception of interest, rather his task is harmonizing the various particular goals of individuals so that the maximum social well-being arises out of the co-ordinated activity of as many of the members of the society as possible. In this sense the legislator creates the institutional conditions within which any additions to the population can realize their own projects, without at the same time pursuing a positive policy of encouraging an increase in the population in order to maximize further the greatest happiness. There is an air of paradox about this problem in that a continuous increase in the population beyond a certain marginal point actually decreases the overall utility. Many contemporaries of Bentham argued that this marginal point had been passed and the only way to return to it was to let nature take its course, and let the poor starve. Bentham neither concurred with the opinions of the Malthusians nor with their policy prescriptions. However, he was sufficiently influenced by their arguments to think that this marginal point at which continued population increase results in a net loss of utility was not that far off, though the precise marginal point was difficult to determine.[18]

[18] Bentham's relationship with Malthusian ideas is obscure. In a number of works, particularly *The True Alarm* (1801), and 'Pannomial Fragments', Bowring, iii. 227–8,

As well as being an efficient condition of free purposive activity the need for subsistence is also the most important species of natural motivation in that it is responsible for individual agents engaging in productive labour. Throughout Bentham's Poor Law writings there is an underlying emphasis on productive labour as the chief means of overall individual interest satisfaction. The need to acquire the means of subsistence is a motivation to act because they provide the material conditions of existence. This motivation to seek the means of subsistence is also necessary in order for the agent to be able to pursue his greater goals. Therefore, the individual has a motivation to engage in productive labour which extends beyond the immediate desire to prevent the pains of hunger and death.

The notion of subsistence as a natural motivation to engage in productive labour connects the pursuit of subsistence with the provision of negative rights to security of expectation. Bentham acknowledged the overriding natural motivation to engage in productive labour in his references to the lone savage hiding his prizes to keep them from other predatory individuals.[19] However, the existence of this lone savage bears little relation to even the poorest in the societies of Europe during the eighteenth century. While the natural motivation caused by the pain of hunger or the contemplation of the pleasure of a good meal is sufficient to encourage the search for the means of subsistence, it is not in itself sufficient to account for the more complex forms of activity that embody the notion of productive labour within a society. Productive labour is a social phenomenon and relies on the stability provided by the formal conditions of social co-operation. The most important of these is the security of expectation provided by a system of law. Security of the material conditions of subsistence is an essential motivating condition for an individual to engage in productive labour. The natural motivation to secure the means of subsistence does not pay any attention to the possessions or entitlements of other people, so that if one individual is stronger than another, the former can secure his subsistence by exploiting the efforts of the latter. Productive labour is the

---

Bentham adopted a Malthusian analysis of the problems posed by population growth. However, Bentham never adopted any Malthusian policy prescriptions. As I have argued in this chapter, Bentham acknowledged a positive title to the means of subsistence, whereas Malthus argued that poor relief ought to be progressively abolished. Rather than abolishing poor relief and leaving the indigent to fend for themselves, Bentham planned an elaborate programme of poor relief based on Poor Panopticons and administered by the National Charity Company. There are other aspects of population policy on which Bentham and Malthus differ. Bentham's relationship with Malthusianism is discussed in L. Campos Boralevi, *Bentham and the Oppressed* (Berlin, 1984), 48–52 and 106–8. She concludes: 'Bentham's ideas on poor relief were as much opposed to Malthus's abolitionist proposals as was "the principle of utility", in his words, opposed to "the principles of asceticism and sympathy". There are very good reasons therefore for believing that Bentham would have criticized Malthus's arguments for the abolition of Poor Laws, as he had criticized Malthus's looking to moral restraint as the only remedy to the evils of overpopulation' (p. 108).

[19] Bowring, i. 308.

means by which an individual can best achieve the guarantee of his own subsistence within society. It is also the means of providing certain goods and benefits which can either facilitate the satisfaction of an individual's ultimate goals or else form a contribution to that end. So the endeavours of each individual, in so far as he is engaged in productive labour, benefits himself, and by contributing to a product which others find useful he is indirectly benefiting others. However, if the benefits that result from sophisticated forms of productive labour are to be achieved some guarantee must be provided for the individuals who are to engage in this form of behaviour that they will be able to benefit as a result of their efforts. Thus, if an individual is to see labour as the means of securing his subsistence and the material conditions necessary for realizing his goals, he must be protected from the possibility of frustration by others. The institution of law prevents an individual from going out and securing his subsistence wherever he can, and this has the effect of rendering productive labour the only efficient means of securing one's subsistence. If productive labour is the only means open to a person to secure subsistence, and subsistence is the primary material condition for any purposive activity, it is necessary to guarantee to that person the uninterrupted enjoyment of the product of his labour. Bentham emphasized the role of security as the means of guaranteeing to a person the product of his labour saying:

The law does not say to a man, 'Work and I will reward you;' but it says to him, 'Work, and by stopping the hand that would take them from you, I will ensure to you the fruits of your labour, its natural and sufficient reward, which without me, you could not preserve.' If industry creates, it is the law which preserves: if at the first moment, we owe everything to labour, at the second, and every succeeding moment, we owe everything to law.[20]

Without such a guarantee the motivation to engage in productive labour would collapse, and the way is again open for an individual to secure his subsistence in whatever way he can, and this has the effect of undermining the stability of society. If the institutions of a stable social order necessarily preclude an individual from securing his own subsistence by means of productive labour, his natural motivations will encourage him to satisfy his needs in ways that threaten social peace. The provision of overall subsistence is, therefore, dependent on the existence of security, but in the same way the existence of security is dependent on the provision of a positive title to subsistence. Without the material conditions of purposive activity an individual cannot act so as to realize his conception of the good, and if society cannot guarantee this most minimal condition of action the interests of society are in conflict with the interests of that individual. Subsistence is a necessary condition of any purposive action including the pursuit of the material conditions of subsistence in the future. However,

---

[20] Bowring, i. 308.

without security, subsistence cannot be pursued in a way that is compatible with other individuals doing the same, for no individual would have any guarantee that he would enjoy the fruits of his labour, and would, therefore, have no reason for engaging in productive labour. Without the motivation to engage in productive labour, one of the major defining institutions of society would disappear, and there would be an impossible strain placed on the peace and stability of society.

Within Bentham's writings on Distributive Law there is an important change of emphasis which corresponds to a widening of Bentham's practical concerns. This is most clear in the case of the increasing emphasis placed on the need for the positive provision of subsistence. One of Bentham's earliest treatments of subsistence is to be found in the 'Principles of the Civil Code'. This work places great emphasis on security as the most important of the four objects of legislation and on the negative status of any title to subsistence. In this work Bentham acknowledged the importance of subsistence as the necessary material component of social happiness, although he only gave it a negative status. He wrote that law can do nothing 'directly' to provide subsistence, at most it can create motives to secure subsistence, but then nature herself has already provided sufficient stronger motives.[21] 'What can be added, by direct legislation, to the constant and irresistible power of these natural motives?'[22] However, while Bentham argued that there is little that direct legislation can add to the already existing natural motives, he nevertheless stressed that the legislator can do inestimable good by securing the product of an individual's labour. Thus:

the law may indirectly provide for subsistence, by protecting individuals whilst they labour, and by securing to them the fruits of their industry when they have laboured: *security* for the labourer—*security* for the fruits of labour. In these cases, the benefit of the law is inestimable.[23]

The emphasis in the above passage, and throughout the treatment of the subject in the 'Principles of the Civil Code', reflects the classical liberal position that the legislator can only act through the negative means of creating laws which prevent individuals from violating the private realm of other individuals, and not by any direct pursuit of the positive provision of subsistence. While Locke and Hume can plausibly be characterized as liberal in the above sense, a thoroughgoing utilitarian like Bentham could not reconcile a purely negative liberal position with the requirement to secure the maximum social well-being. The reason for this is that the disutility arising from the death or starvation of those who are unable to secure the means of subsistence despite the system of law which guarantees to them the product of their labour, is so great that it is unlikely to be

[21] Ibid., 303.
[22] Ibid., 304.
[23] Ibid.

outweighed by the smaller disutility arising from the positive contribution necessary to guarantee the means of subsistence to all. This argument renders it implausible for a utilitarian to advocate no positive provision whatever, for those who are unable to secure their own subsistence.

Despite the emphasis that Bentham placed on the negative title that an individual has to the means of subsistence, he nevertheless acknowledged that utilitarian considerations require a more positive consideration for those who are unable to secure their own subsistence. Thus, later, in the 'Principles of the Civil Code', he wrote:

the title of the indigent, as indigent, is stronger than the title of the proprietor of a superfluity, as proprietor; since the pain of death, which would finally fall upon the neglected indigent, will always be a greater evil than the pain of disappointed expectation, which falls upon the rich when a limited portion of his superfluity is taken from him.[24]

In this passage Bentham accepted that some form of positive provision of subsistence was necessary for the indigent. However, little attempt is made to explore the implications of this provision, or how it would fit into the wider aim of maintaining social stability. It is only in later works on Distributive Law that Bentham began to place greater emphasis on the positive provision of subsistence. This change in emphasis is perhaps a consequence of a deeper insight into the threats posed to social stability by the indigent, which Bentham acquired in the course of his Poor Law writings of 1795 to 1797.

One of Bentham's chief motives for tackling the problem of the English Poor Law was the threat posed to the holders of property by a large economically disenfranchised class. The situation of the poor was made worse during the latter part of the eighteenth century by the war in Europe. The worsening economic situation can only have raised the further problem of the stability of the social order in light of the increasing numbers of able-bodied poor. C. F. Bahmueller in his study of Bentham's Poor Law writings[25] asserts that given the political and economic climate of Britain during the 1790s Bentham's object was twofold: firstly, to mollify the poor and alleviate distress among them, and secondly, to control them, and dampen the fires of revolutionary fervour. Bahmueller's interpretation confirms the thesis that the problem of the provision of a positive title to the means of subsistence is connected with the wider aim of maintaining security of expectation and social stability.

The problem of large-scale poverty and economic disenfranchisement attacks the very heart of a utilitarian social order. The utilitarian rationale of any political institution is that it provides the maximum of social well-being by providing the minimum conditions necessary for each person to

---

[24] Bowring, i. 316.
[25] Bahmueller, *The National Charity Company* (Berkeley, Calif., 1981), 1–2.

pursue his interest. When it fails to provide these minimum conditions its legitimacy evaporates. Given that, the rationale for the system of secured expectations that guarantees to each the product of his own efforts is premissed on the equal ability of all to secure their own good, and not on any status the system of private property and the market is supposed to derive from natural law. When the system breaks down, and large numbers cannot secure their own continued existence, then the overall goal of 'social happiness' dictates the overriding of these impartial mechanisms in favour of positive provision of the means of subsistence. Without this the economically disenfranchised would see a divergence between the secure social order and the overall object of maximizing social well-being. Once this divergence is perceived, those who have been denied the benefits of the existing institutions will see those institutions acting against the social well-being, and thus attempt to overthrow them in favour of whatever other institutions or practices they think will best secure the overall end. The fear is that those who have no longer any faith in the impartial framework for individuals to secure their own ends, will abandon it in favour of a partial conception of the social well-being, and the conflict between these rival conceptions of the overall object of social life will lead to the fragmentation of the social order, and thus, the loss of all the benefits that it provides. The continuation of a stable social order cannot be guaranteed while large numbers of individuals are precluded from the enjoyment of its benefits. Without a stable social order the expectations of all cannot be secured, and this necessarily leads to a diminution of 'social happiness'. It can, therefore, be asserted that the feeling of security which is an important psychological condition of the enjoyment of the freedom provided by the system of secured expectation, is dependent on the guarantee of the means of subsistence or minimal economic security to all the members of society.[26]

The task for the classical liberal is not to sit by and let the market deprive a large number of individuals of the means of subsistence, but is rather to provide for the minimal economic security of each individual in such a way that the equal liberty of all individuals is not violated by the positive provision of the means of subsistence. Bentham thought that this could be done through the means of his Poor Panopticons, which were designed to be centres for the distribution of the means of subsistence: in effect a form of workhouse.

The character of these Poor Panopticons has attracted much controversy.

---

[26] Bentham's commitment to the positive provision of subsistence as a condition of social stability is reflected in the work of later non-utilitarian theorists such as F. A. Hayek. Hayek's commitment to the provision of the means of subsistence is reflected in the following passage: 'The assurance of a certain minimum income for everyone, or a sort of floor below which nobody need fall even when he is unable to provide for himself, appears not only to be a wholly legitimate protection against a risk common to all, but a necessary part of the Great Society in which the individual no longer has specific claims on the members of the particular small group into which he was born' (*Law, Legislation and Liberty*, iii. 55).

Bahmueller has criticized Bentham for the coerciveness involved in making attendance at these Panopticons a condition of receiving relief. Bentham is also criticized for introducing the notion of 'less-eligibility', which involves the conditions within the Poor Panopticons being sufficiently worse than the conditions of the labouring poor so as to discourage the labouring poor from unnecessarily relying on poor relief. Other criticisms that Bahmueller advances against Bentham are that the education offered for the children of the poor amounts to social-engineering, as it lays great stress on the utilitarian virtue of industriousness.[27] Bahmueller's main point is that the indigent suffer a massive loss of liberty and in fact gain nothing to offset that loss, although he also mantains that nothing could compensate such a loss of liberty. The indigent are deprived of their freedom simply because they are not able to secure their own subsistence. Bahmueller contrasts this with the system of outdoor relief which the poor enjoyed in their own homes and which combined subsistence with liberty.[28] If this is the premiss that underlies Bahmueller's charge that Bentham's Poor Law proposals involve a massive loss of liberty for the poor, then his own characterization of the existing state of poor-relief undermines the force of his criticism.

The existing system of poor-relief was not uniform throughout the country, and while in some parts the poor did relatively well, in others they suffered badly. Bentham's intention was to introduce a system that provided an equal and sufficient standard of relief for all. Given this difference in the standard of relief throughout the country it is not possible to see the existing system as consistent with liberty, as opposed to Bentham's system which, according to Bahmueller, opted for administrative efficiency instead of liberty. Bentham's writings on the Poor Law have attracted substantial criticism[29] particularly with regard to Bentham's intentions; much of that criticism has turned on the impossibility of reconciling utilitarian efficiency with liberty. Not all of that criticism has been hostile. Warren Roberts[30] has argued that Bentham did not introduce the notion of 'less-eligibility'; he only intended the standard of subsistence within the Poor Panopticons to be no better than that of the labouring poor. Roberts also argues that while Bentham appeared to sacrifice some freedom for subsistence, there were benefits along with the means to subsistence which must be taken into account when weighing up the costs of Bentham's system of Poor-relief. The

---

[27] For his overall judgement of Bentham's utilitarian system see Bahmueller, *The National Charity Company*, p. 2.

[28] J. Semple, 'Bentham's Haunted House', *Bentham Newsletter*, 11 (1987), 35–44.

[29] See G. Himmelfarb, 'Bentham's Utopia: The National Charity Company', *The Journal of British Studies*, 10 (1970), 80–125, J. R. Poynter, *Society and Pauperism: English Ideas on Poor Relief, 1795–1834* (London, 1969), 117–44, W. Robert, 'Bentham's Poor Law Proposals', *Bentham Newsletter*, 3 (1979), 28–45, and M. I. Zagday, 'Bentham and the Poor Law', in G. W. Keeton and G. Schwartzenberger (eds.), *Jeremy Bentham and the Law* (London, 1948), 68–78.

[30] Roberts, 'Bentham's Poor Law Proposals', p. 30.

Poor Panopticons offered education and training for the younger inmates. This training provided these younger inmates with the ability to improve their chances in the labour market. The Poor Panopticons also provided a system of paupers' banks which were intended to encourage the virtues of thrift and frugality as well as providing a deposit facility for small sums which the existing commercial banks would not accept. Roberts's argument can be contrasted with the position advanced by Bahmueller. Bahmueller argues that Bentham's Poor Law proposals are soul-destroying and oppressive because of the loss of liberty entailed. Roberts, on the other hand, while acknowledging that some freedom is lost by requiring the indigent to enter the Poor Panopticons, nevertheless, argues that within these Poor houses the loss of liberty is only so long as the poor need remain within them, and that through the education and training that is received, the poor are provided with the means necessary to enjoy a wider liberty when they are able to return to the labour market. For Bentham, Bahmueller's claim that the Poor have been deprived of freedom is disingenuous. The indigent have been deprived of the minimum physical conditions of free action, so to them the value of the concept of freedom which underpins Bahmueller's argument is non-existent.

The choice for Bentham is between the continued enjoyment of a purely nominal freedom, which to the indigent is the freedom to starve or turn to crime or the violent overthrow of the system, or the guaranteed enjoyment of the minimum physical conditions of subsistence until such a time as that person is able to return to the market. There is indeed some loss of freedom, but Bentham clearly thought that the gain of continued existence plus the other benefits of education and health-care outweighed this loss. Throughout all of the Poor Law writings Bentham was concerned apart from his administrative interest to balance the positive provision of subsistence against the possible creation of a premium on idleness—that is, to avoid encouraging free-riders, who enjoy the benefits of the social provision of the necessary conditions of purpose action, but incur none of the costs such as having to engage in productive labour. Whatever the argument in favour of Bentham's balance between freedom and subsistence, he is at least clearly distinguished from those Malthusians who advocated the abolition of relief for the indigent, thus in effect introducing the gravest and most severe punishment for something most of the indigent could not be held responsible.[31] What is clear from the debate surrounding Bentham's Panopticon scheme is that it ought not to be read as a blueprint for a Benthamite Utopia, but was designed to address a number of specific social problems and not recast all social relationships.

The arguments of Malthus and his followers would have had quite the

---

[31] 'We are bound in justice and honour formally to disclaim the right of the poor to support' (T. R. Malthus, *Essay on the Principle of Population*, 6th edn. (2 vols., London, 1826), ii. 201).

opposite effect to that desired by Bentham, for by placing the gravest and most severe punishment on an individual whose only crime is to be indigent, they invite that individual to commit some action worthy of the punishment. The Malthusians offered an invitation to the poor to engage in actions that undermine the stability of the social order, simply because it offers them no other hope of securing the means of subsistence, and thus, their own continued existence. The avoidance of just such an eventuality was precisely Bentham's intention. The role of the Poor Panopticons as a means of securing the stability of the social order colours the perceptions of interpreters of Bentham's Poor Law writings, and in part explains why writers such as Bahmueller attribute such a sinister purpose to Bentham's project. Bahmueller appears blinded by the notion that Bentham chose the means of law to realize his utilitarian project, and the idea that law is necessarily coercive only confirms the view that Bentham's intention was to force the indigent into a situation where they no longer posed a threat to society. However, as Postema has argued,[32] placing too much emphasis on law as a means of social control obscures Bentham's real intention which was to prevent law as the constitutive framework of the social world. While it is true that law is necessarily coercive, Bentham did not intend this to imply that the utilitarian legislator would proceed by coercing individuals into realizing some preconceived social good. It is only when an individual chooses to disregard the sphere of another individual that the coercive nature of law is revealed; in this case the threat of punishment is used to make recalcitrant individuals respect the inviolability of others.

The misreading of Bentham's intentions that Bahmueller derives from a misunderstanding of the true character of Bentham's legislative project leads him to see coercion as the primary aim of the Panopticon scheme. However, I have suggested that Bentham chose the system of poor relief as the means through which the positive provision of subsistence would be provided, and that the chief rationale for this positive title was to secure the stability of the social order by providing an alternative to crime or revolution for those who are economically disenfranchised. When it is acknowledged that Bentham's intention was not to punish the poor for their poverty, but rather to provide them with a real alternative to crime and revolution, then there is a sound reason for assuming, with Warren Roberts,[33] that the provision of subsistence should not take place under a regime that is unnecessarily harsh, but rather one that is sufficiently pleasant to pose a real and desirable alternative to starvation or crime and revolution. This aspect of the system of positive provision of the minimal means of subsistence is often obscured by Bentham's other concerns such as administrative efficiency and the need to provide an economically cost-effective system. However, these can only

---

[32] Postema, *Bentham and the Common Law Tradition*, pp. 162–7.
[33] Roberts, 'Bentham's Poor Law Proposals', pp. 41–2.

be the means to the greater utilitarian end of the system which is the positive provision of subsistence as a means to securing the continued stability of the social order.

In some of the later writings on Civil Law Bentham placed the greatest emphasis on the role of the positive provision of subsistence as a means to securing the continued stability of society. In a manuscript composed in 1828 he wrote:

Sooner than continue to labour under this affliction individuals who are experiencing it [the lack of the means of subsistence] will naturally and necessarily, in proportion as they find the opportunity do what depends upon them towards obtaining at the charge of others the means of rescuing themselves from it: and in proportion as endeavours to this purpose are employed, or believed to be intended to be employed security for property is certainly diminished, security for person probably diminished on the part of all others.[34]

In the above passage Bentham made it quite clear that the non-provision of positive assistance for the indigent is inviting social disorder. While in the 'Principles of the Civil Code' great stress was laid on the role of nature as the natural motivation to secure subsistence with only a passing acknowledgement of the need for some positive measures, in these later works the emphasis has changed to an acknowledgement of the need to provide the positive means of subsistence in order to secure social stability. Despite making no further substantial contribution to the debate over the form of poor-relief after 1797, Bentham's analysis of the dangers of allowing a large economically disenfranchised class to develop was incorporated into manuscripts written towards the end of his life in the late 1820s. Bentham saw the dangers of widespread and long-term indigence as a causal factor in the fragmentation of the social order:

The consequence is that, sooner or later in every habitable part of the earth's surface the community will consist of three classes of inhabitants: 1. those for whom with the addition of more or less of the matter of abundance, the matter of subsistence is possessed in a quantity sufficient for the preservation of life and health against death, and disease proceeding speedily to death: 2. those who being in a state in which they are perishing for want of the matter of subsistence are on their way to speedy death: 3. those who to save themselves from impending death are occupied in waging war upon the rich, providing the means of subsistence for themselves at the expence of the security of all, and the matter of subsistence and abundance in the possession of all.[35]

It is the last of the three categories that most concerns the utilitarian legislator because this class poses the greatest threat to the stable social order. However, he ought also be concerned with those individuals in the second category who are also suffering and dying, for this also affects the overall balance of social well-being. These are the arguments, expressly

---

[34] BL Add. MS 33550, fo. 125.   [35] Ibid., fo. 126.

stated in the Civil Law writings which form the premiss for the positive provision of the means of subsistence. However, while it is clear that Bentham unequivocally backed this provision of the means of subsistence in his late Civil Law writings, it is equally clear that Bentham was acutely aware of the difficulties that face any adequate social safety-net. Thus along with providing the analysis upon which the positive provision of subsistence is premissed, the Civil Law manuscripts composed in the late 1820s, which were later incorporated into the 'Pannomial Fragments', are also concerned with striking an adequate balance between guaranteeing the means of subsistence and providing a bounty on indolence.[36]

It can be argued in Bentham's favour that the cost of the loss of liberty on being required to enter the Poor Panopticon in order to receive the means of subsistence was designed to tip the balance away from putting a bounty on indolence or providing encouragement for the unlimited procreation of the poor.[37] But it can be argued in Bentham's favour that he had no one simple answer to the problem of reconciling the provision of the means of subsistence with the placing of a bounty on indolence, for he wrote:

Human benevolence can therefore hardly be better employed than in the quiet isolation of the difficulties and in the reconciliation of a provision for the otherwise perishing indigent with the continual tendency to an increase in the demand for such provision.[38]

The emphasis that Bentham placed on the positive provision of subsistence as a means of securing social stability, is one of the most important contributions of Bentham's Civil Law writings. The importance of this measure lies in the fact that it shows Bentham to be the first recognizably liberal political theorist to see the threat posed to social stability and to the existence of freedom by the continued growth of a large class of the economically disenfranchised. Bentham, therefore, avoided the paradox attributed to the Classical Economists by W. D. Grampp,[39] who wrote:

In urging economic freedom upon the world, the classicists were expressly, or by implication, insisting that all men should have a right to seek their own material welfare in their own way and, moreover, that such a policy was not only morally proper but psychologically necessary ... Yet in their observations on political

[36] UC xxxvii, 51, and BL Add. MS 33550, fo. 125.

[37] At one point in 'Pannomial Fragments' Bentham appears to suggest that a policy of emigration might prove to be the solution to balancing the positive provision of subsistence without creating a bounty on indolence (see BL Add. MS 33550, fo. 126.) However, this flirtation with emigration is no more than a passing thought, for in the same manuscript Bentham acknowledges that emigraiton could at most provide a short-term solution. For a full discussion of Bentham's late interest in emigration and the schemes of Edward Gibbon-Wakefield see D. Winch, *Classical Political Economy and Colonies* (London, 1965), 25–39.

[38] BL Add. MS 33550, fo. 126.

[39] Grampp, 'On the Politics of the Classical Economists', *Quarterly Journal of Economics*, 62 (1948), 714–47.

doctrine and the organization of the state (as distinct from the political organization of the market), they were far from holding democratic views, and although they favoured a representative government, they quite pointedly wished a limited one. In the opposition of these views is one paradox: a free market implies what may be called universal economic enfranchisement, but limitations on representative government deny men the political freedom which is the analogue of a free market.[40]

Of the Classical Economists James Mill advocated a property condition as a qualification for the franchise, while Ricardo showed little concern for the radical extension of the suffrage. Only Bentham accepted the full extension of political rights. Grampp argues that for the Classical Economists the extension of the franchise must be limited, for it could not seriously be extended to cover those without property without threatening the system of economic freedom which is premissed on the ownership of private property. The reason why they could not tolerate the continued extension of the suffrage is, according to Grampp, precisely because the distribution of property which it was argued was necessary for the system of economic liberty was the cause of social disorder among the poor or those without property. Bentham alone did not place any strict property condition on the extension of the suffrage, and in principle he saw no sufficient reason why it should even be restricted to males.[41] But more importantly in this context Bentham alone also saw the threat to the stable social order posed by the economically disenfranchised. His response to the threat to social stability was not to limit the suffrage to those who owned property in order to protect it from the indigent, instead he argued that the only permanent solution was to secure to each individual the means of subsistence. He also believed that the ownership of property should be extended to all by taking positive measures to reduce great disparities in inherited wealth. Bentham was alone in seeing that there is a serious incoherence in arguing that the legislator can only interfere in the system of economic liberty by sacrificing liberty, if the legislator's non-interference in the system of economic liberty necessarily results in the build-up of social forces which will eventually destroy the system of private property and the operation of the market.

For Bentham there were no absolute natural rights to freedom or to property, and thus the criticism of legislative action on the grounds that it interfered with economic liberty, when its aim is to secure the stable social order of which the economy is part, was simply an example of the confused thinking that resulted when absolute claims to liberty or property rights were made.

The importance of subsistence within the Civil Law writings is also the key to understanding the role of equality within the hierarchy of legislative goals. This fact has often been obscured by Bentham's intemperate criticism

---

[40] Grampp, 'On the Politics of the Classical Economists', p. 714.
[41] F. Rosen, 'Bentham on Democratic Theory', *Bentham Newsletter*, 3 (1979), 46–61, and *Jeremy Bentham and Representative Democracy* (Oxford, 1983), 131–2.

of 'Levelling Systems'. Once the rhetoric has been removed it is clear that equality plays a crucial role in the hierarchy of legislative goals for the same reasons as subsistence. To defend any substantive conception of equality as part of Bentham's concept of utility is at first sight an unpromising task. Throughout the Civil Law manuscripts Bentham appears to question the role of equality as a value or object of legislation. In an appendix to the 'Principle of the Civil Code' entitled 'The Levelling System', Bentham wrote:

Inequality is the natural condition of mankind; subjection is the natural state of man. It is the state [into] which he is born: it is the state in which he always has been born, and always will be, so long as man is man. It is the state in which he must continue for some of the first years of his life, on pain of perishing. Absolute equality is absolutely impossible.[42]

In other passages from the 'Principles of the Civil Code' Bentham wrote:

Equality ought not to be favoured, except in cases where it does not injure security; where it does not disturb the expectations to which the laws have given birth; where it does not derange the actually established distribution.[43]

Or again: 'The establishment of equality is a chimera: the only thing which can be done is to diminish inequality.'[44] The above passages give conflicting impressions of the role of equality within Bentham's moral and political theory. The expressed hostility to the pursuit of equality found in these and other passages has led one critic to argue that Bentham's contribution to debates over the role and value of equality was in fact to turn away from the traditional discussion and concentrate instead on equalization.

In his paper 'Bentham's Theory of Equality',[45] Parekh presents Bentham's concern as the equalization of benefits—in particular wealth—in accordance with the dictates of diminishing marginal utility, rather than any concern with equality as a substantive value or a necessary component of the theory of justice. Parekh goes on to argue that the concern with equalization has little to do with the traditional concern with equality as a substantive goal; equalization is dictated by diminishing marginal utility. However, other utilitarian conditions limit the applicability of diminishing marginal utility, so that even on Bentham's terms equalization plays only a minor role within his utilitarian system. Parekh's main ground of attack is that this concern with equalization only obscures the fact that 'In Bentham's view there is no prima facia case for equality and fairness in the distribution of benefits and burdens',[46] and he continues that this lack of concern with equality as a substantive value shows that 'The way Bentham understands the greatest happiness principle has profound anti-liberal and anti-egalitarian implications.'[47] Parekh makes substantial and wide-ranging criticisms of

---

[42] UC lxxxviii, 69.   [43] Bowring, i. 303.   [44] Ibid., 311.
[45] B. Parekh, 'Bentham's Theory of Equality', *Political Studies*, 18 (1970), 478–95.
[46] Ibid., p. 494.   [47] Ibid., p. 495.

Bentham's utilitarianism in his paper, which, if correct, seriously undermine any attempt to defend Bentham's utilitarianism as a theory of distributive justice. Nevertheless, there is sufficient evidence to show that Parekh's is neither the only possible interpretation of Bentham on equality nor the most plausible one.

Throughout the above discussion of the positive provision of the means of subsistence there was a strong implication of equality; if subsistence is a necessary condition of maximizing social well-being then it is clear that social happiness implies an equal title to the means of subsistence, even to those who as criminals are denied an equal title to freedom. The equal title to the means of subsistence is a sufficient reason for arguing that Bentham's concern with equality cannot be reduced to projects of equalization dictated by diminishing marginal utility. Bentham's claim for an equal title to the means of subsistence is borne out in a manuscript passage where he wrote:

In regard to subsistence the case is that considered apart from, and accompanied by, abundance, equality is essentially and included in the very conception of it: for as consistently involved with the supposition no man can in this case have more of the means of subsistence than another, so consistently with his existence no man can have less.[48]

And later: 'Subsistence taken in the strict sense, there is not in this case a place for degrees in the scale of equality: for by the supposition no inequality has place in this case.'[49] The Civil Law writings of the 1820s emphasize the connection of equality with the positive provision of the means of subsistence.[50] The positive provision of the means of subsistence is not a consequence of a programme of equalization. It involves a substantial commitment to equality as part of social happiness, and this commitment to equality undermines Parekh's claim that for Bentham equality meant no more than equalization.

The necessity of providing for the equal access to and provision of the means of subsistence implies that the principle of utility entails a principle of distributive justice. Therefore, Bentham is not subject to one of the main criticisms levelled against utilitarianism by Rawls.[51] A complete analysis of the character and role of Bentham's theory of distributive justice will be left to a later chapter. However, the claims made so far go some way to corroborating Rosen's assertion that Bentham can avoid Rawls's criticism of utilitarian theory.[52]

Parekh misses the point of Bentham's theory of equality because he sees the pursuit of equalization as distinct from and as an alternative to a substantive theory of equality. However, the pursuit of equalization, even

---

[48] UC clx, 160.   [49] Ibid., 161.
[50] BL Add. MS 33550, fos. 52 and 143.
[51] J. Rawls, *A Theory of Justice* (Oxford, 1972), 25.
[52] Rosen, *Jeremy Bentham and Representative Democracy*, p. 220.

when it is dictated by considerations of diminishing marginal utility, is not an alternative to, but a necessary component of, a substantive theory of equality. Any theory of equality which is designed to rectify an existing social arrangement in which it did not previously apply must necessarily make some attempt at equalization, that is rectifying the existing distribution of benefits and burdens such that the free exchanges of those goods in the future will reflect the just distribution. It is as a means of rectifying the existing distribution that Bentham can be seen to advocate equalization of the minimal conditions of subsistence. However, it must be emphasized that equalization is only a means to ends which are dictated by substantive equality. The plausibility of Parekh's interpretation is derived from the fact that equality does not feature directly as a component of an individual's real interest in the way that security of expectation and subsistence do. In a late discussion of the four ends of legislation Bentham wrote that 'Equality is not itself, as those other three are, an immediate instrument of felicity.'[53] What he intended by this claim is not that equality is not as important as the other components of social happiness, but rather that equality is a component in a way that is distinct from the other three. Thus far it has been argued that security and subsistence are immediate instruments of felicity because they provide the conditions within which an individual can form and pursue his interests. Abundance, on the other hand, plays an equivocal role as an immediate component of felicity. In one sense it simply refers to the sum total of the means of subsistence in society, and might be termed the collective means of subsistence. However, it also refers to the individual matter of wealth over and above that sufficient for immediate subsistence, and this is borne out by the fact that Bentham sometimes regards the term abundance and opulence as synonymous.[54] When abundance is understood as the individual matter of wealth over and above that sufficient for immediate subsistence, then there is no difficulty in arguing that abundance forms part of the immediate instruments of felicity: firstly by providing the stock from which the positive provision of the means of subsistence can be drawn, and secondly, in the case of each individual, because the greater the sum of wealth of an individual, the more that person will be able to secure his own ends. Equality differs from these other components of social well-being in that it is a relational benefit. It is not a necessary condition of one person's being secure in his rights that all others are similarly secure, but one person cannot stand in a relationship of equality with all others unless they stand in the same relationship to him. Equality is a good derived from a particular distribution of benefits and burdens in society. Therefore, equality is not a necessary condition of purposive action in the way that security, subsistence, and abundance are.

Equality is linked to security of expectation as an indirect component of

[53] UC clx, 161.
[54] Bowring, i. 304.

the conditions necessary for a stable social order. The role of equality as a condition of social stability has already been seen in the discussion of subsistence, where it was argued that the equal title to the means of subsistence was a condition of long-term social stability, and therefore connected to the primary goal of security. However, it would be wrong to think that equality is simply a distributive implication of the positive provision of subsistence. In a number of manuscripts Bentham encouraged the pursuit of equalization programmes that make no reference to the provision of the means of subsistence. Thus he wrote:

it will be found that the plan of distribution applied to the matter of wealth will be as most favourable to universality of subsistence and thence in other words to the maximization of happiness, in which while the fortunes of the richest—of those whose situation is at the top of the scale is greatest, the degrees from the fortunes of the least rich and those of the most rich are most numerous in other words the gradation most regular and invisible.

The larger the fortunes of the richest are, the smaller will be the number of those whose fortunes approach nearest to this high level: the smaller therefore the number of those form whose masses of property the largest defalcation could by propriety be made:[55]

Here Bentham argues that in a situation of great inequality the burden of providing the means of subsistence will fall heaviest on the shoulders of those few individuals who have substantial accumulations of wealth. In order to render the burden more equal it would be better to have a less marked disparity in incomes within society: thus his point about having a numerous gradation of income and wealth, rather than having a few enormously wealthy individuals and a great many poor. Underlying Bentham's concern is the fear that if there is such a great disparity of incomes in society then there is a great pressure towards social instability for two reasons: firstly, the concentration of wealth and power in too few hands is likely to result in both not being used for the benefit of all; and, secondly, this could result in the threat of the economically disenfranchised attempting to restructure the social order for their benefit. Thus Bentham's desire to have a great variety of incomes and an invisible gradation between the lowest and the highest incomes is premissed on the contribution such a policy would make to the reduction of social instability. There does also seem to be some recognition that the concentration of the responsibility to supply the positive means of subsistence on a small portion of society is unfair.

Bentham emphasizes his commitment to the pursuit of equality as a direct condition of social stability in the following passage:

Equality requires that though it is at the expence of all the other members of the community, the means of those whose income is composed of the wages of labour be

[55] BL Add. MS 33550, fo. 137.

maximized. Reason. Of these composed the vast majority of the whole number of the members of the community.

Exceptions excepted Equality requires that the profits of stock be minimized. Reason. Because the net profits of stock is composed of the mass or say portion remaining to the employer of the stock after deduction made of the wages of the labour applied to it.[56]

His intention here is to foster the pursuit of productive labour, which he saw as the best way for each individual to secure his own means of subsistence. Also the rewards for labour are an appropriate means of distributing benefits and burdens within society, for they refer to an individual's own efforts, and not something from which he has benefited as a matter of birthright. If most people are required to work for their subsistence, while others are able to enjoy vast benefits without any efforts, then there remains an incentive for the labouring poor to cease labouring and prey on the wealthy. The law can prevent this by creating crimes and punishing them, but the only long-term and effective means of removing this threat to social order is the creation of an integrated and equal society, where those inequalities that exist are the result of labour.

Bentham did not advocate the complete levelling of all incomes.[57] He argued that 'Absolute equality is absolutely impossible',[58] and that absolute equality is only found in the realm of physics.[59] However, he did argue that inequalities of wealth and power must have a clear utilitarian justification. Therefore, he could consistently allow for those inequalities of wealth and income which were the result of individual effort, and were necessary in order to sustain economic activity, while subjecting to equalization those portions of income that were unearned, and did not contribute to the incentive to continue labouring. The existence of large unearned incomes at times when there are also large numbers who are impoverished or excluded from the benefits of the market due to unemployment, poses a danger to the continued stability of the social order. Thus in the interests of securing expectations Bentham is able to justify the pursuit of programmes of equalization. Therefore, a connection between security and equality can be established, even though the two ends are often presented as being incompatible. A connection can be established between those redistributive programmes designed to encourage labour and the wider egalitarian concern with personal dignity and lifestyle through the conditions of equality sufficient to guarantee social stability.

It might be argued that a condition of substantive equality within a community is that each member is able to see that all other members of the community enjoy no special privilege which gives them a status above that of any other member of the community. If some members of the community

---

[56] BL Add. MS 33550, fo. 138.   [57] UC lxxxviii, 52–81.
[58] Ibid., 69.   [59] Ibid., clx, 161.

enjoy substantial unearned incomes then not only is equality of wealth lacking in the community, but so is equality of status, because those individuals are guaranteed the realization of their projects independently of the system which is justified on the ground that is the efficient means of securing the realization of an individual's desires and projects. The fact that some do not depend on their own endeavours within the labour market for the realization of their projects creates a situation where the identification of the system as the sole and sufficient condition for individual well-being is undermined.

The chief condition of social stability is that each sees the institutions of the stable social order as the necessary means of the realization of the ends and goals of all the members of society whatever those may happen to be. When this identification breaks down, the stability of the social order is undermined. The best means of ensuring this identification with the institutions of a market society is to encourage the conditions within which every individual is dependent on them for the realization of their goals and projects—by securing the wages of labour, and redistributing in the long term all unearned benefits, even those which are a return on capital.

While Bentham clearly had a substantial commitment to the goal of redistribution of wealth to foster individual labour and initiative, this has been regarded as a serious weakness of his theory by some critics, for reasons that have been developed recently by philosophers such as Nozick.[60] In a recent paper Schwartz identifies Bentham's commitment to the equalization of wealth and incomes as a major anti-liberal component of his utilitarian theory.[61] The problem that Schwartz identifies in Bentham's commitment to the equalization of incomes is the familiar Nozickean problem of patterned principles of justice, whereby the maintenance of the pattern implies an intolerable interference with freedom, such that the positive pursuit of equality actually undermines freedom. Surprisingly, given Schwartz's criticism of Bentham on this point, Bentham appears to acknowledge those very arguments, whereby the unrestricted pursuit of equality would actually destroy the very benefits that the programme of restribution is supposed to equalize. There are many passages in his writings where he is critical of claims for the unrestricted pursuit of equality;[62] nevertheless, he still advocated policies of equalization. How did he reconcile the two? The key to understanding the relationship between the freedom implied by security of expectation, and the positive pursuit of redistributive policies is to be found in equality's role as one of the conditions of social stability. The policies of redistribution that Bentham advocated were, I have argued, geared to the task of securing social stability.

[60] R. Nozick, *Anarchy, State, and Utopia* (Oxford, 1974), pp. 149–67.

[61] P. Schwartz, 'Jeremy Bentham's Democratic Despotism', in R. D. Collinson-Black (ed.), *Ideas in Economics* (London, 1986), 128.

[62] See UC lxxxviii, 77–9, clx, 161, lxi, 9, BL Add. MS 33550, fo. 137.

His hostility to unrestricted policies of redistribution based on first-order considerations of diminishing marginal utility, can be explained by the fact that they cannot be reconciled with the other three goals of legislative policy, and will eventually undermine the existence of a stable social order and its benefits. It is only when equality itself becomes a threat to that same stability that it ought to be abandoned in favour of security. Schwartz later acknowledges that Bentham introduces the 'disappointment-preventing principle' in order to reconcile the egalitarian implications of the principle of utility with the maintenance of security of expectations. However, he concludes that Bentham made no attempt to develop his principle and, therefore, that it fails to save the argument. Schwartz is wrong, however, to give the impression that Bentham does not develop the 'disappointment-preventing principle' at all, for while it would have been more helpful had Bentham dealt with it in greater detail, it will be seen in a later chapter that it is still possible to determine how it is supposed to function within his theory of justice.

The third object of legislation discussed in this chapter can be dealt with briefly as it receives the shortest treatment of the four ends of legislation within the Civil Law writings. The good of abundance, as I have already argued, fits into the conditions of social happiness in two ways: firstly, as an individual good, where it refers to the surplus of the material conditions of interest satisfaction over and above that required for immediate subsistence; in the second case, as a collective good, by providing a fund from which can be drawn that which is necessary to secure the positive provision of subsistence and to finance the institutions necessary to maintain security of expectation. It is in this second sense that abundance makes its contribution to social happiness, and it is with abundance in this second sense that I shall be concerned in what follows.

Throughout this chapter I have tried to show that the four ends of legislative policy are different modifications of a single end—social happiness—which is the sole object of the legislator's concern. Understood in this way it is possible to see how the four ends of legislative policy are all concerned with the one overall goal, that of providing a secure and stable pattern of expectations within which any individual can both develop and realize his conception of well-being. Abundance fits into this project because it provides the means for the long-term material security of a stable social order.

Bentham writes of abundance as if it were merely the means of subsistence considered as a collective good:

Included in the mass of the matter of abundance the mass of subsistence. The matter of wealth is at once the matter of subsistence and the matter of abundance. Subject matter of sole difference, the quantity less in the case of subsistence; greater in the case of abundance.[63]

[63] BL Add. MS 33550, fo. 127, punctuation added.

However, abundance is an important component of social happiness, because it provides the material conditions of security. All of those institutions within a society that are geared towards maintaining security, such as those of law and government, as well as all those bodies which give execution to security, such as the courts and the military, are dependent on the means of abundance which through taxation and loans to the government guarantee their provision. Bentham acknowledged that all aspects of public policy and preventive police were to be funded from the means of abundance. He was also equivocal over the question of whether these public services should be provided by private or government agencies. Prisons, public health, the armed forces, and the courts are all public goods in that they contribute to social happiness. Their provision is essential for the happiness and stability of a sophisticated and civilized society, irrespective of the origin and ownership of these utilities. Bentham's emphasis on abundance as an essential condition of a civilized life and social happiness were merely the recognition of something that was the common currency of those writers he acknowledged as influences. Adam Smith in *The Wealth of Nations*, Montesquieu in *The Spirit of the Laws*, and Hume in a number of his essays all saw the pursuit of abundance as an essential condition of a civilized and happy state. For example, Hume wrote:

The greatness of a state, and the happiness of its subjects, how independent soever they may be supposed in some respects, are commonly allowed to be inseparable with regard to commerce; and as private men receive greater security, in the possession of their trade and riches, from the power of the public, so the public becomes powerful in proportion to the opulence and extensive commerce of private men.[64]

In the same way as the good of abundance or opulence is connected with commerce by Hume, Smith, and Montesquieu, Bentham also placed great weight on commerce and industry as the means of providing the abundance necessary to sustain social life at a civilized and stable level. Thus it is that of all the four components of social happiness, abundance is that for which the legislator can do least. In the 'Principles of the Civil Code' Bentham argued that it would be superfluous for the legislator to attempt to legislate for the pursuit of abundance, because natural motivations were sufficient to guarantee its supply:

Wants and enjoyments, these universal agents in society, after having raised the first ears of corn, will by degrees erect the granaries of abundance, always increasing and always full. Desires extend themselves with the means of gratification; the horizon is enlarged in proportion as we advance; and each new want, equally accompanied by its pleasure and pain, becomes a new principle of action . . . And what more is

---

[64] D. Hume, *Essays, Moral, Political and Literary*, ed. T. H. Green and T. H. Grose (2 vols., Oxford, 1963), i. 288–9.

required than the force of these natural motives for carrying the increase of wealth to the highest possible degree?[65]

Bentham consistently denied that the legislator had any direct means of encouraging the pursuit of abundance,[66] beyond those motivations which nature has already supplied. Therefore, within the Civil Law writings there is little treatment of the nature of the policies by which abundance can be maximized. His most sustained treatment of those policies which have reference to the good of subsistence is to be found in his economic writings, and here his concern is wholly negative; he advocates the removal of 'useless and expensive encouragements given under the instance of benefit to trade',[67] and the general object of his policies are the removal of impediments to trade and industry. Such positive encouragements to trade were at best superfluous and at worst pernicious:

The trade thus encouraged is either an advantageous trade in comparison with others not encouraged, or an unadvantageous one: if an advantageous one in itself and without the encouragement the encouragement is unnecessary and useless: if an unadvantageous one, it is pernicious. If the legislator in the plenitude of his wisdom happens to know of a more advantageous branch of trade than is known to any man whose business it is to trade, let him but point it out, and if it be really so, he need not be apprehensive of not betaking themselves to it: instruction which costs nothing, will answer every good purpose of a bribe.[68]

Abundance can only be encouraged indirectly by removing impediments to trade and industry, enforcing contracts, and by minimizing interference in the private sphere of individuals so as to leave them to contribute to the quantity of abundance through their own projects and plans. Thus in the famous *Defence of Usury*[69] Bentham argues for the removal of restrictions on the lending of money for interest by allowing private individuals to set their own money bargains governed only by mutual self-interest. However, throughout Bentham's writings it is clear that the chief means for guaranteeing sufficient abundance is provided by the provision of security. Just as subsistence is best achieved through the guarantee of the uninterrupted enjoyment of the fruits of labour, so also is the means of abundance. The pursuit of abundance is inextricably connected to security of expectation, for it is by providing the secure conditions within which an individual can engage in the direct pursuit of his projects, that industry and commerce flourish. Abundance, therefore, forms a part of social happiness not only because it provides the material conditions necessary for social stability, but also because it is a product of security of expectation and social stability. One important implication of this connection between security and abundance is that social stability requires a system of economic

---

[65] Bowring, i. 304.   [66] UC xxxvii, 52.

[67] Ibid., c. 182.   [68] Ibid.

[69] W. Stark (ed.) *Jeremy Bentham's Economic Writings* (3 vols., London, 1952–4), i. 121–207.

liberty, for this is both a condition on the maintenance of social stability, and a consequence of security of expectation.

One consequence of the argument so far is that Bentham's concept of social happiness or utility appears to pull in two opposite and incompatible directions. The requirements of social stability involve the direct pursuit of policies for the redistribution of wealth, whereas the conditions necessary for abundance, without which there could be no positive provision of subsistence or security, require a system of economic freedom. There are two questions that arise from this; the first is concerned with how Bentham balances the egalitarian and libertarian claims of his concept of utility; the second is concerned with what light the above explanation of the nature of social happiness throws on the character of his Political Economy. The answer to the first of these questions will be found in the details of Bentham's theory of property and the role of the 'disappointment-preventing principle' in his theory of distributive justice. The answer to the second question concerning the character of Bentham's Political Economy will be dealt with in the next section.

II

Writing at the end of the eighteenth and the beginning of the nineteenth centuries, Bentham has been seen by some to stand at an important crossroads for the tradition of liberal political thought, which has its origin in the writings of Locke and extends through to the nineteenth and twentieth centuries. Despite historicist criticism of such an ahistorical interpretation of political thought,[70] a recent commentator has described Bentham as effecting a rupture in the tradition of liberal political thought which came down to him via Locke, Montesquieu, Adam Smith, and the Scottish Enlightenment, by creating a 'system of thought which legitimated the interventionist and statist tendencies which grew even stronger throughout the latter half of the nineteenth century in England.'[71] For those who saw a conflict between two forms of liberalism, classical and revisionist, or else those who were the ideological opponents of both forms of liberalism, the labels *laissez-faire* or collectivist became terms of abuse or praise depending upon which side of the ideological divide they stood. A. V. Dicey saw Bentham as a classical nineteenth-century economic liberal and a thoroughgoing advocate of *laissez-faire*.[72] Leslie Stephen also characterized

---

[70] See in particular Q. Skinner, 'Meaning and Understanding in the History of Ideas', *History and Theory*, 8 (1969), 3–53, 'Conventions and the Understanding of Speech Acts', *Philosophical Quarterly*, 20 (1970), 118–38, 'Some Problems in the Analysis of Political Thought and Action', *Political Theory*, 2 (1974), 277–303; also J. Dunn, 'The Identity of the History of Ideas', *Philosophy*, 43 (1968), 85–104, and J. G. A. Pocock, *Politics, Language and Time* (New York, 1971).

[71] J. Gray, *Liberalism* (Milton Keynes, 1986), 30.

[72] Dicey, *Lectures*, p. 44.

Bentham as a theorist of *laissez-faire* economic liberalism.[73] More recent writers, such as Henry Simons,[74] have praised Bentham for his *laissez-faire* attitude to economic policy. However, others who, like Simons, favour a *laissez-faire* policy have seen Bentham as the originator of an interventionist brand of liberalism which they regard as paving the way for socialism. Into this category fits J. B. Brebner who saw Bentham as 'the formulator of state interventionism for collectivist ends'.[75] The remainder of this chapter presents a number of considerations which show the inappropriateness of describing Bentham as either a defender of *laissez-faire* economics or as the originator of collectivism.

While many of the economic policies which Bentham advocated tend to lend support to those who want to characterize him as an advocate of *laissez-faire*, those who have wished to characterize him as a founder of collectivism have concentrated on his utilitarianism. Since Halevy,[76] it has been customary to see two conflicting principles at work within Bentham's moral theory: the first is an egoistic principle which maintains that each individual will pursue his own interests; the second is the principle of utility itself which enjoins each to pursue the maximum social well-being. Petrella[77] has recently used a version of this argument to support the claim that Bentham's work embodies a transition from eighteenth-century classical liberalism into the anti-liberal and bureaucratic forms of government which characterized the nineteenth century. He argues that on one level Bentham's moral theory requires a large degree of liberty and tends towards *laissez-faire*, whereas at another level, that of the principle of utility, the pursuit of the maximum social well-being is incompatible with the extension of individual liberty. On the first level the individual is the final arbiter of his own well-being, and in order to pursue that, he needs a stable pattern of institutions which facilitate personal liberty and the development of stable expectations. On the second level it is argued that the direct pursuit of the greatest happiness of the greatest number is incompatible with the sort of stable established institutions which are necessary for personal freedom. The principle of utility must remain responsive to changes in the overall balance of utility. Therefore, it cannot be constrained by considerations of personal liberty and respect for rights. While a series of institutions designed to allow individuals the secure pursuit of their own interests will result in an undesigned objective dictated by the individual decisions taken within those institutions, the principle of utility

---

[73] Stephen, *The English Utilitarians*, p. 310.

[74] H. C. Simons, *Economic Policy for a Free Society* (Chicago, Ill., 1948), 104–5.

[75] Brebner, 'Laissez-faire and State Intervention in Nineteenth Century Britain', p. 60.

[76] E. Halévy, *The Growth of Philosophic Radicalism*, trans. M. Morris (London, 1972). A version of the thesis of the natural convergence of public and private interests has been advanced by D. Lyons, *In the Interest of the Governed* (Oxford, 1973), 19–106.

[77] F. Petrella, 'Benthamism and the Demise of Classical Economic *Ordnungspolitik*', *History of Political Economy*, 9 (1977), 215–36.

actually dictates the outcome by directing the impersonal processes within an economy to the end of maximizing social well-being, and this necessarily involves the sacrifice of liberty.

According to Petrella, Bentham is a collectivist because he intends the imposition of a ready designed outcome on political and economic life, rather than creating conditions within which the final outcome is the impersonal product of the countless decisions of free individuals in society.[78] Petrella's argument is particularly important in the case of the Civil Law writings because it appears to mirror the conflict that is thought to exist between the libertarian concern for security and the egalitarian concern for redistribution. Whereas a system that gave absolute priority to security of expectation would be compatible with true individualism, Bentham gave a high priority to redistributive policies and this undermines true individualism in favour of some patterned principle of justice or social design.

The weakness in Petrella's argument is that Bentham did not intend that the maximum social well-being should be pursued by means of global utility calculations. Instead the legislator achieves the maximization of social well-being by means of indirect strategies premissed on the utilitarian value of security of expectation. Therefore, like the system of natural liberty, these strategies do not prescribe the substantial outcome of social interaction, but are solely concerned with the formal conditions within which the maximum social well-being can arise. The pursuit of utility only conflicts with the security of expectation sufficient for each individual to pursue his own interests, if security of expectation is seen to be distinct from the goal of maximizing utility, as Petrella's argument implies. However, there still remains the problem posed by the requirement to pursue egalitarian redistributive policies, for this still suggests that Bentham's commitment to liberty is subordinated to a previously conceived pattern of distributive justice. If Bentham did intend the realization of a pattern of distributive justice then he still falls foul of Petrella and Hayek's argument, for he was still determining the end result of social action rather then leaving that to the free actions of individuals. However, by connecting the pursuit of equality with security Bentham was able to retain a commitment to liberty, and to avoid the charge that he was attempting to determine the substance of the social good. Thus Bentham was not a collectivist in the sense in which Hayek or Petrella implies.

While there is good reason to argue that Bentham is not a collectivist in the technical sense used by Hayek, there is also good reason to argue that Bentham is not a collectivist in its less technical sense where it used to refer to the opposite of *laissez-faire*. Bentham has been described as 'the

---

[78] For this distinction see F. A. Hayek, 'Individualism: *True and False?*', in *Individualism and Economic Order* (London, 1949).

formulator of state intervention for collectivist ends',[79] because of his policies of poor-relief. Unlike the Malthusians Bentham was not prepared to let the poor starve; neither was he prepared to rely solely on the system of private charity. He believed that leaving the provision of poor-relief to charity would not only put an unfair burden on those of a benevolent nature, but that it would put a premium on selfishness.[80] This would contribute to a fragmentation of the social order by discouraging the provision of poor-relief, which was precisely what he sought to avoid.

However, though Bentham argued for a centralized national provision of poor-relief through the National Charity Company, this does not imply that he intended the provision to be organized and controlled by the government. The National Charity Company was to be organized as a joint stock company similar to the East India Company and the individual Poor Panopticons were to be self supporting in the long run, and any profit that resulted from the system would in part be paid as a premium to the shareholders. The point of giving the National Charity Company the status of a joint stock company was precisely so that it would not constitute an increasing burden on the rate and taxpayer who financed the previous parish poor-relief system. The effect of the status of the National Charity Company was that it did not constitute a collective good which depended on the sacrifice of individual freedom to sustain it, whereas the criticism of Bentham by Gray[81] and Brebner[82] is precisely that the provision of a collective welfare system is incompatible with an individual's freedom to dispose of his time and property as he wishes. Thus in so far as Bentham does accommodate a realm of economic liberty within his political morality, that economic liberty is not undermined by the positive provision of limited social welfare as some critics have suggested.

However, while Bentham cannot appropriately be described as a collectivist in any informative and uncontroversial way, neither can he be described as an advocate of *laissez-faire*, at least not in the sense in which the Classical Political Economists might be so described. As T. W. Hutchison[83] has argued, one of the main features that distinguishes Bentham from the other Classical Economists is that he approached economic policy through the agenda of the four ends of legislative policy of the Civil Law which are constitutive of the principle of utility. Hutchison argues that Smith began with the notion of the beneficence of a free market and then constructs around this the institutions necessary to sustain it. He has also shown that Bentham's concern with equality as an end of economic policy has no important parallels among any of the other liberal Classical

---

[79] Brebner, 'Laissez-faire and State Intervention in Nineteenth Century Britain', p. 60.

[80] Bahmueller, *The National Charity Company*, p. 19.

[81] Gray, *Liberalism*, p. 30.

[82] Brebner, 'Laissez-faire and State Intervention and Nineteenth Century Britain', p. 60.

[83] T. W. Hutchinson, 'Bentham as an Economist', *Economic Journal*, 66 (1956), 288–306.

Political Economists; the writings of Smith and Ricardo contain no similar discussion of equality or distributive justice.

Despite the eloquent defence of Bentham as a Classical Economist in the field of economic policy by Lord Robbins[84] little can be gained by trying to force him into either a collectivist or a *laissez-faire* mould, and this is because these are essentially later nineteenth-century categories. His economic concerns, in so far as these can be distinguished from those of his legislative project, have more in common with the economic writings of Hume and Adam Smith than with positive economic theories being developed by Ricardo and McCulloch in Bentham's later years. Bentham's economic writings are primarily concerned with practical questions of fiscal policy arising out of the national debt. This is in line with Hume whose economic writings are also concerned with questions arising from the management of the national debt. The eighteenth century saw the rapid increase in the size of the national debt, and this raised a whole variety of questions about the propriety of mortgaging the future, as well as the technical questions surrounding the problem of debt management. While Hume and to some extent Smith were concerned with the propriety of the national debt,[85] Bentham was largely concerned with the more technical problems of debt management and the control of the supply of money, as well as with how the cost of government could be reduced.

Bentham's economic concerns naturally took him out of the sphere of purely economic reality, and placed his contribution to economic thought within the sphere of economic policy where it is closely connected with more purely political concerns as well as constitutional theory and the theory of government practice. Against this background of the national debt and the increasing cost of government, it is hard to see Bentham's economic thought in the same light as that of Ricardo, McCulloch, or even James and John Stuart Mill. It should not, however, be thought that because Bentham's economic writings were concerned with problems arising from the national debt that these writings are anachronistic in the light of Ricardo and the development of Classical Economics. All that is implied in stressing the eighteenth-century character of the problems with which Bentham was concerned is that his economic thought was governed by practical problems facing government rather than with the construction of a scientific theory.

The main reason why it is inappropriate to characterize Bentham's economic writings in nineteenth-century terms is that he did not construct a positive economic theory, and this was because he did not recognize the

---

[84] L. C. Robbins, *The Theory of Economic Policy in English Classical Political Economy*, 2nd edn. (London, 1978).

[85] See D. Winch, *Adam Smith's Politics* (Cambridge, 1978). An exploration of the issues of debt management and the extension of public credit, which concerned Hume, Smith, and Bentham is provided by J. O. Appleby, *Economic Thought and Ideology in Seventeenth Century England* (Princeton, NY, 1978), and P. G. M. Dickson, *The Financial Revolution in England: A Study in the Development of Public Credit 1688–1756* (London, 1970).

economy as an autonomous sphere of action. The social world was constituted by the law which supplied the ground rules of all individual interaction by providing the focus of expectation which makes individual coexistence and co-operation possible. The primary role of law in Bentham's work distinguishes it from that of Hume or Adam Smith: for Hume property provides the framework of social reality, and in the case of Smith the mechanism of the market provides a system of natural liberty which sets a framework for the positive law. Thus in the case of Smith the sphere of natural liberty constrains what the legislator can do with regard to commerce and economic activity. In Bentham's case there are no constraints placed on the legislator's activity by the need to respect the regime of natural liberty. However, this does not mean that the legislator is allowed to act without constraint; he ought to act in accordance with the dictates of utility, and this requires that a wide sphere of liberty ought to be tolerated so as to facilitate the maximization of abundance. Thus Bentham grounds a sphere of economic liberty directly on the dictates of the principle of utility, and not on the need to recognize an autonomous realm of action such as the system of natural liberty. In so far as one can identify the economy within Bentham's writings, it is part of the social reality that is constituted by law. It is not surprising, therefore, that the principles which determine the utilitarian model of social life and the utilitarian model of economic life should be found in the same place, namely the principles of Civil Law.

While Bentham cannot adequately be described as the founder of 'state interventionism for collectivist ends', or as an apostle of *laissez-faire*, there is still a sufficient reason for describing Bentham's economic thought as liberal.[86] The justification for this is to be found in the relation these have with his utilitarian legislative project. By providing the conditions for the realization of individual conceptions of well-being, the legislator makes no distinctions between the quality of individuals' interests, and he is neutral or impartial between these interests. The same system of security of expectation is constitutive of the sphere of economic liberty. Thus, while the principle of utility does not determine the pursuit of any one individual end, but is rather concerned with providing the conditions in which all individuals can secure their interests, so in the economic realm the principle of utility does not determine the final outcome at which all economic activity should be directed. Rather it provides the framework within which the maximum of social well-being will be pursued through the free action of individual agents. It is this neutrality between individuals' interests which encapsulates the spirit of liberalism, and in so far as this is reflected throughout Bentham's writings on economic subjects, he can be described as an economic liberal.

---

[86] For a discussion of Bentham as an economic liberal see P. J. Kelly, 'Utilitarianism and Distributive Justice: The Civil Law and Foundations of Bentham's Economic Thought', *Utilitas*, 1 (1989), 62–81.

6

The Security-Providing Principle

THE emphasis placed in the last two chapters on the importance of securing expectations and maintaining social stability as the conditions of maximizing social well-being, appears to give Bentham's argument a conservative character. However, to see his political morality in this light would be a grave error for he was not simply concerned with social stability as such (though in times of crisis he preferred the stability of the social order however conceived to the threat of anarchy),[1] but rather with the stability of a pattern of expectation which provides a framework of certainty within which each individual can secure his own conception of well-being.

If Bentham's concern was the total eradication of contingency from social life[2] then the sphere of personal inviolability left to each person would be so small as to preclude any freedom of choice and action. Yet, if he was not concerned with establishing a realm of certainty throughout political and social life, then it remains to be shown just how far he intended the legislator to go in fixing patterns of behaviour by securing expectations.

The object of this work is to identity a principle of right which distributes to each person a sphere of personal inviolability. These spheres of personal inviolability ground those expectations which are the necessary conditions of interest formation and personal continuity and coherence over time. This chapter will argue that Bentham was not concerned with securing all expectations by means of positive law. Instead he intended to create a series of rights which demarcate an individual's sphere of personal inviolability. This realm is determined by identifying a class of harms which affect the development and pursuit of any person's interests, and this category of harms is the subject-matter of private offences. These spheres of personal inviolability, taken together, give rise to a pattern of expectations which is necessary for the co-ordination of individual actions, and thus, to maximize social well-being. In the course of this chapter it will become clear that Bentham's peculiar conception of property played an important role in his theory of distributive justice and in determining an objective concept of harm, and part of this chapter will be concerned with defending Bentham against the charge made by Long[3] that he was unconcerned with questions

---

[1] Bowring, i. 311 and 358–64, and UC lxxxviii (a), 52–81.

[2] See C. F. Bahmueller, *The National Charity Company*, (Berkeley, Calif., 1981), 1–11, and S. R. Letwin, *The Pursuit of Certainty* (Cambridge, 1965), 127–88.

[3] D. G. Long, 'Bentham on Property', in A. Parel and T. Flanagan (eds.), *Theories of Property: Aristotle to the Present* (Waterloo, 1979).

of distributive justice and simply interested in following Blackstone in defending the socio-economic status quo. It will also be agued that Bentham's extended use of property as corresponding to an individual's sphere of personal inviolability shows that his theory is not as narrowly instrumentalist as Ryan suggests in his recent book *Property and Political Theory*.[4] The first part of this chapter will be concerned with explaining the function of these spheres of personal inviolability within Bentham's theory of distributive justice.

I

The most important implication of the argument so far, is that the individual conditions of interest formation and realization can only be obtained within the context of a particular form of social structure. The most important of the conditions of interest formation and realization is a realm of individual freedom embodied within a pattern of secured expectations, and this can only be obtained within the context of an overall pattern of secured expectations which guarantees a realm of personal inviolability to each individual in society. The long-term provision of the means of subsistence also depends on a secured pattern of expectations within which each individual can secure his own subsistence through productive labour, and where the flourishing of productive labour will provide the abundance from which the positive provision of the means of subsistence can be supplied to those who are unable to secure their own. The legislator cannot pursue the maximum social well-being by means of direct global utility calculations without undermining the conditions of interest formation. Thus the legislator's task is the institution of a principle of right which embodies the equal distribution of a sphere of personal inviolability. The form this structure takes is determined by a formal principle of distributive justice which Bentham calls the 'security-providing principle',[5] and the rest of this chapter will explain the nature of this principle.

The 'security-providing principle' is a principle of justice in virtue of the fact that it determines the pattern of rights and titles which give substance to the realms of personal inviolability which follow from the conditions of interest formation and realization. These spheres of personal inviolability mark the boundaries between individuals, and thus determine an important class of constraints both on the sort of interests agents can legitimately develop and on the ways they can pursue them. Perhaps of more importance from Bentham's point of view, the 'security-providing principle' puts constraints on how the utilitarian legislator ought to act if he is to maximize

---

[4] A. Ryan, *Property and Political Trust* (Oxford, 1984), 91–117, and 'Utility and Ownership', in R. G. Frey (ed.), *Utility and Rights* (Oxford, 1985), 175–95.
[5] UC lxi, 47, and BL Add. MS 33550, fo. 55.

social well-being. The 'security-providing principle' is a formal principle because it sets out the ideal utilitarian rules which demarcate those spheres within which individuals are able to secure their own interests. The principle of justice not only provides spheres of personal inviolability which in turn provides the social conditions for maintaining the separateness of persons, but it also provides the conditions for social interaction, and thus the social conditions of personal identity and continuity. This latter function of the principle of justice is largely ignored by radical individualists and libertarians such as Nozick[6] and Hospers,[7] who defend the claims of the individual against the community without recognizing any role for the community and social interaction as a major condition of interest formation and consequently as a condition of the development of a sense of self. While Bentham is often seen as a radical individualist, the emphasis he places on the importance of expectation embodies the insight that a secured pattern of expectations is a necessary condition of personal continuity and coherence over time, and this is certainly antithetical to the atomistic and individualistic received interpretation of his moral theory.

Revisionists such as Postema[8] have interpreted Bentham's legislative project as constituting what he calls the 'social reality' within which individuals develop and pursue their own particular interests. However, while Postema places great emphasis on the role of security within Bentham's utilitarian theory, he sees no place for a substantive principle of justice within his thought. The only concession Bentham makes to justice in Postema's view is to interpret the concept as simply a category of particularly weighty utilities based on secured expectations. While there is some justice in Postema's interpretation, it ignores the fact that the principle of utility, despite appearances to the contrary, is not a direct source of obligation, because obligations are dependent on the threat of sanctions.[9] The 'security-providing principle' is a source of obligations because in distributing rights and titles it also determines the punishments appropriate for their violation. The 'security-providing principle' translates the dictates of utility into a system of obligations and duties. Because the rights and titles distributed by the 'security-providing principle' are legal rights and titles, the main sanction that provides for their obligatory character is the legal sanction. However, the political or moral sanction exercised through the public opinion tribunal also plays a part in ensuring that government functionaries act in accordance with the dictates of justice. Thus while the

---

[6] R. Nozick, *Anarchy, State, and Utopia* (Oxford, 1974).

[7] J. Hospers, *Libertarianism* (Los Angeles, Calif., 1971), and 'The Nature of the State', *Personalist*, 59 (1978), 398–404.

[8] G. J. Postema, *Bentham and the Common Law Tradition* (Oxford, 1986), 147–190.

[9] See H. L. A. Hart, 'Natural Rights: Bentham and John Stuart Mill', and 'Legal Duty and Obligations', in *Essays on Bentham* (Oxford, 1982), 79–104 and 127–61; also P. M. S. Hacker, 'Sanction Theories of Duty', in A. W. B. Simpson (ed.), *Oxford Essays in Jurisprudence*, 2nd ser. (Oxford, 1973).

'security-providing principle' is derived from direct considerations of utility it is not strictly the same thing as the principle of utility as Postema implies.[10] Nor is it strictly true to argue that the principle of utility is a principle of justice. The principle of utility is the criterion for determining a utilitarian principle of justice, but it is not the direct source of obligations and duties; these are derived from the sanctions which accompany the principle of justice. What Bentham does in the Civil Law writings is outline two principles, which while derived from considerations of utility, provide a system of duties and obligations which serve his utilitarian ends. The two principles of justice are the 'security-providing principle' and the 'disappointment-preventing principle' and it is by means of these two principles that the legislator brings about the overall end of maximum social well-being.

As a formal principle the 'security-providing principle' can be contrasted with Bentham's substantive principle of justice, the 'disappointment-preventing principle', which is concerned with realizing and maintaining the requirements of the formal principle within a particular society. The substantive principle of justice, the 'disappointment-preventing principle' will be dealt with in more detail in the next chapter, but it is appropriate to point out here that it requires a prior formal principle[11] both to guide its application, and to determine the realm of legitimate expectations which it is supposed to protect. Bentham's use of a principle of distributive justice which determines the structure of social interaction is another characteristic example of his moral foundationalism which distinguishes him from the tradition of Hume and Smith—a tradition which is carried on by contemporary philosophers including F. A. Hayek. Hume and Smith confine their concern with justice to commutative justice, or the justice of exchanges and contracts, and ignore the justice or fairness of the distribution of holdings on the basis of which these exchanges are made. They have an evolutionary or conventional account of the origin of property titles which are justified in general utilitarian terms. Therefore, the principles of commutative justice are divorced from the justification of the institution of property within which they function. As a consequence of separating the justification of the institution of private property and the justification of the rules which regulate its operation, the rules of commutative justice are not required to serve even an indirect utilitarian end. A further consequence of Bentham's foundationalism is the criticism that he is a rationalist[12] because he attempted to impose a rational order on

---

[10] Postema, *Bentham and the Common Law Tradition*, pp. 149–59.

[11] On the priority of distributive justice over other forms of justice see H. Steiner, 'The Concept of Justice', *Ratio*, 16 (1974), 206–25.

[12] The term is used here in a perjorative sense, rather than a technical sense. For the basis of this perjorative use see M. Oakshott, *Rationalism in Politics* (London, 1962). The influence of Oakshott's anti-rationalism can be seen most clearly in D. J. Manning, *The Mind of Jeremy Bentham* (London, 1968). Manning's Bentham is presented as a paradigm case of the

a social structure which is beyond the comprehension of any one human understanding.[13] However, Bentham's theory of distributive justice does have the intuitive appeal of utilitarian theories generally, in being able to reform institutions which appear to result in grossly unjust distributions of power and wealth. Conventionalists such as Hume who appeal only to the utilitarian benefits of having the institution of property as opposed to not having it, are unable to justify alternative systems of property distribution even when it is quite clear that the present system results in massive disutility for most of the society. Bentham's achievement was to develop the reforming strengths of utilitarianism, without undermining the value of a system of private property.

II

In Chapter 4 it was argued that for each individual to pursue his own conception of well-being the legislator must distribute and maintain a realm of liberty or personal inviolability. However, as I pointed out at the end of that chapter the concept of liberty creates problems, because it is a descriptive or objective concept. As Bentham understands liberty in a negative sense, whereby it simply involves the absence of constraint, the maximization of liberty cannot be the legislator's object, because the straightforward maximization of a negative liberty neither involves distributive questions nor does it involve normative questions concerning the priority of certain forms of liberty. The straightforward maximization of liberty in this negative sense could in principle be achieved by concentrating an enormous liberty of action in the hands of a tyrant and leaving his subjects virtual slaves.[14] This is an unsatisfactory account, for it ignores the fact that part of the value of liberty resides in its distribution, and secondly that the freedom to realize one's own life-plan is prima facie more valuable than the tyrant's freedom to exploit and terrorize his subjects. Bentham's solution to these problems was to locate the value of liberty within the normative framework of his principle of utility, and use the principle of utility as the criterion for determining the forms of liberty sufficient for each person to realize his own well-being. He also abandoned the use of the term liberty in favour of security of expectation because this latter concept

'rationalist' which Oakshott criticizes. Manning criticizes Bentham for arguing that society is rationally comprehensible. He argues that according to Bentham once society is understood and individual motivations can be enumerated, it is possible to reconstruct society in accordance with a blueprint which will resolve all political disputes. However, Manning's argument bears little or no resemblance to Bentham's philosophy of politics.

[13] F. A. Hayek, 'Individualism: *True* and *False?*' in *Individualism and Economic Order* (London, 1949).

[14] For a recent version of this argument see H. Steiner, 'Individual Liberty', *Proceedings of the Aristotelian Society*, 76 (1975), 33–50, and 'How Free: Computing Personal Liberty', in A. Phillips-Griffiths (ed.), *Of Liberty*, Royal Institute of Philosophy Lecture Series, 15 (1983), and 'Liberty and Equality', *Political Studies*, 29 (1981), 555–69.

embodied the idea of the subordination of liberty within the normative framework of utility, and a notion of the priority of that form of liberty, which derives its value from being essential to the realization of an individual's well-being.

While the legislator's overall task is maximizing social well-being his substantive task is not one of maximizing, but distributing the realization conditions of well-being. But as has been suggested already, security of expectation is not sufficiently precise an end for the legislator to pursue, for the legislator were to secure all expectations, he would virtually annihilate liberty. This is quite contrary to Bentham's intention in the following passage:

> what is necessary to show is that by the legislative arrangements necessary to afford such security against maleficent acts affecting person, pain will not be produced in such quantity as will cause it to outweigh the pleasure that would have been produced by the maleficent acts so prevented.[15]

Bentham's point is clearly that the legislative arrangements necessary to afford security must be constrained by the overall utilitarian justification of those arrangements. Therefore, the legislator must be able to distinguish between that pattern of expectations which is essential for the development and pursuit of each individual's interests, and those which are not integral to personal continuity and coherence.

Within his political morality there are two levels of expectation. He argued that for every pleasure of fruition there is a pleasure of expectation.[16] The pleasure of fruition is the pleasure that is derived from an individual's goal or object coming to fruition. However, in the case of many projects individuals adopt, the realization of those objects is possible only in the distant future and after much effort. If pleasure of fruition was the only causally efficient motive, it becomes difficult to explain why one individual would put off a present pleasure for one that is in the distant future and accompanied by a difficult and laborious apprenticeship. Bentham avoided this problem with the notion of pleasure of expectation which derives its value from its contribution to the overall end pursued, but at the same time is a source of pleasure, and thus a continuing motivation because it ultimately contributes to the realization of the overall end. This pleasure of expectation depends on regularities in behaviour such that the pursuit of a particular action will in all probabilty lead to the realization of its ultimate end, and thus, the pleasure of fruition. The pleasure of expectation also accounts for the motivatation to engage in productive labour, because productive labour is the means of realizing a whole variety of different goals or projects in the future. These pleasures of expectation accompany every interest and desire that a person may have: there are in effect as many pleasures of expectation as there are possible pleasures of fruition.

---

[15] BL Add. MS 33550, fo. 119.   [16] UC lxi, 28.

However, within this enormous body of pleasure of expectation it is possible to identify a particular core of expectations with which the legislator ought to be concerned, and these are defined as an individual's legitimate expectations.

This second level of expectations, or legitimate expectations, is a general class that individuals presuppose in being able to formulate any particular end, and in being able to pursue any particular action. They are general in the sense that they do not refer to any particular end or goal, but are necessary for the pursuit of all goals and projects. The legislator's task is not to pursue one particular conception of the good, but rather the distribution of a pattern of secured expectations within which all individuals are free to pursue their own ends. By concentrating on securing only this class of expectations the legislator is able to remain neutral between various particular conceptions of what is pleasurable. The question remains as to how Bentham identified this class of expectations?

Legitimate expectations are conceived in terms of the absence of certain categories of harm, that is harm against the person, property or possession, beneficial condition in life, and reputation. The grounding of these legitimate expectations depends on the distribution of a pattern of rights which protects person, possession, beneficial condition in life, and reputation. It is because the pattern of rights which the legislator secures forms some protection against these four categories of harm that the 'security-providing principle' can be described as a harm principle.

This class of expectations is particularly important because it provides the conditions within which each individual can develop and pursue his own particular conception of well-being, and in order to secure this core of legitimate expectations the legislator has to secure each individual against a particular class of harms. The realm of freedom or personal inviolability which is embodied in the idea of security of expectation is based on protection from this class of harms. The form of harm principle that is being attributed to Bentham is similar to that attributed to J. S. Mill by Berger, Lyons, and Gray.[17] All these writers argue that Mill's principle of liberty is based on a system of rights which secures for each individual a realm of personal inviolability within which he can pursue his own particular conception of the good. None of Berger, Lyons, and Gray explores in any depth the question of how far Mill's concept of liberty and justice was influenced by Bentham's utilitarian theory, though other writers such as Rees[18] and Hollander[19] have argued that Mill's philosophical debt to

[17] F. R. Berger, *Happiness, Justice and Freedom* (Berkeley, Calif., 1984), and J. Gray, *Mill On Liberty: A Defence* (London, 1983), and D. Lyons, 'Mill's Theory of Morality', *Nous*, 10 (1976), 101–20, 'Mill's Theory of Justice', in A. I. Goldman and J. Kim (eds.), *Values and Morality* (Dordrecht, 1978), 1–20, and 'Benevolence and Justice in Mill', in H. B. Miller and W. H. Williams (eds.), *The Limits of Utilitarianism* (Minneapolis, Minn.), 1982, 42–70.

[18] J. Rees, *John Stuart Mill's* On Liberty (Oxford, 1985).

[19] S. Hollander, *The Economics of John Stuart Mill* (2 vols., Oxford, 1985).

Bentham and James Mill is greater than the impression created by his supposed break with his forebears would suggest.

Bentham identified the four categories of harm against which the legislator is to provide security early in his career. In *An Introduction to the Principles of Morals and Legislation* and *Of Laws in General* he did develop the connection between them and the limits of the legislator's authority.[20] The four categories of harm are contained within the four components of private offences,[21] and an offence is any 'maleficent' act, the performance of which merits punishment.

In *An Introduction to the Principles of Morals and Legislation*, chapter 16, Bentham identified five classes of offences which concern the utilitarian legislator. These are: private offences, semi-public offences, public offences, self-regarding offences, and heterogeneous offences. Semi-public offences are those which are concerned with unassignable individuals, that is individuals who are not named, but suffer harm as the members of some assignable class such as a particular neighbourhood or religious or ethnic group. Public offences are like semi-public offences in referring to unassignable individuals, but in this case the individuals who suffer harm do so as members of an indefinite multitude such as a community or state. Self-regarding offences are based on the four basic categories of harm, but these offences differ from private offences in that the agent is also the victim of these offences. The final category of offences are those which concern offences against falsehood and against trust. The argument of this chapter will focus on the category of private offences because they are essential for determining the realms of personal inviolability on which Bentham's theory of distributive justice is based. In so far as the class of basic harms embodied within the category of private offences constitute the basic conditions of social interaction, they are prior in importance to the other classes of offence. The reason for this priority is because they constitute the basic conditions of social interaction on which more complex forms of social organization which semi-public and public offences refer to, are premised.

According to the principle of utility all acts which foster pain rather than pleasure are wrong, but for this it does not follow either that a person ought to be prevented from doing the act or that he should be punished for so acting. Not all 'maleficent' acts constitute offences, but only those who are deserving of punishment, and only those actions which, on utilitarian grounds are detrimental to the interest of the community. At the beginning of *An Introduction to the Principles of Morals and Legislation*, chapter 16,

---

[20] The four classes of harm are found in *IPML*, chap. 16, 'Division of Offences', it is also to be found in *OLG* (CW), pp. 200–4, the companion work to *IPML*, and a variety of manuscripts. See e.g. BL Add. MS 33550, fos. 55, 117, UC c, 173 and lxi, 30. In these later manuscripts the four categories of harm most commonly feature as an illustration of the scope and boundaries of the legislator's role in providing security; see BL Add. MS 33550 fo. 117.

[21] *IPML* (CW), pp. 191–4.

Bentham distinguished between acts which ought to be classed as offences on utilitarian grounds, and those which are or may be considered offences in any given legal system:

It is necessary, at the outset, to make a distinction between such acts as *are* or *may* be, and such as *ought* to be offences. Any act *may* be an offence, which they whom the community are in the habit of obeying shall be pleased to make one: that is, any act which they shall be pleased to prohibit or to punish. But, upon the principle of utility, such acts alone *ought* to be made offences, as the good of the community requires should be made so.[22]

The sovereign legislator is technically free to make offences of whatever acts he chooses, but according to Bentham, a utilitarian legislator will only make offences of those acts which are detrimental to the community. The utilitarian legislator does not rely on the claims of a majority vote in order to determine what is detrimental to the community, rather he relies on an objective conception of harm. Those actions which constitute a threat to the interests of an agent independently of the substance of his ultimate goals are the basis of Bentham's objective concept of harm. Thus, an act that is detrimental to the community is one that would interfere with the most basic interests of an agent irrespective of his substantive goals.

While Bentham's argument in *An Introduction to the Principles of Morals and Legislation*, chapter 16, is presented as an analytical division of offences, it nevertheless embodies his utilitarian intention of freeing the law from imposing subjective moral judgements. His division of offences precluded a certain important class of offences that are found in many legal systems, and these are offences based directly on attempts to enforce morality. There is, for example, no allowance made for offences which consist of holding certain beliefs or for being a certain kind of person where this does not involve direct interference with another person. Bentham did include a class of 'offences against religion' under the category of public offences,[23] but he made clear that in so far as these can be offences at all, they were such because of the damage they did to the community, and not because a particular individual is harmed by holding erroneous religious beliefs. Within a utilitarian system of law it is quite possible for there to be offences against religion in the strict sense of offences against the possibility of some engaging freely in religious practices without suffering harm from others. What a utilitarian legal code could not include are offences arising from not holding religious beliefs, holding incorrect religious beliefs, or of refusing to participate in religious observance. A Benthamite code of laws would certainly preclude the enforcement of adherence to a particular religious creed or a particular set of non-utilitarian moral beliefs. It is also quite clear from Bentham's later writings on religion that he was not in

---

[22] Ibid., pp. 187–8.
[23] Ibid., p. 264 n.

favour of affording institutions of religion a legal protection, and in the long run he was concerned with undermining or exposing religious belief and discouraging religious practice as these gave rise to sinister interests. These controversial goals were not, however, the concern of his theory of justice.

The four basic harms included under the category of private offences do not make allowances for harms derived from beliefs and practices that do not affect one's own person, property, reputation, or beneficial condition in life. The fact that a person's neighbour might hold religious beliefs that he finds obnoxious, or engages in a lifestyle[24] that he finds immoral is not sufficient for those beliefs and practices to become grounds for a private offence. Unless an action affects the person, property, reputation, or beneficial condition in life of a particular individual it does not constitute a private offence. Thus the division of offences precludes the class of arguments for the enforcement of morality that relies on a person feeling so offended by another's acts or beliefs that these constitute a harm to that person. The concept of harm underlying the category of private offences is based on actions which violate legitimate expectations, and these preclude concepts of harm that are derived from moral or religious beliefs. Legitimate expectations are those expectations necessary for a person to form his own lifestyle and pursue his well-being. They are the conditions necessary for the formation of interest, and therefore cannot be premissed on prior conceptions of the good. Much recent Mill scholarship[25] has attempted to account for the distinction between self- and other-regarding actions[26] in terms of a sphere of vital or basic interests. It is only acts which threaten this sphere of basic interests which ought to be the concern of the law. Thus if an individual's actions do not damage the interest or infringe the basic sphere of personal inviolability of another, it is inappropriate to prohibit those actions no matter how much others may dislike them. The problem for Mill scholars was to make sense of a sphere of purely self-regarding actions, for it had become an accepted criticism of Mill that all actions affect others at some level. On the received view it was argued that any action could constitute a real harm to someone whose moral principles turned that action into an offence. The solution that the revisionists sought in the case of Mill

---

[24] A recent attempt to defend the enforcement of morality, particularly in the case of the prosecution of homosexuals, relies on the argument that the existence of homosexuals within society is a cause of such annoyance as to justify its criminalization. So long as the 'reasonable man' within a society, after looking at the question 'calmly and dispassionately', feels that it is 'a vice so abominable that its mere presence is an offence', then it may be suppressed according to P. Devlin in *The Enforcement of Morals* (Oxford, 1965), 17. Bentham rejected the notion that subjective feelings should masquerade as moral judgements and thus justify an act being considered a criminal offence.

[25] Berger, *Happiness, Justice and Freedom*, pp. 241–50, Gray, *Mill on Liberty*, pp. 57–9, and Rees, *John Stuart Mill's* On Liberty, pp. 137–55.

[26] Mill, *On Liberty*, in *Essays on Politics and Society* (The Collected Works of John Stuart Mill), xviii. 223–4.

was one that Bentham had already adopted in *An Introduction to the Principles of Morals and Legislation* and in the writings on Civil Law.

Bentham sought an objective account of harm which was neutral between various conceptions of the good or various subjective moralities. Thus he provides an account of harm as those actions which violated person, property, beneficial condition in life, and reputation. This conception of harm which underlies the category of private offences is independent of any particular interests or moral beliefs. However, the idea of a class of objective harms raises serious problems because the concept of harm is generally thought of as being irreducibly normative. It derives its meaning from the context of the normative discourse within which it functions. Since the flourishing of analytical philosophy in the latter part of this century there have been many attempts to strip particular concepts both in the realms of moral theory and political thought of their normative connotations and reveal their objective meaning. This tendency can in part explain the attempts of contemporary political theorists such as Feinberg[27] and Oppenheim[28] to provide objective accounts of the meaning of certain important political concepts: in Feinberg's case an attempt is made to defend a libertarian harm principle on the basis of an analysis of objective harms which determine the limits of legislative authority. This tendency among contemporary philosophers to derive an objective account of certain key political and moral concepts has also influenced historians of political thought. In the case of Bentham, Long[29] has laid great emphasis on the role of Bentham's definitional writings as the key to understanding the role and meaning of liberty within his political thought: he argues that Bentham provides a descriptive analysis of liberty which is wholly negative, and in a later work[30] he argues that Bentham premisses his work on the role of property with an attempt to provide an objective analysis of its meaning. The problem for Bentham's theory is how he can be defended against the charge of providing stipulative definitions which are far from uncontroversial. If Bentham's intention was to eradicate confusion by providing an objective moral language, how is it that many of his analyses remain controversial? Long attributes to Bentham the twentieth-century idea that once certain concepts have been analysed it is possible to construct a rational political morality. However, Bentham did not think a morally objective language would provide the key to solving political problems, his solution was always the principle of utility, and therefore any concern with definitions cannot be more than a secondary task guided by the principle of utility.[31] Bentham's concern with definition must be viewed in the light of

[27] J. Feinberg, *The Moral Limits of the Criminal Law* (4 vols., Oxford, 1984–8).

[28] F. Oppenheim, *Political Concepts* (Oxford, 1981).

[29] D. G. Long, *Bentham on Liberty* (Toronto, 1977).

[30] Id., 'Bentham on Property', pp. 221–54.

[31] Postema shows that Bentham connected the roles of utilitarian censor with the definitions of the expositor in his paper: 'The Expositor, the Censor and the Common Law', *Canadian*

his primary commitment to the principle of utility. Much the same position has been adopted by revisionist critics of J. S. Mill in interpreting his use of a notion of objective harm.

The notion of objective harm used by Feinberg relies on the idea that it is possible to isolate a realm of harms so basic that they must be common to any moral code. However, it is by no means easy to isolate such a class of basic harms, for even the most obvious candidate for objectivity—physical violence to the person—is far from problematic.[32] It may appear strange to argue that the sufferings of a Christian martyr before the Roman lions do not constitute a real harm to that person, but it is by no means contradictory. Given Christian moral teaching as understood by the early martyrs, to suffer a glorious death as a witness to Christ, no matter how horrible it may have appeared to others, was a positive good. In the case of other harms such as the loss of liberty the notion of an objective harm becomes even more difficult to free from the moral constraints that surround it. Horton[33] uses the example of Dostoevsky's Sonia in *Crime and Punishment*, who urges Raskolnikov to confess his crime and desire punishment to show that even the loss of liberty does not provide an unproblematic notion of harm. Sonia urges Raskolnikov to desire punishment not because she wants him harmed: she is concerned with Raskolnikov's well-being and wants him to desire punishment as a benefit—a means of reconciling himself with humanity. However strange these examples may seem they are certainly not contradictory. Thus the notion of harm is irrevocably embedded within the context of normative discourse.

If harm is a term that is irreducibly normative, what sense is to be made of Bentham's notion of an objective concept of harm which is embodied in the category of private offences? In order to salvage his intention and defend his objective, it is necessary to distinguish two senses within which a term can be objective: the stronger and the weaker. In the stronger sense, a concept such as harm is objective when it can be analysed fully outside of the context of normative discourse, that is when it can be given a meaning independent of any particular moral theory. Both Feinberg and Oppenheim are concerned with providing objective analyses of certain concepts in this stronger sense of being independent from all hidden normative implications. However, given the two examples above it seems impossible to provide a completely objective definition of any concept used in moral and political discourse. Either these strong objective analyses will require the implausible

Journal of Philosophy, 9 (1979), 643–70. Postema's point is that the whole of Bentham's legislative project was premissed on the wider task of the utilitarian reform of the legal system; see also id., *Bentham and the Common Law Tradition*, pp. 147–336.

[32] J. Horton, 'Toleration, Morality and Harm', in J. Horton and S. Mendus (eds.), *Aspects of Toleration* (London, 1985), 113–35.   [33] Ibid., p. 122.

denial of certain perfectly acceptable uses of the term or else they will introduce normative considerations without acknowledging them. Feinberg's theory is of the latter kind for it imports a normative theory under the guise of a liberal or neutral conception of the good as preference satisfaction, and this necessarily precludes conceptions of the good which draw moral distinctions between the values of certain kinds of preferences.

The weaker sense of objective harm acknowledges the fact that harm cannot be analysed independently of the normative contexts within which it functions. It accepts that a particular conception of morality has priority over other rival theories, but it is still objective or neutral in that it does not presuppose any particular conception of an individual's good within that anti-perfectionist morality. It is not objective or neutral between moral theories for it precludes the notion that there can be an objective hierarchy of preferences based on a moral conception of human nature. An action constitutes an objective harm in this weaker sense if it interferes with the realization of any individual's conception of well-being irrespective of its substance. In the weaker sense the notion of objectivity does not imply freedom from normative constraints, but is nevertheless neutral between particular individuals' conceptions of their welfare. The whole complex structure of Bentham's thought is founded on the principle of utility; this underlies all of his methodological and definitional writings just as much as it underlies his moral and political theories. It is, therefore, wrong to argue that his intention was to provide objective analyses of key terms as the first task in his project of legislative reform. I have already argued that, contrary to Long's theory, Bentham was largely concerned with analyzing terms such as liberty in the way he did in order to further his legislative project.

It is clear that while Bentham's writings do pre-empt certain developments in the philosophy of language one should not try and force him into the categories of twentieth-century philosophy. Bentham did not try and derive theories from conceptual analysis, he was quite clear that concepts could only be given precise meanings within a propositional structure. Given the importance he attached to 'paraphrastic' analysis and the priority of the proposition or sentence as the basic unit of meaning, he could not have attempted to derive a moral theory simply from conceptual analysis nor could he have intended that conceptual analysis provide the basis for an objective moral language. His hostility to the use of certain terms is not based on the view that they are meaningless, but rather on the view that the theories from which they derive their sense cannot be rationally justified. According to Bentham, utilitarianism forms the only rational basis for moral theory. Only when moral and political concepts can be given a utilitarian value can they also be given a determinate moral sense. In the same way, though the division of offences in *An Introduction to the Principles of Morals and Legislation*, chapter 16, does not directly reflect a utilitarian concept of the bounds of legislative activity, it does reflect a particular conception of the social function of the law.[34] The conception of the social function of law underlying Bentham's legal and political theory is of law as the condition of ordered social interaction. The offences under the law are those actions which frustrate ordered social interaction by destroying those expectations on which an ordered social reality depends. This conception of law does not see it as a means of moral perfectionism: it precludes those conceptions of the law which attempt to impose a morality and to bring about the moral perfection of a people. For Bentham law remained indifferent between various conceptions of welfare so long as they were compatible with an ordered social existence. This anti-perfectionism is reflected in his hostility to the criminalization of homosexuality. In a number of manuscripts[35] he argued against the proscription of homosexuality on the grounds that matters of taste were none of the law's business so long as they did not result in harm to others. The fact that others might take exception to one's tastes does not provide adequate grounds for the legal interference with that person. Thus homosexual acts between consenting adults do not constitute harms, and therefore ought not to be considered offences. His commitment to the liberty of taste and his defence of homosexuality at a time when sodomy was still a capital offence, are evidence that a Benthamite utilitarian code of laws was intended to be neutral between various conceptions of the good.[36] This defence of liberty of taste in the sphere of personal morality is a further illustration of the liberal spirit of his utilitarian thought. Bentham's concept of the social function of the law implies both the virtue of toleration, which since Locke was the paradigmatic virtue of the Enlightenment, and the moral scepticism which underlies the importance of toleration.

By precluding perfectionist legislation Bentham's conception of the social function of the law made an important advance towards a liberal conception of harm. However, the absence of perfectionist legislation is not in itself sufficient to guarantee a liberal polity. Its absence simply means that those laws designed to punish the non-subscription to any set of moral or religious doctrines are precluded from the categories of harm that Bentham incorporates under the heading of offences. It is clear that the category of public offences allows from the punishment of those acts which are contrary to the generally held religious practices of a society when such acts are

---

[34] The idea that Bentham's legal positivism reflects a particular conception of the law and its social function is forcefully argued by Postema in *Bentham and the Common Law Tradition*, particularly chap. 5.

[35] See UC lxviii, 10–18, lxxii, 187–205, lxxvii, 90–100, lxxiv(a), 1–25, and clxi(a), 1–19.

[36] For a full discussion of Bentham's thoughts on homosexuality see; L. Crompton, *Byron and Greek Love: Homophobia in Nineteenth Century England* (Berkeley, Calif., 1985), 38–62 and 251–83; also L. Crompton, 'Jeremy Bentham's Essay on "Pederasty": An Introduction', *Journal of Homosexuality*, 3 (1978), 383–7, and 'Jeremy Bentham's Essay on "Pederasty": Part 2', *Journal of Homosexuality*, 4 (1978), 91–107; see also L. Campos Boralevi, *Bentham and the Oppressed*, chap. 3, and Bahmueller, *The National Charity Company*, pp. 171–3.

judged to threaten the social order. The two sorts of above offences are different in that public offences against religion do not make any claim on the authentic beliefs and commitments of an individual, whereas perfectionist legislation does. Nevertheless, both perfectionist moral legislation and moral legislation which is justified through the need to maintain public order by protecting from harm those practices which a particular conception of morality deems essential for the maintenance of social stability require a considerable curtailment of liberty. There is also the more serious problem posed by the category of self-regarding offences which appears to allow the legislator to interfere in the life of an individual when that person is not acting in accordance with a conventionally accepted standard of behaviour. If Bentham is to be defended on the grounds that he has a liberal conception of utilitarianism, it must be shown that he can reconcile these two hard cases with the liberal intentions of his theory.

The issue of moral and religious legislation which comes under the category of public offences need pose no real problem for Bentham, for he clearly denied that such legislation is essential for the continued stability of the social order.[37] The utilitarian legislator's concern in the sphere of public offences is the same as his concern in the sphere of private offences, that is a category of objective harms. In the case of public offences an objective harm is one that is not derived from the dictates of a particular conception of the good, but is a harm to the community independent of the good pursued by its particular members. Bentham denied that a uniform religious practice duly enforced is a necessary condition of social stability, because such a view is not entailed by his formal theory of justice which prescribed the necessary conditions of social interaction. Utilitarianism may well recognize that religious belief and practice is central to the lives of many, but for Bentham it is so solely in virtue of the choices that certain individuals make, and not because of the objective truth of particular religious doctrines. For Bentham there are no grounds for imposing religious doctrines on anyone who does not authentically subscribe to them. His theory does, however, allow religious legislation which prevents particular groups from being interfered with in the pursuit of their religious beliefs so long as these beliefs respect the personal inviolability of others. Bentham's long-standing hostility to religion, with its anti-utilitarian emphasis on asceticism, and to the established Church of England, as a source of sinister interest, which is developed in a number of works,[38] confirms his antipathy towards an

---

[37] In the last chapter it was argued that the conditions of social stability are all formal. They involve a positive right to subsistence and progress towards material equality. Bentham would certainly have rejected the idea that even inauthentic adherence to a set of moral or religious beliefs as essential for social stability.

[38] *Church of Englandism and its Catechism Examined* (London, 1818), and *Not Paul, but Jesus* (London, 1823).

enforced national religion as a condition of social stability. Therefore, legislation concerning religion which is accommodated within Bentham's utilitarian code of laws more properly falls within the categories of semi-public and private offences.

The class of self-regarding offences poses a much more serious threat to the liberal character of Bentham's utilitarian theory. This category includes the whole class of paternalistic laws which, it is argued, undermine the individual's choice and responsibility for his own life. The category of self-regarding harms is the same as that which makes up the class of private offences—the only difference being the source of those harms, in this case the agent himself. Therefore, the law can in principle intervene on the grounds of preventing harm to the individual when the individual acts in such a way which damages his property, his reputation, or his beneficial condition in life. Such interference may undermine any notion of freedom to experiment or take those risks which are essential for economic advancement and social happiness. The problem with paternalistic legislation, based on utilitarian principles, is that once it is acknowledged that the legislator may interfere with an individual's freedom when his acts are injurious to his own person, property, beneficial condition in life, or reputation, it becomes difficult to provide a criterion by which it is possible to distinguish those harms which are intended and those which are the unintended consequences of free actions. Both the intended harm and the unintended harm resulting from failed speculation may be equally acutely felt, so the resulting pain cannot provide a criterion for distinguishing within the class of self-regarding harms. The choice is between preventing individuals from acting against the conditions of their own pleasure, and thus restricting individual freedom, or else allowing individuals to act in ways that may harm the conditions of their own interest because to preclude such actions would hinder economic and social advance.

The acknowledgement of a category of self-regarding offences recognizes that there are ways in which an individual can harm himself in the same way as the actions of another can harm him. This is a necessary consequence of a notion of objective harm that is based on the consequences of actions rather than the origin of those actions. However, on the question of what significance should be attached to the category of self-regarding harms, Bentham's position is much closer to that of J. S. Mill than to any paternalistic version of utilitarianism. Even in *An Introduction to the Principles of Morals and Legislation* Bentham suggested that little if anything will actually fall within this class:

As to the questions, What acts are productive of a mischief of this stamp? and, among such as *are*, which it may, and which it may not, be *worth while* to treat upon the footing of offences? these are points, the latter of which at least is, too unsettled, and too open to controversy, to be laid down with that degree of confidence which is implied in the exhibition of properties which are made use of as the groundwork of an arrangement. Properties for this purpose ought to be such as shew themselves at first glance, and appearance to belong to the subject beyond dispute.[39]

In this passage he suggested that two conditions must be met in order for an act to constitute a self-regarding offence; firstly, it must be a harm against person, property, beneficial condition in life, or reputation, and secondly, even if it does constitute a harm, one must consider if it is appropriate to render it an offence by imposing punishments. On the second of these conditions he argued that in order to qualify as an offence it should be beyond dispute that punishment is appropriate. However, he acknowledged that little, if anything, would actually fall within this class. An important passage from *An Introduction to the Principles of Morals and Legislation*, chapter 17, emphasizes how inappropriate punishment was as a means of preventing self-regarding offences:

With what chance of success, for example, would a legislator go about to extirpate drunkenness and fornication, by dint of legal punishment? Not all the tortures which ingenuity could invent would compass it: and, before he had made any progress worth regarding, such a mass of evil would be produced by the punishment, as would exceed, a thousand-fold, the utmost possible mischief of the offence. The great difficulty would be in the procuring evidence; an object which could not be attempted, with any probability of success, without spreading dismay through every family, tearing the bonds of sympathy asunder, and rooting out the influence of all the social motives. All that he can do then, against offences of this nature, with any prospect of advantage, in the way of direct legislation, is to subject them, in cases of notoriety, to a slight censure, so as thereby to cover them with a slight shade of artificial disrepute.

It may be observed, that with regard to this branch of duty, legislators have, in general, been disposed to carry their interference full as far as is expedient. The great difficulty here is, to persuade them to confine themselves within bounds. A thousand little passions and prejudices have led them to narrow the liberty of the subject in this line, in cases in which the punishment is either attended with no profit at all, or with none that will make up for the expense.[40]

Given these doubts about the propriety of punishing self-regarding actions which result in harm to the agent, it is clear that Bentham did not envisage the legislator second-guessing each individual's actions, and preventing those which he decides are inconsistent with the agent's freedom. There will, however, be some cases in which it is clear that an individual's acts will harm his own person, property, beneficial condition in life, or reputation, but even in these cases he suggested direct legislative interference would produce more harm than good and so should be avoided. In these uncontroversial cases, self-regarding harms can best be prevented by education and 'private deontology' which aims to inculcate those motives which will help the individual pursue his own projects in ways that do not

---

[39] *IPML* (CW), pp. 195–6.
[40] Ibid., pp. 290–1.

destroy the conditions of necessary for their ultimate realization. Like J. S. Mill after him, Bentham thought coercion was an inappropriate way of preventing self-regarding harms. Both writers did not, however, deny that the utilitarian legislator could exhort, encourage, and educate people to act in ways which did not undermine the necessary conditions of interest realization.

The concept of liberty and the value of freedom as a condition of social happiness and progress is given a higher profile in the work of J. S. Mill then in that of Bentham. However, it should be clear that the substantive commitment to freedom is crucial in both Bentham's and Mill's theory of justice. It is impossible to show just how far J. S. Mill might have been influenced by Bentham's category of private offences in setting the boundaries to his own conception of objective harm, but it is certain that the conditions of liberty in Mill's theory of justice resemble Bentham's conditions for the realization of individual well-being. The remaining task of this chapter is to consider Bentham's choice of the four basic harms that function within the category of private offences and how these harms undermine legitimate expectations.

III

The class of legitimate expectations which marks the boundaries of an individual's sphere of personal inviolability depends upon the absence of four basic classes of harm. Each of these basic classes of harm constitutes a violation of legitimate expectations. Thus legitimate expectations are based on the absence of harm to the person, property or possession, beneficial condition in life, and reputation. However, though property or possession is included within the list of sources of legitimate expectation Bentham also used the concept of property to encompass all the sources of legitimate expectations with the exception of person, and in one place he even included person as a source of expectations within the broad concept of property. Of the four sources of legitimate expectations he says they are, 'four objects which however disparate in their nature, have according to the usage of language been sometimes comprised under the common term *possessions*.'[41] In his later writings Bentham excludes legitimate expectations which are based on the absence of harm to the person as a component of this extended sense of property.[42] Two questions arise from Bentham's use of the concept property to encompass this class of legitimate expectations: why does he describe these sources of legitimate expectations as components of property or objects of possession? and why did Bentham ultimately exclude legitimate expectations, which had their source in the absence of harm to the person, from this broad concept of property?

[41] UC c, 173.
[42] Ibid., lxi. 30–1, and BL Add. MS 33550, fo. 117.

A clue as to why Bentham used such a wide concept of property is to be found in the 1829 'Article on Utilitarianism',[43] where he wrote:

In thus holding up to view *property*—that being the appellation employed by him, though the *matter of wealth* would have been the more determinate and better defined one—in thus holding it up to view in connection with *injustice*, the opposite to *justice*, Locke showed that on that occasion he had missed sight of so many other valuable subjects of possession.[44]

Elsewhere he wrote:

Property the only thing entitled to be the object of care to government! Possessors of property accordingly the only persons entitled to be represented in and by a representative body forming part and parcel of the sovereign authority![45]

In the first passage Bentham criticized Locke for placing too much emphasis on property in the narrow sense of wealth at the expense of other objects of possession, and in the second passage we see why he criticized Locke.[46] Bentham interpreted Locke as arguing that justice is concerned solely with property, and consequently, that the government's concern should only extend so far as the concern for property. What underlies his position is the idea that justice is concerned with the forms and limits of social interaction, that is, with the rules which mark out spheres of personal inviolability and individual liberty as the conditions of social interaction. Justice and property are also linked by Hume, Blackstone,[47] and Smith.[48] It was a commonplace of eighteenth-century social theory that property played the part of the primary constituent of an ordered social world. Bentham suggested in the passages from the 1829 'Article on Utilitarianism' that Locke was the chief source of this idea. However, Bentham was concerned to emphasize that property was a fictitious term which only derived a determinate sense from a particular theory. It is not immediately clear what is meant by asserting that justice is solely concerned with property. If by property Locke, Hume, Blackstone, and Smith simply meant pecuniary wealth, Bentham argued they were wrong to suggest that justice was solely concerned with property, for property in this restricted sense certainly did

---

[43] *Deontology* (CW), pp. 289–318.
[44] Ibid., p. 314.   [45] Ibid., p. 315.
[46] The following is not intended as an endorsement of Bentham's interpretation of Locke's theory of property. Bentham's concentration on money in his account of Locke's theory of property is reflected in C. B. Macpherson's interpretation of Locke as an ideologist for Capitalism and a 'possessive individualist'. See *The Political Theory of Possessive Individualism: Hobbes to Locke* (Oxford, 1962). Macpherson's account and Locke's theory of property has received extensive discussion in J. Tully, *A Discourse on Property: Locke and his Adversaries* (Cambridge, 1980), and J. Waldron, *The Right to Private Property* (Oxford, 1988).
[47] For the relationship between justice and property in Blackstone see F. G. Whelan, 'Property as Artifice: Hume and Blackstone', *Nomos*, 22 (1980), 102–25.
[48] For Hume and Adam Smith on justice and property see K. Haakonssen, *The Science of the Legislator* (Cambridge, 1981).

not exhaust the concerns of justice as the forms and limits of social interaction. The rules which determine social interaction form a body of rights which extends beyond the realm of corporeal property: that is private property in money, clothing, or machinery. Bentham argued that the rights which determined social interaction included rights which determined one's status and position in society as well as the conditions necessary for changing that position. These rights were closely connected but not synonymous with the idea of corporeal rights. This class of incorporeal property rights which determines an individual's social role is as important in fixing public limits on certain types of action as are the restrictions on interference with private property, partly because it can provide the basis for certain property titles, and partly because it is equally important in providing the space within which an individual can pursue his own well-being.

Bentham's extended concept of property was intended to include all those rights which determined the conditions of social interaction whether they referred to corporeal or incorporeal property, because it was with the whole class of such rights that justice was concerned. However, given that Bentham intended the notion of justice to refer to the forms and limits of social interaction, why did he still try and bring that varied body of rights under the notion of property? The reason that these rights are described as articles of property is that they are individual rights; they are held by particular individuals against all other members of society and they facilitate an individual's pursuit of his own well-being in the same way as corporeal property rights. As objects of property or possession these rights refer to the control of an external realm within which an individual is able to act. This external realm is given a particular shape by the individual agent's projects, so that while these rights fix the boundaries against interference from others they do not fix the uses of that external realm for the possessor, and this is analogous to the ways in which private property rights function. Private property rights determine how others ought to act with respect to one's own property rights, but they do not determine the uses to which that property ought to be put by the owner. This does not imply that there are no constraints on the uses of private property. Bentham was quite clear that the notion of absolute property rights was absurd:

As to a right of ownership absolutely unlimited, it is what, can never consistently with utility subsist with relation to any thing whatsoever. To establish any such rights would be to give allowance to almost every sort of crime. If for instance a man's right to a log of wood which he has been cutting were absolutely unlimited, [he] should have a right among other things of employing it as a weapon, in the shape of a club to beat out any man's brains, as a sceptre, a symbol of loyalty to employ in the usurpation of kingly powers: converting it into a priapus [he] might employ it in giving pain to the modest part of the community: converting it into an idol, [he] might wound the religious feelings of those in whom the worship of idols is an object of abhorance as a spear to fall upon it, and put an end to [his] own existence.[49]

Private property rights do not prescribe a particular use to which they must be put, and it is this which is analogous to the components of property in the wider sense of the term as used by Bentham.

It is now possible to see that the reason why he excluded those rights which refer to the protection of the person from his extended sense of property is that they do not function in the same way as the rights to protection of possession, beneficial condition in life and reputation. While rights to the protection of the person are necessary conditions of any purposive action, they are nevertheless rights which function by placing a boundary around the individual's person which is inviolable. They do not enable the agent to take control of an external realm and mould it to his own projects as they provide a realm around the individual which is so basic that it cannot be modifiable by that individual's actions in the same way that property rights are modifiable. The rights which protect the person differ from property rights in the sense that they consist solely of prohibitions on the actions of others. They do not provide a flexible realm within which an individual can act, instead they secure the individual so that he can act. Property rights on the other hand determine the realm within which the individual can act and it is the use to which these property rights are put that determines the structure of the realm of action of a particular individual. In the course of acting, an agent can alienate certain rights through contracts with others. Thus, he can change and modify the structure of his realm of action. Rights to the person are inalienable, and therefore they do not feature in the extended concept of property.

The significance of Bentham's extended sense of property for his formal principle of justice is that it is the most significant of the sources of legitimate expectations which are at the core of his theory of distributive justice. The absence of harm to possessions, beneficial condition in life, and reputation is a more important source of legitimate expectations then the absence of harm to the person. While the absence of harm to the person is the source of a set of expectations which are fundamental to any actions, it is those expectations which derive from the absence of harm to possession, beneficial condition in life, and reputation which do most to shape the social realm within which an individual can develop and realize his own conception of well-being. The absence of physical harms to the person is the source of a fundamental set of legitimate expectations, because security against physical interference is an essential condition of any action whatever. This basic set of legitimate expectations is the source of a class of indirect pleasures, that is, pleasures that depend on the forbearance of others, rather than on any particular actions of the agent himself. All

---

[49] UC xxxii, 161 (punctuation added).

purposive action presupposes as a condition of non-frustration the protection of the individual agent from the violent actions of the others. While it has been argued that within some moral schemes physical violence need not necessarily constitute a harm, it is nevertheless true that in the absence of a substantive conception of the good, the legislator can assume that physical violence threatens all individuals in the pursuit of their interests.

Without a body of rights protecting the person there can be no legitimate expectations because the absence of security of the person means that the individual is constantly at the mercy of all others, and his life will be 'solitary, poore, nasty, brutish, and short'.[50] It is only when an individual is freed from the constant need to protect his own existence that he can begin to develop expectations which are premissed on his continued existence in the future. As Hobbes pointed out, without security of the person:

there is no place for industry; because the fruit thereof is uncertain; and consequently no Culture of the Earth; no Navigation, nor use of the commodities that may be imported by Sea; no commodious Building; no Instruments of moving, and removing such things as require much force; no Knowledge of the face of the Earth; no account of Time; no Arts; no Letters; no Society.[51]

Bentham's position is similar to that of Hobbes, in that he also argued that freedom from the constant threat of violent interference by others is a necessary condition of legitimate expectations, and thus of interest formation. However, the legitimate expectations that are secured by those rights protecting the person do not provide a very wide realm of personal inviolability. The absence of the threat of violence is essential if the individual agent is to be able to form projects which come to fruition in the future. Interest formation requires more than simply the freedom to move about unhindered in society. Interest formation and realization presupposes the ability to impose some order and control upon the world and this requires complex institutions and practices. Underlying these institutions and practices through which man can impose some order and control are the components of Bentham's extended sense of property.

The expectations derived from Bentham's extended sense of property are some of the most important sources of legitimate expectation, because they provide the conditions of social interaction by marking out an external realm in which the individual agent is able to act unhindered by others. Among the sources of expectation which mark out this external realm, private property is the most important. Bentham's defence of the rights of property in many of his works seems to place him among those libertarians who argue that private property is the most basic condition of liberty and

[50] T. Hobbes, *Leviathan* (Harmondsworth, 1968), 186.
[51] Ibid.

autonomy. Contemporary libertarians such as Nozick[52] and Hospers[53] even argue that private property is a condition for marking out the separateness of persons, and that to violate or attempt the redistribution of property is to sacrifice one individual to the good of others, and this is to fail to acknowledge their dignity. Bentham's strong defence of private property certainly appears to place him within this tradition. In a striking passage from the 'Principles of the Civil Code', Bentham wrote:

In consulting the grand principle of security, what ought the legislator to direct with regard to the mass of property which exists?

He ought to maintain the distribution which is actually established. This, under the name of justice, is with reason regarded as his first duty: it is a general and simple rule applicable to all states, adopted to all plans, even those which are most opposed to each other. There is nothing more diversified than the condition of property in America, England, Hungary, Russia: in the first country the cultivator is proprietor; in the second he is farmer; in the third he is attached to the soil; in the fourth he is a slave. Still the supreme principle of security directs the preservation of all these distributions, how different soever their natures, and though they do not produce the same amount of happiness.[54]

No doubt such an argument is behind Long's claim that Bentham was not concerned with distributive justice but only with maintaining the socio-economic status quo.[55] However, this passage is not representative of Bentham's considered opinions as will be seen later in discussing the 'disappointment-preventing principle' where it will be argued that he accommodated the possibility of redistributive policies based on a utilitarian theory of justice within a system of respect for private property. What the passage does show is the great weight he attached to the importance of private property as a source of expectations. Even in a grossly unjust distribution of private property, the pattern of expectations derived from it does shape the social realm within which individuals can form and secure their own ends, as long as they enjoy some property. Property rights, for Bentham, provide the material conditions of free purposive action. They enable the individual agent to exercise exclusive control over a portion of the social realm by giving him control over certain objects which he can use in constructing his own ends and in realizing his own happiness. Exclusive control over a portion of the social world is essential in order to realize the potential for action protected by rights against the person.

Property rights in this narrow sense which include rights to corporeal objects such as tools, clothing, personal possessions, and money enable the individual to act freely in the world in pursuit of his projects. The reason why private property has become so important as a condition of freedom

[52] Nozick, *Anarchy, State, and Utopia*, pp. 28–53.
[53] Hospers, *Libertarianism*, pp. 52–4, 61–80.
[54] Bowring, i. 311.
[55] Long, 'Bentham On Property', p. 244.

within liberal thought is that the objects of private property, while they may constrain the number of options an individual has available, do not prescribe the choices of action he must ultimately make. The exclusive control over a portion of the social realm provided by private property rights enables an individual to act in ways that are not precluded by others trying to make use of the same material objects. Therefore, if the exercise of one person's liberty is not to be undermined by the same liberty of another, then each person must be able to control a certain portion of the social world.[56] This is achieved by private property which gives exclusive control of that portion of the social realm embodied within the articles of possession by excluding others from the simultaneous use of those objects. The apportioning of a realm of private property as a component of a sphere of personal inviolability is also a condition of the co-ordination of private action which is essential for the maintenance of social stability. The private property rights of each person mark out limits on the use that can be made of certain objects in the social realm by others. Private property not only enables the owner to form and pursue his own goals and interests by providing him with the physical components of purposive action, the realm of private property also guides the expectation of others by prohibiting those actions which necessarily interfere with another's property.

The possession of property rights creates legitimate expectations both for the owner and for other members of society. The private property holdings of others help to give shape to the expectation that an individual can develop with a given society, and thus to his interests. The connection between private property and expectation turns on the fact that these objects embody exclusive control of a portion of the social realm. Also they do not necessarily prescribe any one use, and an individual can incorporate a whole variety of uses within his ends and projects. Similarly they persist over time so that individuals can lay them aside for future use, thus creating expectations about their enjoyment. Alternatively, he can use them now as part of the means to some future end, with their use based on the expectation that they will contribute to the realization of that end. Even when an object of property is an end in itself, it remains a potential source of expectation so long as it remains in existence.

Bentham's discussion of private property as a source of expectation is not confined to fixed objects of property such as fixed capital, it is also concerned with more liquid types of property such as money. Money is the greatest source of expectation within the category of private property for it is the most liquid type of property, and thus the one which enables the greatest flexibility in use. Money can be an end in itself, but ordinarily it

---

[56] A similar argument is made by H. Steiner, in 'Individual Liberty', *Proceedings of the Aristostelian Society*, 76 (1975), 33–50, and 'The Structure of a Set of Compossible Rights', *Journal of Philosophy*, 74 (1977), 767–75.

serves as a means to a much wider variety of ends than fixed objects of property, its value being derived from the liquidity. The possession of money gives rise to expectations of use without involving any specification of the uses to which it must be put. Fixed objects of property can in principle be put to a whole variety of uses, but often only as a result of sale or exchange can they realize the interests of the owner. Property in money also has the added advantage that it can extend a person's realm of freedom: individuals are able to trade some of their property, thus restricting their freedom in some area in order to extend it in another by entering into contracts with others and by means of exchanges. Money serves as a means of marking out a realm of exclusive control, because it enables the possessor to take control of those components he needs in order to realize his own projects. But unlike fixed objects of private property, the liquidity of money enables a greater responsiveness to changes in the circumstances of action.

In the 'Principles of the Civil Code',[57] Bentham argued that property 'is the right which has overcome the natural aversion to labour', and most discussions of his justification of private property revolve around its function as a necessary condition of continuing productive labour. In his book *Property and Political Theory*, Alan Ryan argues that Bentham offers a purely instrumental justification of private property rights. The system of private property is a necessary condition of guaranteeing productive labour in the future, and this ultimately results in the maximum social happiness.[58] It is certainly true that Bentham argued that private property rights guarantee continued productive labour. He acknowledged that the returns on labour are the material conditions of realizing interests, and consequently that unless one is allowed to enjoy the fruits of one's labour then one is unable to build up expectations about future enjoyments which are the motivation to continue labouring. However, it is wrong to see the connection between private property and the motivation to engage in productive labour as entailing a narrowly instrumental account of the value of property. For Bentham, the value of property resided in its connection with freedom and its function as a basic source of expectation. Thus, private property is a condition of personal continuity and coherence, because it is through the formation of expectations that a person is able to build up a distinctive conception of himself which persists over time. When his broader conception of property is taken into account it is clear that he did not have any narrowly instrumental justification of the value of property.

Though Bentham recognized that private property was a necessary condition of interest realization he did not maintain that it was the sole sufficient condition. While property rights help mark out the boundaries between individuals in the social realm, they do not provide the full set of conditions within which an individual can develop his own interests. Those

---

[57] Bowring, i. 309.
[58] A. Ryan, *Property and Political Theory* (Oxford, 1984), 244.

contemporary libertarians, such as Nozick, who see private property as the sole sufficient condition for free purposive action and the sole public criterion marking the boundaries between individuals, ignore the fact that autonomous action requires more than simply the control of material objects in the world. The libertarians have a fragmented understanding of the social conditions of interest formation and purposive action, for they fail to see that interpersonal co-ordination cannot be based solely on property relations without abandoning the notion of community altogether. A large body of rights which are a basic source of expectation are based on status with regard to other individuals, and on regularities in behaviour based on status. The body of rights respecting these conditions of expectation is as important in the developing of projects and goals as private property in the narrow sense.

For Bentham, property relations are the outcome of complex patterns of social interaction which are derived from reputation and standing within society. In his wider conception of property, Bentham includes beneficial condition in life and reputation. These are both sources of expectation based on the regular provision of services. In *An Introduction to the Principles of Morals and Legislation*, chapter 16, he argued that the services one had grown to expect from others constitute an important component of property because they give rise to expectations, and provide the means for developing and realizing interests. Expectations based on beneficial condition in life arise from those services a person derived from particular relationships, as Bentham indicates:

An offence, therefore, the tendency of which is to lessen the facility you might otherwise have of deriving happiness from the services of a person thus specially connected with you, may be styled an offence against your condition in life, or simply your condition. Conditions in life must evidently be as various as the relations by which they are constituted . . . In the mean time, those of husband, wife, parent, child, master, servant, citizen of such or such a city, natural-born subject of such or such a country, many answer the purpose of examples.[59]

Those expectations derived from reputation do not depend on the particular relationships between individuals, but rather on services derived from the people at large. Bentham wrote:

An offence, therefore, the tendency of which is to lessen the facility you might otherwise have had of deriving happiness or security from persons at large, whether connected with you or not by any special tie, may be styled an offence against your *reputation*.[60]

The importance of beneficial condition in life and reputation as sources of expectation rests on the fact that purposive action depends as much on personal interaction as on the accumulation and disposal of property.

[59] *IPML* (CW), p. 193.
[60] Ibid.

Unlike the libertarian individualists, Bentham recognized that man is a creature of society, and thus the formation and realization of his interests depends as much on the actions of others as on his own actions. Beneficial condition in life is important because it is the basis of services which as the source of expectation has become the premiss of purposive actions and property relations. An individual's condition in life is as much a condition of the realization of his interests as is his property. For one's status as a husband, wife, employee, or public functionary helps to shape the world within which one acts and gives rise to expectations as crucial to the maintenance of personal continuity and coherence, as are property rights. Condition in life gives rise to expectations which project a conception of the self into the future, for one's individual personality is shaped by one's status within society, and by the particular social relationships one enjoys. Unlike the individualist libertarians, Bentham did not employ an abstract conception of the person, which takes interests as given. He recognized that interests were premissed on expectations which in turn were the product of social interaction. Private property in the narrow sense they employ might well be a sufficient condition for the realization of interests, but it is certainly not a sufficient condition for the formation of interests. Bentham's concern was with the conditions necessary to form and realize interests.

It might be argued, however, that condition in life appears to constrain an individual's freedom within a sphere of responsibilities whereas property rights facilitate great freedom. This emphasis on the security of condition in life should not lead to a conservative interpretation of Bentham's thought, because condition in life is only one of the components of property, and as such it works in conjunction with the other components. Although an individual's condition in life does give shape to his interests, it is nevertheless possible for a person's condition in life to change as a result of his own actions. The way in which a person comes to acquire and dispose of his property will create the circumstances within which his condition in life can change. He can enter into and conclude contracts which modify his condition in life and give rise to new expectations which in turn shape his interests.

Reputation is similar to beneficial condition in life in that it is a basis for services from others. However, in this case these services do not depend on particular individual relationships, but instead depend upon an individual's standing in the eyes of others. Whether a person is trusted and whether others are prepared to enter into contracts with him, depends upon his reputation. Therefore, reputation affects how a person is able to exercise his liberty and realize his interests. The services one derives from reputation such as trust and respect influence the sorts of undertakings one can engage in with others. If a person's reputation for probity could not become the object of security, he would not be able to form interests that are premissed on the expectation of changing one's social position through contracts. And without the possibility of extending one's sphere of action through contracts that sphere of action would become extremely limited. Similarly, others will not be prepared to sacrifice their own condition and property unless they can count on a person's reputation. Reputation is a public creation derived from the expectations of all others which are based on a person's past conduct and condition in life, and it helps guide others in the formation of their interests and projects. In this way it functions as a component of property in the wider sense.

Bentham did not presuppose abstract individuals who developed their interests independently of society, which they then hope to realize within the context of social interaction. Individuals form and realize their interests within the context of social interaction. All but the most basic or natural interests are premissed on patterns of expectation which develop only within the context of social life. In this way Bentham's theory differs from those libertarian theories which give property the highest priority as a condition for the exercise of freedom. He is concerned not solely with the conditions necessary for the realization of ends which are taken as given, but he also recognizes that property as a source of expectation is a condition of individual well-being. Therefore, Bentham is not a crude individualist who fails to appreciate the importance of social interaction as a condition of the formation of goals and projects. When in *An Introduction to the Principles of Morals and Legislations*, chapter 1, he described the interest of the community as 'the sum of the interests of the several members who compose it'[61] he implied that the interest of the community is nothing other than the sum of particular individual interests. However, this does not entail a strong individualism which maintains that individuals have interests independently of the community. In fact, Bentham's emphasis on the pursuit of maximum well-being implied that an individual's interest could only be secured at the same time as those of everyone else, because they are all intricately interwoven in an elaborate pattern of mutually dependent expectations.

In this chapter it has been argued that person, property, beneficial condition in life, and reputation must be secured because they provide those basic sources of expectation which are essential in order to develop and pursue interests. To see why personal continuity or personal identity is so intimately connected with expectation, it is necessary to remember that Bentham has a Humean conception of the self. For him as for Hume the self is composed of the collection of experiences, sensations, and perceptions of a particular individual. However, on introspection, a particular individual who seeks that which connects those experiences as his own, will find nothing but a collection of perceptions, experiences, and sensations, including the experience of introspection. There is nothing about a person's

[61] *IPML* (CW), p. 12.

inner life that can be abstracted from that body of experience in order to provide an enduring object of experience. The self which is the subject of experience at the age of ten will be noticeably different from the subject of experience at twenty-five and again at sixty-five. Given this fact, the question remains as to what aspect of experience common to all these sensations and perceptions can be appealed to as a means of unifying them under the category of one person? The British Empiricist tradition forgoes any Kantian appeal to a 'transcendental unity of apperception', and therefore has two choices: either abandon the search for some ordering condition of those experiences or else provide an external ordering condition.

Bentham was among those who sought the ordering conditions of experience in the social realm in the basic sources of expectation. Expectation provides the link between various subjective experiences which enable an individual to form a conception of himself projecting into the future.[62] Those components of the extended sense of property which enable the individual to control a portion of the social realm are also the source of those expectations which give unity to individual experience, and thus provide some enduring concept of the self. His reliance on the external conditions of personal identity did not provide a full conception of the self which unified an individual's experience throughout his life. It was not his intention to provide such a conception. However, he did manage to provide the possibility of substantial unity within an individual's experience. The degree of unity within experience provided by these external conditions of personal continuity depends on the sort of projects pursued, and the further into the future expectation stretches, the greater the unity of experience. Some projects such as marriage and certain forms of employment provide substantial continuity within an individual's experience for most of that person's life. Thus contrary to the standard objection to utilitarianism that it fails to take seriously the separateness of persons, the body of rights which demarcate an individual's sphere of personal inviolability also provide public criteria for respecting the separateness of persons.

The above arguments reinforce the importance of the four basic sources of expectation as conditions of personal continuity and coherence, and thus as the conditions for the formation and realization of interests. However, concentration on expectation as the justifying condition of rights to person, property, beneficial condition in life, and reputation leaves two problems for a theory of distributive justice: firstly, how do people acquire property rights, and, secondly, how are these rights distributed. The answer to the first question will clarify how the second is to be answered.

Bentham clearly justified private property as a major condition of the formation of expectations which give unity to existence, and as a realization

[62] Bowring, i. 308.

condition of individual well-being which is premissed on those expectations. The discussion throughout this chapter has concentrated on the importance of private property as a source of expectations, but while this does not indicate what sorts of thing ought to be secured by rights within a utilitarian theory of justice, it does not provide a criterion for the just acquisition of the objects of those rights. How these property holdings are obtained in the first instance is not of direct concern to Bentham. Underlying his theory of distributive justice is his own rejection of natural-rights arguments. Thus the ways in which individuals acquire property holdings are a matter of convention just as private property itself is the product of convention. The justification of any particular pattern of distribution will therefore depend on its overall consequences. In the next chapter it will be argued that Bentham disagreed with Hume and Smith that because the original grounds of property acquisition were conventional the legislator ought to be indifferent to the actual distribution of property holdings.

In 'Principles of the Civil Code'[63] he identified present occupation, prescription, succession, and consent as four conventional grounds for acquiring property rights. These four rules are similar to those used by Hume in the *Treatise*,[64] which suggests that Bentham was unconcerned with providing an elaborate theory of property acquisition such as that in Locke's *Second Treatise*. Neither did he have a historical entitlement theory of justice which is premissed on a theory of property acquisition. What matters for his theory of distributive justice is not how people acquire the rights which determine their sphere of personal inviolability, but how those rights ought to be distributed in order that the maximum social well-being is achieved.

The pattern of rights which embodies equal spheres of personal inviolability is that which maximizes social well-being. In the case of rights to protect the person, condition in life, and reputation, it is clear that these are equally necessary for all individuals to form and realize their own interests and projects and they need to be equally protected. The same pattern of rights will protect any person irrespective of their substantive goals. Thus the equal pattern of rights protecting person, condition in life, and reputation grounds an equal title to security of the person, condition in life, and reputation.

The case of private property is rather more complicated. The protection of private property is equally important to all because without it one would be unable to enjoy property as an exercise condition of liberty. However, given that the overall object of the legislator is to secure the maximum social well-being, and that he is unable to determine which particular interests are the most valuable, he therefore, has to provide the conditions in which each

---

[63] Bowring, i. 326–36.
[64] Hume, *Treatise*, III. 2. iii. 505.

can pursue his own conception of the good. This entails not simply equal rights to the protection of property, but equal rights to private property. The legislator has no good reason for favouring one set of interests over another. He can only provide for the maximum of social well-being when he provides equal freedom for each individual to secure his own interest. This equal freedom requires equal access to property, which remains the major exercise condition of liberty. This does not deny that some interests require the use of more of the means of property than others. In a situation where the legislator has no good reason for giving some interests a greater weight than others, equally he has no good reason for giving more of the means of property to some than to others. Similarly, if the mass of property is concentrated in a few hands this means that the majority has little scope for pursuing their own conceptions of the good, and this results in a smaller amount of social well-being.

In the case of person, beneficial condition in life, and reputation, he argued that the provision of equal spheres of personal inviolability entails the distribution of equal liberties, that is rights to protection from interference with these objects. In the case of property Bentham argued both for equal liberties, that is to say equal rights to the enjoyment of acquired property, and for equal rights to the objects of property, because the end in view is the maximum of substantive liberty as a condition of securing interests. The overall object of the legislator is not the maximization of liberty, but the maximization of social well-being. Therefore the legislator must distribute an equal pattern of liberties which facilitates ordered social interaction. In this sense law does not limit liberty it actually creates it by creating the conditions within which individuals can form and pursue their interests. As I have already argued, Bentham chose to call this sort of liberty security, because it necessarily involves distributive considerations which are derived from the principle of utility. Thus by distributing security the Benthamite legislator is not simply redistributing liberty that already exists, he is also creating the conditions of social interaction. However, the distribution of a pattern of liberties only entails equal security in the enjoyment of property not equal access to property which must be entailed if everyone is to be given the equal chance to realize their own ends. Bentham's utilitarian theory appears to be pulling in two opposite directions: firstly, in the direction of equal liberties which involve the equal enjoyment of property rights, and secondly, in the direction of equality of property as a means of guaranteeing the maximum of social well-being. In the next chapter I shall be concerned with how he pursued these egalitarian implications of the 'security-providing principle' within the context of his substantive theory of justice.

7

The Disappointment-Preventing Principle and Substantive Justice

In two recent revisionary accounts of Bentham's political morality[1] it has been acknowledged that he used the 'disappointment-preventing principle' as a principle of distributive justice. The view that this principle provides all that Bentham intended by a theory of justice is supported in the following passage where he wrote:

Civil more expressively termed distributive justice assumes and makes reference to the distribution made or proposed to be made of the several external objects of value, the several objects of general desire, the several objects corresponding to the several quarters in which as above security is capable of being wounded.

This being understood, thereupon have that which according to Mr Bentham is the first principle of Civil justice. It is that which he calls the *disappointment prevention principle*.[2]

However, the 'disappointment-preventing principle' is only one of the principles which constitute Bentham's theory of distributive justice.[3] The other is the 'security-providing principle' which prescribes the forms and limits of social interaction sufficient for each individual to realize his own end without interference from others. In order to defend the substance of this interpretation of his theory of distributive justice it is necessary to reconcile the importance that has been attached to the 'security-providing principle' with Bentham's claim that the 'first principle of Civil Justice'[4] is the 'disappointment-preventing principle'.

Despite the fact that Bentham appeared to identify the 'disappointment-preventing principle' as the sole principle of distributive justice[5] there are still good reasons for arguing that it is only one part of his theory of distributive justice. The 'disappointment-preventing principle' has only recently begun to figure in the discussion of Bentham's theory.[6] Rosen connects the 'disappointment-preventing principle' with the pursuit of

---

[1] G. J. Postema, *Bentham and the Common Law Tradition* (Oxford, 1986), 159 and 415–21, and F. Rosen, *Jeremy Bentham and Representative Democracy* (Oxford, 1983), p. 106.

[2] UC lxi, 51 (punctuation added).

[3] See Chap. 6, above.   [4] UC lxi, 51.

[5] Ibid., 53. Bentham refers to the 'Disappointment-preventing principle' in previous manuscript pages as the principle of distributive justice.

[6] P. Schwartz, 'Jeremy Bentham's Democratic Despotism', in R. D. Collison-Black (ed.), *Ideas in Economics* (London, 1986), 74–103.

equality. However, his concern is primarily with Bentham's democratic theory and the *Constitutional Code* so he does not develop the connection between the principle and Bentham's utilitarian theory of distributive justice in any great depth. Postema gives the principle a more systematic treatment from the perspective of Bentham's utilitarian theory of adjudication. While Postema connects the 'disappointment-preventing principle' with Bentham's utilitarian theory of justice he confines his attention to the function of the principle within Bentham's legal theory, and this results in a partial understanding of the role and importance of the principle within his wider political morality. Postema's account of the role of the 'disappointment-preventing principle' fails to capture precisely those broader insights which are suggested by Rosen. Schwartz on the other hand is not a revisionist Bentham scholar and his concern in the paper 'Jeremy Bentham's Democratic Despotism' is to criticize Bentham's constitutional theory and Rosen's account of the *Constitutional Code*. Schwartz offers no substantial discussion of the principle other than saying that it is inadequately developed, and therefore will not save Bentham's utilitarian theory from liberty-destroying policies of redistribution.

All of the above commentators have fostered the impression that the 'disappointment-preventing principle' is the sole principle of distributive justice within Bentham's utilitarian theory. These authors have succeeded in refocusing attention on the role of justice within Bentham's utilitarian theory, and as such they have gone some way to defending him against the charge that he is a crude act-utilitarian, which was implicit in the received interpretation of Bentham's moral theory.[7] However, the emphasis placed on the 'disappointment-preventing principle' as the sole and complete principle of distributive justice is misleading and even the interpretation of Bentham's moral theory offered by revisionists such as Rosen and Postema is incomplete.

Part of the reason why Bentham's theory of distributive justice has not received a full and comprehensive discussion is that many important components of his theory are buried in previously unpublished manuscripts. The 'disappointment-preventing principle' is first mentioned in 'A Commentary on Mr Humphreys' Real Property Code' which appeared in the *Westminster Review* in 1826. But in this work, Bentham offered little explanation of the connection of the principle with his utilitarian theory of justice. No doubt partly for this reason the 'disappointment-preventing principle' has featured so little in the discussion of Bentham's theory until very recently. He did, however, discuss the 'disappointment-preventing

---

[7] For a standard interpretation of Bentham on justice see H. A. Bedau, 'Justice and Classical Utilitarianism', *Nomos*, 6 (1963), 284–305. Bedau argues that Bentham has a dual theory of justice which involves the direct pursuit of utility and obedience to the rule of law. However, he also maintains that these two positions are ultimately irreconcilable, and, therefore, Bentham's theory of justice is fatally flawed and cannot accommodate many of our intuitions about an adequate theory of justice.

principle' in his Civil Law writings, many of which remain unpublished manuscripts. These manuscripts form the basis of my claim that the 'disappointing-preventing principle' is only one aspect of his theory of distributive justice, for they substantiate the connection between this principle and the 'security-providing principle'. In an 1828 manuscript, Bentham wrote: 'To security alone has justice any direct application: to the security providing principle',[8] and elsewhere he wrote: 'A modification of the security-providing principle, applying to security in respect of all modifications of the matter of property, is the disappointment-preventing principle.'[9] Bentham makes the same point in manuscripts that were incorporated into 'Pannomial Fragments' where he wrote:

Disappointment preventing principle. This is a modification of the security-providing principle. The use of it is to convey intimation of the reason for whatever arrangements come to be made for affording security in respect of property and the other modifications of the matter of prosperity, considered with a view to the interest of the individual possessors.[10]

Despite the fact that all of these manuscripts date from the last few years of Bentham's career the connection of the 'security-providing' and 'disappointment-preventing' principles does not represent a substantial change in the character of his theory, although his use of the terminology of disappointment in developing his theory of justice is novel. It is unclear why Bentham adopted this new terminology late in his career. Rosen suggests that it is possible that Bentham's renewed commitment to radicalism, which is to be found in his thought from 1809 onwards, is reflected in the new formulations of the principle of utility and its connection with equality found in the *Constitutional Code*.[11] Bentham's radicalism in the later years of his life may have prompted him to rethink the substance of his principle of utility and even use a different terminology to capture what he thought implicit in his utilitarian political morality. Whatever reason Bentham had for adopting the language of the 'disappointment-preventing principle' it is clear that he intended it to be seen as a modification of the 'security-providing principle'. The 'security-providing' and 'disappointment-preventing' principles appear at about the same time within his theory. Bentham provided little substained or detailed discussion of these principles and how they were supposed to operate, nevertheless, it is possible to piece together from the Civil Law manuscripts how he intended these principles to function within his theory.

This chapter will concentrate on the 'disappointment-preventing principle' as Bentham's substantive principle of justice, that is as the principle which guides the legislator in creating the conditions within which each individual can develop and realize his own well-being. The 'disappointment-preventing

---

[8] UC lxi, 47.   [9] Bowring, iii. 213.
[10] BL Add. MS 33550, fo. 57, also fo. 143.
[11] Rosen, *Jeremy Bentham and Representative Democracy*, p. 104.

principle' is a substantive principle because it prescribes the way in which the legislator ought to act in pursuit of the ultimate conditions of distributive justice which are set out out by the formal principle.

Those commentators who have concentrated on the role of the 'disappointment-preventing principle' as the sole principle of distributive justice have failed to recognize that by itself this principle is as indeterminate as a direct requirement to maximize utility. By itself it implies no priority rule which helps distinguish between trivial and important disappointments. Bentham's concern was with those disappointments that arose from frustrated expectations which originated from recognized social norms and institutions. However, not all existing social norms and institutions can be justified in terms of utility. Therefore, if the 'disappointment-preventing principle' is concerned simply with preventing the disappointment of expectations that arise out of institutions and practices that have little utilitarian justification, then it becomes detached from consideration of justice and Bentham's utilitarian theory no longer provides a standard for social reform. The 'disappointment-preventing principle' was the means by which he intended the most fundamental reform of government and the law to be carried out. However, it did not prescribe the direction in which that reform should proceed—that was prescribed by the 'security-providing principle'. Therefore, the 'disappointment-preventing principle' depends on the formal principle of justice in order to determine the end to which it should be applied and the way in which that end should be achieved. The two principles are intimately connected and only when they are regarded together do they convey the substance of Bentham's theory of distributive justice.

The substantive principle of justice is required in order to bring about the state of affairs prescribed by the formal principle of justice, because the legislator was not starting from an original position in which there were no rights or titles—a situation in which they are already existing patterns of expectation give rise to expectation utilities. His position is closer to that of Hume and Smith than Rawls or contemporary social contract theorists. Hume and Smith justified political institutions such as property and contract on the grounds that they contributed to overall welfare, but they did not justify particular obligations, rights, or titles in terms of utility. For both Hume and Smith the nature of property titles and the distribution of property within a state were a matter of convention and had no direct utilitarian justification. Though Hume is often included in histories of utilitarianism[12] his theory is at best a form of rule-utilitarianism which

[12] See J. P. Plamenatz, *The English Utilitarians* (Oxford, 1966). A. Quinton, *Utilitarian Ethics* (London, 1989), and D. D. Raphael, 'Bentham and the Varieties of Utilitarianism', *Bentham Newsletter*, 7 (1983), 3–14. Plamenatz, however, argues that little was added to the theory of Utilitarianism between the time of Hume and J. S. Mill. The implication being that Bentham made no significant contribution to utilitarianism and he simply popularized the doctrine.

places the greatest emphasis on the utilitarian justification of institutions. His theory is certainly distinct from the forms of utilitarianism advocated by Bentham or J. S. Mill.

A contemporary social contract theorist such as Rawls does not accept the normative force of existing social institutions and practices; rather he constructs a hypothetical original position in which rational individuals contract from a position of ignorance into a pattern of rights and titles which will, given certain epistemological constraints, provide the best prospects for each agent. This hypothetical social contract provides the moral justification for certain forms of rights and titles and the basis of the principles which distribute these rights.

Like Hume and Smith, Bentham acknowledged the conventional origin of the means of property acquisition as well as the form of distribution that a Benthamite legislator would face at any given time. He wrote that 'Property and law were born and die together. Till there was law there was no such thing as property: take away law property is at an end'.[13] What this shows apart from the dependency of property on law is that property as an institution is something that grow up within civil society. It is not something that the law recognized, but is something that the law creates. Therefore, the institution of property is not based on the principle of utility nor on a system of natural rights[14] but is the product of artifice and convention. Despite this similarity Bentham's theory differed from that of Hume and Smith in that he developed a theory of distributive justice within his utilitarian moral theory, whereas they accommodated distributive questions within their theories of history and rejected the foundationalist method of Bentham's philosophy.

The principle of utility through the means of the 'disappointment-preventing principle' is applied to the distribution of property within society in order to bring that existing distribution into line with one which embodies the maximum social well-being. For Hume and Smith, distributive justice is always a matter of commutative justice. Any question of the justice of an overall distribution of property in a society for Hume and Smith can be reduced to the question of whether or not the rules of property acquisition and contract were upheld in arriving at the present pattern of property holdings. For Bentham such an approach would be unacceptable despite the weight he attached to security of property.[15] He accepted that any given pattern of expectations and distribution of property implied a distribution of utilities, and that interference with it must result in a loss of utility on a large scale. However, a distribution of property which precludes a majority of agents within society from realizing their interests must

---

[13] UC xxxii, 157.   [14] Ibid., 156–7.

[15] 'In consulting the grand principle of security what ought the legislator to direct with regard to the mass of property which exists.

He ought to maintain the distribution which is actually established. This under the name of justice' (Bowring, i. 311).

necessarily entail a lesser amount of social well-being than a distribution which enabled each agent to realize his interests. The Benthamite legislator has to strike a delicate balance between respect for the existing pattern of expectations which entails a certain degree of social well-being, and the movement to a distribution which enables a greater degree of well-being. Despite Plamenatz's endorsement of Leslie Stephen's claim that 'the essential doctrines of utilitarianism are stated [by Hume] with a clearness and consistency not to be found in any other writer of the century' and his own claim that 'from Hume to J. S. Mill the doctrine [of utilitarianism] received no substantial alternation',[16] it is clear that Bentham's use of the 'disappointment-preventing principle' as a means of utilitarian reform is a major advance on the theories of his predecessors.

The main reason why Bentham's theory of distributive justice cannot involve a simple commitment to the protection and maintenance of the existing distribution, whatever its net consequence, is that he was also committed to the provision of the material conditions of freedom. A distribution of property that concentrates the major portion of property in the hands of the few not only creates the conditions of social unrest, but also limits the effective freedom of the majority. Bentham was not simply committed to the provision of the legal framework within which each individual could form and realize his own conception of the good. He was also committed to creating the conditions within which each had access to the material conditions of interest realization, and ultimately this involves the progressive equalization of property holdings. This commitment to creating the conditions within which each individual has the material conditions of freedom is an essential part of Bentham's theory of justice, and it is something that is completely lacking in the theories of his predecessors. His version of utilitarianism is not open to the charge made against preference-utilitarian theories of justice by Ronald Dworkin,[17] who argues that a just distribution cannot simply consist in people having what they want, for what they want is a function of the existing distribution, and therefore the existing distribution is self-perpetuating.[18] A person who is

---

[16] Plamenatz, *The English Utilitarians*, p. 22.

[17] Dworkin, 'Liberalism and Justice', in *A Matter of Principle* (Oxford, 1986), p. 204.

[18] Bentham's rejection of a straightforward interest satisfaction account of justice is borne out by his analysis of the interest of the community. He argued that the interest of the community is the 'sum of the several members who compose it' (*IPML* (CW), p. 12). However, he did not argue that the community interest is the sum total of what individuals want at any given time. This would be the equivalent of the preference-utilitarian theory that Dworkin criticizes. Rather Bentham argued that 'A thing is said to be in or *for* the interest of an individual, when it tends to add to the sum total of his pleasures: or, what comes to the same thing, to diminish the sum total of his pains' (*IPML* (CW), p. 12). What this implies is that an individual's real interest is what objectively tends to add to the sum total of his pleasures and what is the necessary conditions of purposive action. Given these necessary conditions of purposive action an individual is free to form and develop his own projects. Therefore, the

deprived of the effective means of extending his interest beyond the immediate requirement of subsistence can be easily satisfied by the provision of the means of subsistence. That individual may be formally free to form interests and pursue them, but without the possibility of access to the means of interest realization that freedom remains nominal. To satisfy the interests of a community, the majority of whom are constrained by material circumstances to the pursuit of basic subsistence, is not to give the claims of these people equal weight with that of substantial property owners. This is because those who have access to the material conditions of freedom or purposive action are unconstrained in their formation and realization of projects and goals within that range of options opened to them by the amount of property they hold. Those who are constrained by material circumstances to the pursuit of basic subsistence are effectively unfree in that their interest is given, and they have no other real choices before them. If the object guiding the Benthamite legislator is the maximizing of social well-being it cannot be argued that the continuation of a distribution that deprives the majority of the material conditions sufficient to form and realize effective interests is justifiable. This does not imply that the realization of each person's well-being necessarily requires an equal amount of property. Obviously some interests require more of the material conditions of purposive action than others. However, the progressive equalization of property will extend the range of projects that can be pursued, and increase overall social well-being.

This chapter will show just how Bentham hoped to reconcile the egalitarian and reforming implications of the 'disappointment-preventing principle' with his commitment to security of expectations and stability of property as a condition of prosperity, and the ultimate source of the material conditions of purposive action. Before turning to this question I will briefly consider the question of whether the appearance of the 'disappointment-preventing principle' in Bentham's thought in the late 1820s amount to a substantial modification in his utilitarian theory.

I

The 'security-providing' and the 'disappointment-preventing' principles first made their appearance in Bentham's thought in the late 1820s. After the 'disappointment-preventing principle' first appeared in 'A Commentary on Mr Humphreys' Real Property Code', it began to appear frequently in many

---

satisfaction of the interests of each individual would be the end in view of a utilitarian theory of justice. However, in the circumstances in which Bentham found himself it was not the case that all individuals were free to form and pursue their own interests. Therefore, the satisfaction of the desires of all individuals would not necessarily entail the realization of the community interest for in such circumstances not all individuals' desires represent freely chosen interests.

of Bentham's later works, most notably the *Constitutional Code*,[19] the 'Article on Utilitarianism',[20] and the late manuscripts which were incorporated into the 'Pannomial Fragments'.[21] As Schwartz[22] points out, Bentham failed to develop in any detail the justification of this principle within his thought. The fact that he placed such importance on it suggests that it represents an important development of his utilitarian theory. In his study of the *Constitutional Code* Rosen connects Bentham's use of the 'disappointment-preventing principle' with the project of radical reform.[23] He writes: 'The 'disappointment-prevention' principle, which is developed in his later writings, is discussed as a principle of justice especially relevant to cutting government expenditure in the name of reform.'[24] Rosen also connects the appearance of the principle with Bentham's reconsideration of the principle of utility that followed Macaulay's attack on utilitarianism in the *Edinburgh Review* in 1829.[25] Throughout his study of the *Constitutional Code*, Rosen stresses the fact that the appearance of the 'disappointment-preventing principle' is a late modification of Bentham's thought which is developed in response to the requirements of radical reform. The justification of Rosen's claim is very plausible. Firstly, there is the chronological connection between the appearance of the principle and Bentham's commitment to radical reform, and secondly, there is the logical connection between the principle and the requirements of radical reform. Bentham's constitutional reforms involved the institution of new offices and responsibilities as well as the abolition of sinecures and many superfluous offices. The problem that he faced was that the abolition of superfluous offices would violate the expectations of those whose interests had become vested in their continuation. These violated expectations create a utilitarian cost which if sufficiently great outweighs the prima facie case for reform. Although only a small number of place-holders may have suffered frustrated expectations, the precedent set is that the legislator is free to interfere in the existing pattern of expectations for only small incremental gains in overall utility. According to Rosen, Bentham attempted to avoid this problem by remunerating and compensating dispossessed place-holders in order that their expectations need not be violated, and that the net loss in utility is reduced. The 'disappointment-preventing principle' is the basis of these policies of compensation and remuneration, and its object is to protect the overall pattern of expectations from the radical reform proposals that he advocated.

[19] *Constitutional Code* (CW), ix. 17. A 39. Rosen argues that the 'disappointment-preventing principle' only appears in those parts of the *Code* added in 1830; see the discussion, *Jeremy Bentham and Representative Democracy*, p. 104.

[20] *Deontology* (CW), p. 308.   [21] BL Add. MS 33550, fos. 48–144.

[22] Schwartz, 'Jeremy Bentham's Democratic Despotism', p. 129.

[23] Rosen, *Jeremy Bentham and Representative Democracy*, p. 15.   [24] Ibid.

[25] Macaulay's Critique of James Mill's *Essays on Government*, is reprinted together with the responses from the *Westminster Review* in J. Lively and J. C. Rees (eds.), *Utilitarian Logic and Politics* (Oxford, 1978).

Schwartz has also argued that the 'disappointment-preventing principle' was a late addition to Bentham's thought which was suggested by the need to respond to the circumstances of reform.[26] Other writers on Bentham have, while acknowledging the late appearance of the principle within his thought, claimed that it was simply a new version of his commitment to security of expectation.[27] Rosen has responded to this criticism by arguing that while the 'disappointment-preventing principle' is undoubtedly connected to the general aim of securing expectations, the use that he made of the principle is enough to show that it reflects a new development in his thought. However, it is precisely this new approach to security of expectation that, according to Rosen, is embodied in the 'disappointment-preventing principle' which I suggest was already to be found in much earlier writings.

Rosen's argument is that Bentham used the principle to justify measures of remuneration and compensation for those who suffered as a result of reform. It is this connection between the requirements of reform and the need for security of expectation which according to Rosen takes the 'disappointment-preventing principle' beyond the simple commitment to security of expectation. Bentham developed a position that is similar to the 'disappointment-preventing principle' much earlier in his career. None of the manuscripts is dated, but it is clear they were all written long before Bentham's conversion to radicalism in 1809.[28] It is likely that these manuscripts date from the mid-1780s because some of them form material that was incorporated into Dumont's *Traités de législation civile et pénale*[29] and many of the other Bentham manuscripts that Dumont used in the *Traités* were written in the 1780s.

Bentham's earlier thoughts on disappointment prevention occur within the context of a discussion of the application of the principle of utility in a way that would bring about social reform. He began:

The want of the regard due to the existing interests of individuals is one of the most powerful causes as well as in many instances the perfectly sufficient warrant of the opposition made to plans of *reformation*: and so serious is the objection, so considerable the sum of evil which thus comes to be set against the sum of good expected from such measures, as in many instances to have no balance in point of utility in favour of them.[30]

---

[26] Schwartz, 'Jeremy Bentham's Democratic Despotism', p. 129.

[27] Long, 'Bentham on Property', p. 242.

[28] UC c, 96–186. It is not possible to put a precise date on the manuscripts but *Catalogue of the Manuscripts of Jeremy Bentham* (London, 1962) dates them at *c.*1776 and describes them as 'Legislation—Seen by Dumont, and made use of by him in *Traités de législation*'. Many of the manuscripts were certainly incorporated into the *Traités de législation* and this would suggest that they could not have been written much later than the end of the 1780s. However, the particular manuscripts which refer to the threat of disappointed expectations are not included in the *Traités*.

[29] *Traités de législation, civile et pénale* ed., P. E. L. Dumont (3 vols., Paris, 1803).

[30] UC c, 177.

In this passage Bentham clarified the problem faced by utilitarians in dealing with given patterns of expectation and the concomitant utilities derived from them. Any reform policy, whether it is derived from the direct application of the principle of utility or from an intermediate principle will necessarily involve the violation of some expectation, and consequently result in some loss of utility. Bentham's answer to this problem in these early writings is similar to the 'disappointment-preventing principle'. He wrote:

Policy therefore concurs with justice the probability of success as well as the advantage of succeeding in presenting on every such occasion a religious regard to the existing interests of individuals affronted by the change. To carry that regard to the pitch which utility requires, two rules ought to be laid down.

1. Where indemnification can be made to the individuals in question, to make such indemnification a condition precedent to, or at least concomitant with reform, and to take care that it be a full and adequate one.

2. If in the nature of the case such indemnification can not be made, not to attempt the reform, unless there be individuals whose advantage immediately derived from the reform will be more than equal to any equally immediate detriment that can result to the individuals demnified by it.

The expensiveness of the indemnification so long as the nature of things admits of the possibility of its being made can never form an adequate objection against the making it. If the benefit of the reform will not pay for the charge of indemnification, it is not an advantageous one on the whole.[31]

In this passage Bentham stressed the need to remunerate and compensate those who suffered frustrated expectations due to a policy of reform. He also argued that the expense of compensation should not be the immediate concern. The legislator should be especially concerned with the appropriateness of the level of compensation offered. If the cost of compensation is too great then that shows that the net benefit that will supposedly result from the reform policy is not as great as that which arises from maintaining the secured pattern of expectation. This reflects Rosen's view of the 'disappointment-preventing principle' which was designed to protect vested-right-holders by offering them compensation and remuneration.[32] The above passage also reflects the view that compensation will reduce opposition to reform. This is another of the benefits that Rosen associates with the 'disappointment-preventing principle'.[33]

In addition Bentham associated the need for remuneration and compensation with the requirement to protect existing expectations and prevent the pain of disappointment.[34] He gave two examples of areas where reform was appropriate, but where it was also necessary not to violate expectations. The first example arises out of government encouragement in the field of trade:

---

[31] Ibid., 177–8.
[32] Rosen, 'Jeremy Bentham and Representative Democracy', p. 102.
[33] Ibid., p. 102.   [34] UC c, 183.

Every encouragement bestowed upon this or that particular branch of Trade with the sole view of the benefit to trade (and which is not necessarily employed in the procurement of national subsistence, or profitably employed in the advancement of national defence), is so much money or money's worth thrown away . . . The trade thus encouraged is either an advantageous trade in comparison of the others not encouraged, or an unadvantageous one: if an advantageous one in itself and without the encouragement, the encouragement is unnecessary and useless: if an unadvantageous one, it is pernicious.[35]

There is a clear case for the reform and removal of these useless encouragements to trade. However, he continued, 'because the encouragement ought not to have been given, it follows not that it ought without more ado immediately be taken away.'[36] His solution to the problem of balancing the utility of maintaining the existing pattern of expectations against the utility of reform is to apply utilitarian principles in a way that prevents disappointment, thus:

No reform ought therefore to be attempted in the way of abolition of useless encouragement (in the way of trade) but on condition of taking adequate provision for indemnifying the persons engaged by means of such encouragement in the branch of trade in question from whatever loss appears likely to ensue from the withdrawing of the encouragement.

In the view of affording this indemnification the most obvious and most frugal course that can be taken is to postpone the withdrawing of the encouragment to a certain period more or less distant, and giving the earliest warning of that period:[37]

The second case which Bentham considered is that of unnecessary offices, sinecures, and excessive salaries. This emphasizes his concern for cutting government expenditure and the economy of office which is reflected in the later writings on constitutional reform, particularly in the *Constitutional Code*. Again this is something that Rosen considers to be distinctive of the 'disappontment-preventing principle' as a later development in Bentham's thought.[38] In the case of these unnecessary expenses of government, Bentham wrote:

Finance expence of, resulting from excessive salaries to public offices, salaries annexed to superfluous or useless offices, or sinecures i.e. pensions of favour, salaries without office. That reform in every one of these instances is desirable is not scarcely to be disputed.[39]

However, despite the obvious case for reform, Bentham still acknowledged the need to compensate those who suffered loss of office, writing:

The loss by the abolition of places for life can be no otherwise be adequately compensated than by the grant of pensions of at least equal value. But what is more

---

[35] UC c, 182.
[36] Ibid., 183.　　　　　　　　　　　　　　　　　　[37] Ibid., 184.
[38] Rosen, 'Jeremy Bentham and Representative Democracy', pp. 15, 93, and 101.
[39] UC c, 185.

neither can places said to be held during pleasure be compensated on terms any thing if at all inferior.[40]

Bentham thought that failure to appreciate the need to employ compensation and remuneration in the pursuit of policies of reform sprang from a failure to understand the egalitarianism implicit in the principle of utility. He is not here referring to the possibility of bringing about a more equal distribution of property, but to the equality captured by what J. S. Mill calls Bentham's dictum, 'Each is to count for one and nobody to count for more than one'.[41] Bentham does not use the exact words of the supposed dictum attributed to him by J. S. Mill, nevertheless it is quite clear that this is exactly what he intended, for he wrote:

What seems very frequently not to occur in these zealous promoters of the public good in the ardour of their zeal is that as a faggot is comprised of sticks, so is the public of individuals: that one individual is as large a portion of the public as another individual: and the happiness of the one as much a portion of the happiness of the public as is the happiness of the other.[42]

Bentham's point is that in order to take seriously the greatest happiness of all concerned, the reform-minded legislator must pay as much attention to the disappointment of those who are deprived of superfluous benefits by a reform measure, as those whose happiness depends on the reform of existing institutions. This is precisely what Bentham intended to achieve by means of the 'disappointment-preventing principle'.

The reason for quoting so extensively from these previously unpublished manuscripts is that they show in the clearest terms that he was aware of the problems of reconciling a policy of reform with a respect for expectations. This shows that Bentham's later adoption of the 'disappointment-preventing principle' from 1826 onwards does not mark a substantial development in his thought. However, while this suggests that Rosen is wrong to see the 'disappointment-preventing principle' simply as a response to a series of theoretical and practical problems thrown up by his commitment to radical reform from 1809 onwards, he is not wrong in rejecting Long's claim that the principle is simply Bentham's commitment to security of expectation in a new guise.[43] The reason for this is that the 'disappointment-preventing principle' and the requirement to minimize disappointment in the early manuscripts both reflect a response to the tension within utilitarian theory between securing the existing pattern of expectations and the need for reforms which facilitate the maximum social well-being. Long fails to see the importance of reform within Bentham's utilitarian theory. His interpretation captures only one aspect of Bentham's utilitarian theory and it is

---

[40] Ibid., 186.
[41] Mill, *Utilitarianism*, in *Essays on Ethics, Religion and Society* (The Collected Works of John Stuart Mill, x), 257.   [42] UC c, 179.
[43] Long, 'Bentham on Property', p. 242.

for this reason that he can argue that Bentham's utilitarianism does not provide a criterion of distributive justice.

Long argues that Bentham's concern was to maintain the economic status quo: 'everything as it should be Bentham'.[44] These early manuscripts are especially important in that they show that he was not as committed to the absolute protection of any given distribution of property, as some passages from the 'Principles of the Civil Code' would suggest.[45] They also show that he was aware of the problems involved in constructing a utilitarian theory of justice early on in his career. What these early manuscripts do not emphasize in the same way as the later writings on the 'disappointment-preventing principle' is the connection between the concern with the prevention of disappointment and the requirements of a utilitarian theory of justice. The fact that Bentham placed more emphasis on this connection in the later writings does not constitute the addition of anything that was not already implicit in his earlier thought. However, it does bring to the fore the radical nature of Bentham's reform project and the role of the pursuit of material equality within that project, which is totally absent from the 'Principles of the Civil Code'.[46]

The next section will concentrate on how Bentham used the 'disappointment-preventing principle' within his theory of justice, and how he balanced the claims of liberty or security with his commitment to increasing material equality as a means of realizing greater freedom.

II

The spheres of personal inviolability distributed by the 'security-providing principle' are the product of the equal distribution of rights to person, property, beneficial condition in life, and reputation. These rights mark out the boundaries of those spheres within which individuals are able to form and pursue their own conceptions of interest. Therefore, the wider these spheres of personal inviolability are drawn, the greater the freedom there is for each individual to form and realize his own projects. The 'security-providing principle' prescribes that the law embodies the equal distribution of those rights protecting person, property, condition in life, and reputation. The objects of such an equal distribution is that no individual necessarily enjoys a greater realm of freedom than any other. However, Bentham is not simply concerned with the formal conditions of freedom, but also with the substantive or material conditions within which each can pursue his own conception of well-being. This entails that the legislator is required to maintain the security of property in its narrow sense, because this is the primary efficient condition of freedom. By securing rights to private

---

[44] Long, 'Bentham on Property', p. 247.
[45] Bowring, i. 311.
[46] Ibid., 297–364.

property the legislator enables individuals to develop conceptions of interest and to pursue well-being. These rights to private property, along with rights protecting condition in life and reputation, form the framework within which each can pursue his own projects. However, while it is sufficient that the legislator provide rights protecting condition in life and reputation, it is not sufficient that he merely protect the given distribution of property. If the object of the formal principle of distributive justice is to identify that pattern of expectations which enables the maximum of social well-being to be obtained, then the legislator must prescribe an equalization of property. Only by pursuing the equalization of property can the securing of property rights have any direct contribution to the maximum of social well-being. It is also the case that only by means of this equalization of property holdings can the spheres of personal inviolability which are distributed by the 'security-providing principle' have any substance.

In advocating an equal distribution of the material conditions of purposive action the 'security-providing principle' provides what some contemporary philosophers describe as a patterned principle of justice.[47] It promotes a pattern to guide legislative actions and social interaction in order that the best state of affairs should result. The significance of patterned principles of justice is that they provide a guide or a picture of the end-state of social interaction. So long as social arrangements are designed in such a way that this end-state or pattern is realized then the distribution is just. This seems a fair description of the 'security-providing principle', which advocates an equal distribution of property as that state of affairs most conducive to justice as the maximum of social well-being. Patterned or end-state principles of justice ignore what J. R. Lucas has called 'process values'.[48] Process values are concerned not with the end-state or the overall consequences of action but rather with the procedures by which that end result obtains. Consequently they incorporate the concept of desert which is the primary focus of many non-consequentialist theories of justice. These considerations are most appropriate in the case of determining the legal treatment of offenders, where the procedure for dealing with a case is as important as the ultimate outcome. Process values have also been introduced in considering the justice of the distribution of property and economic benefits. In this case it is argued that what is of primary importance is not the outcome of the distribution, but whether or not the particular holdings which make up the overall distribution have been arrived at by appropriate or fair means. The charge laid against utilitarianism and Bentham's theory of justice is that because it is concerned with that distribution which has the best consequences, it is an end-state or patterned principle of justice and ignores process values. This is the charge implicit in

---

[47] Nozick, *Anarchy, State and Utopia*, pp. 155–60.
[48] J. R. Lucas, *On Justice* (Oxford, 1980), 72–3.

Schwartz's criticism of the egalitarian tendencies of Bentham's utilitarianism. Schwartz argues that one of the major defects of the theory of utility is that it lends itself to unwarranted assumptions about equality through redistribution.[49] He refers to the egalitarian implications of diminishing marginal utility as evidence of this tendency in Bentham's thought.[50] These are considered at the end of 'Pannomial Fragments', where Bentham wrote:

> Thus it is, that if the effects of the first order were alone taken into account, the consequence would be, that, on the supposition of a new constitution coming to be established, with the greatest happiness of the greatest number for its end in view, sufficient reason would have place for taking the matter of wealth from the richest and transferring it to the less rich, till the fortunes of all were reduced to an equality, or a system of inequality so little different from perfect equality, that the difference would not be worth calculating.[51]

The basis of Schwartz's criticism of the egalitarian tendencies of Bentham's utilitarianism is that it ignores process values and existing entitlements in favour of an end-state. The Benthamite legislator is never faced with an original position in which everything is previously unowned, therefore any attempt at pursuing equality must always be at the expense of those who already benefit from the original distribution. While Schwartz draws attention to certain difficulties facing Bentham's utilitarian theory, his overall criticism of Bentham is misdirected. Bentham did not advocate the direct pursuit of a crude maximizing act-utilitarianism. He recognized the greater utilities that are derived from a secured system of expectations. Therefore, the requirements of the theory of justice have not been given in terms of the direct pursuit of incremental gains in utility, but in terms of securing a pattern of expectations within which each individual can form and pursue his own conception of interest. However, he was not simply concerned with securing any given pattern of expectations. The ultimate aim of Bentham's theory of justice was to secure a pattern of expectations that embodied the equal provision of the material and formal conditions of interest realization and this necessarily entails the progressive equalization of property holdings. Schwartz emphasizes that this reforming aspect of Bentham's theory of distributive justice with its egalitarian implications, is necessarily antagonistic to the notion of process values and the existing distribution of freedom and property.

There are two opposing tendencies inherent in Bentham's theory of justice. Firstly, private property holdings and liberty are already distributed throughout any given social order. Any social order breeds certain patterns of expectation and these generate expectation utilities. So long as these expectations have been the consequence of some accepted procedure of

---

[49] Schwartz, 'Jeremy Bentham's Democratic Despotism', p. 128.

[50] Bentham discusses the egalitarian implications of diminishing marginal utility at Bowring, i. 304–7, and iii. 228–30.

[51] BL Add. MS 33550, fo. 136 (Bowring, iii. 230).

distribution and acquisition there is a prima facie reason that the utilitarian should take these utilities into account in judging the appropriateness of reform measures. Secondly, a given pattern of expectations may well embody expectation utilities, but if these are outweighed by the benefits that would accrue to those who may be precluded from realizing their interests, there is also a prima facie reason for utilitarian reform. Bentham was the first utilitarian theorist to recognize these two tendencies within utilitarian theory and the first to attempt to reconcile them using the two principles embodied in his theory of justice.[52]

Bentham was not prepared to ignore those utilities that are derived from an existing pattern of expectations. However, the need to take into account the expectation utilities derived from any given distribution has created additional difficulties for his theory. Unlike Rawls and contemporary social contract theorists who argue that those utilities arising out of an unjust distribution are irrelevant in judging the overall justice of that distribution,[53] Bentham is required to take these expectation utilities into account. This places him in the unfortunate position of having to take account of the expectation utilities of slave owners against the utilities of freed slaves in determining whether or not slavery should be abolished. Bentham certainly thought there was a good utilitarian case to be made against slavery. However, he has no prima facie reason for excluding from consideration the disappointment suffered by slave-owners who would lose their property and income as a result of abolition. Therefore, in determining how the dictates of the 'security-providing principle' ought to be actualized Bentham argued that all costs have to be weighed equally. Thus he wrote:

as a faggot is comprised of sticks, so is the public of individuals: that one individual is as large a portion of the public as another individual: and the happiness of the one as much a portion of the happiness of the public as is the happiness of the other.'[54]

This simply implies that equal utilities are treated equally which is not itself sufficient ground for substantive equality of property. However, formal equality is a foundation for the rejection of moral perfectionism and a basis for toleration. Bentham's reliance on utility as the sole criterion of value conflicts with most common moral intuitions which would rule out of consideration the benefit of unjust social arrangements. His only solution to this problem is to rely on the fact that the utilities of those who would benefit from the reform of unjust social institutions will outweigh the utilities of those who benefit from the existing institutions. Thus in the case

---

[52] This is directly contrary to Plamenatz's claim in *The English Utilitarians* that 'from Hume to J. S. Mill the doctrine [utilitarianism] received no substantial alteration' (p. 22). Plamenatz fails to see these two conflicting tendencies within utilitarian theory. The first tendency is best represented by Hume and the second by Godwin.

[53] J. Rawls, 'Justice as Fairness', *Philosophical Review*, 67 (1958), 164–94.

[54] UC c, 179.

of slavery the legislator has to take into account the expectation utilities based on the property rights of slave-owners, just as he has to consider the interests of the slaves. What underlies his position is the view that if the slave-owners are not directly responsible for the institutions of which they are the beneficiaries then the disappointment they suffer is as worthy of consideration as that of anyone else. This was why Bentham not only took account of the expectation utilities of those who are the beneficiaries of unjust social institutions, but also advocated that they should be compensated and remunerated in the event of the reform of those institutions.

The difficulties posed by end-state principles of justice are not, however, confined to unique redistributions. Redistributions required to bring the existing pattern of property rights into line with that advocated by justice involves a single violation of the system of property. However, once the pattern or end-state is achieved and individuals are left free to exercise their liberty, the pattern of property holdings necessarily changes back to one of inequality. It can be argued that these inequalities are legitimate in so far as they are the result of free purposive actions by individuals in pursuit of their projects. This might justify inequalities that result among a closed group of individuals starting from a position of equality, but it is an unconvincing argument when it is extended to a whole society. While at any given moment a society is made up of a fixed number of individuals, over any given period of time within which action takes place, that number of individuals changes. New individuals are born and others die, none of whom benefited from the original distribution, but all have an equal need for property as a means of pursuing their own interests. The initial justification of the end-state was that it provided the conditions for each person to pursue his own conception of well-being. However, when individuals make use of the freedom provided by the end-state, there is a need to re-establish that distribution of property rights. Thus, instead of a single attack on the original distribution of property rights, the end-state requires a continual interference with liberty and property. This continual interference with property rights has the effect of severely restricting an individual's liberty because it constrains him in the ways in which he can act in exercising of his property rights. As Nozick[55] and Buchanan[56] argue, patterned or end-state principles of justice are incompatible with property rights. In the case of Rawls's difference principle, which is their primary target, they argue that because a system of previously just legitimate expectations loses its legitimacy due to new information about how to maximize the benefit of the worst off, there can be no real property rights. Thus, a continual interference with the distribution of property rights in the name of justice also has the effect of threatening expectations, because no

[55] Nozick, *Anarchy, State, and Utopia*, pp. 160–4 and 167–74.
[56] A. Buchanan, 'Distributive Justice and Legitimate Expectations', *Philosophical Studies*, 28 (1975), 419–25.

individual can project himself into the future through the continuity of his projects, and the pursuit of his goals. Without secured expectations individuals are unable to organize rationally their lives and secure their well-being. The main consequence of this is that industry, on which the future well-being of society is based, is seriously undermined. The disutility that would result from a substantial lessening of industriousness weighs heavily against the claims of reform. Therefore, the cost of bringing about the pattern of distributive justice appears to vitiate the claims of the 'security-providing principle'. The case of this principle is similar to that of Rawls' difference principle in that once the distribution of property departs from initial equality, the justification of those unequal titles disappears in favour of another equal distribution.

The problem of end-state principles only arises in the case of Bentham's 'security-providing principle' when that is seen as the sole component of his theory of distributive justice. However, it is only one aspect of his theory of distributive justice. The other aspect of his theory, the 'disappointment-preventing principle' is concerned with translating the direction of reform into practical measures that aim at the equalization of property without violating the expectations derived from security of property. While the 'security-providing principle' defines the direction in which the Benthamite legislator should aim, it is simply concerned with that social arrangement which results in the maximum of social well-being, and takes no account of the utilities derived from the existing distribution of property. However, as I have already argued, because the Benthamite legislator is faced with a given pattern of expectation the complete principle of distributive justice must take into account disappointment resulting from upsetting that pattern while moving towards the distribution prescribed by the 'security-providing principle'. The 'disappointment-preventing principle' functions by specifying the three main directions in which the Benthamite legislator can pursue a utilitarian policy without undermining expectations.

In the first case he can in certain circumstances override the interests of particular individuals and require the submission of a portion of their property as a contribution to the social good. He is allowed to do this even when the individual property-holder desires not to make a direct contribution to this chosen social good. This policy can be justified on the grounds that the end pursued is an objectively necessary component of the individual's interest. Such a policy is allowed in *An Introduction to the Principle of Morals and Legislation*, where Bentham wrote: 'A thing is said to promote the interest, or to be *for* the interest, of an individual, when it tends to add to the sum total of his pleasures: or, what comes to the same thing, to diminish the sum total of his pains.'[57] While an individual property-holder might object to paying taxes that finance the military, judiciary, and police force, it

---

[57] *IPML* (CW), p. 12.

can, nevertheless, be argued that it is within his interest that he contributes to their provision for they protect those institutions of which he is a beneficiary.

Throughout his career Bentham argued that there were certain public goods which were so important to the well-being of the community that the legislator was justified in interferring with property rights in order to provide for them. These public goods include the provision of defence against external enemies and internal disorder, the provision of protection against physical calamities, and the support of a system of justice and police.[58] In each case he specifically included the essential components of the maintenance of security which benefit each person. Without the provision of external and internal security, the benefits of property would be negligible. Similarly, without a judicial system and the criminal law, the institution of property should not function as there would be no way of settling contested titles or prosecuting unjustified interferences. Although these public goods are undeniably of benefit to the community, the provision of these goods depends upon legislative interference with the given distribution of property, and with security of expectation. For this reason the 'disappointment-preventing principle' is involved in determining whether it is appropriate for the legislator to pursue such a policy. The legislator has to take into account the disappointment that will result from his actions, and whether that is counterbalanced by the benefits that will accrue to the whole community from such policies. In the 'Principles of the Civil Code' some policies are justified as 'Sacrifices of Security to Security'.[59] This means that only certain reasons justify interferences with property. The legislator cannot simply redistribute property on the grounds of an incremental gain in utility. Nevertheless, he can interfere with property as a means of contributing to greater security. Sacrifices of security to security do not constitute significant causes of disappointment, whereas a policy of redistribution aimed at an incremental gain in overall utility does constitute such a cause. Sacrifices of security to security counteract the disappointment, because they demonstrate that the legislator's intention is the overall protection of property. While there is a cost in depriving members of the community of a portion of their property there is an equivalent gain in the security of their remaining property. The form and direction of this policy illustrate that the legislator's intention is to maintain security. This diminishes the threat of alarm caused by his actions. Overall expectations are not undermined because the policy is directed at the continued protection of property, and the institution of property can function normally. However, if the legislator violates property for a utilitarian reason, not concerned with the maintenance of security, his action would have serious consequences for the stability of expectation. An

[58] Bowring, i. 313.
[59] Ibid.

action which violates security of property for a reason other than the maintenance of security sets a precedent for interference with property where an incremental gain in utility will result, and this is incompatible with the maintenance of security of property.

While the Benthamite legislator may interfere with property in order to provide greater security, Bentham clearly believed that this policy is acceptable only in a narrow class of cases where there can be no doubt that the overall aim of the policy is the extension and maintenance of security of expectation. The direct services which the legislator provides are only those concerned with the maintenance and protection of security. Though Bentham was a supporter of what are now called social-welfare measures, such as the positive provision of subsistence, he believed that these could be founded by charitable companies.[60] However, there are circumstances in which direct interference with property is justified in order to help the indigent. Such measures are only appropriate in cases of approaching social catastrophe, where some direct action is necessary to prevent the overthrow of the system of secured expectations. Such social catastrophe is extremely infrequent, and would not be a consideration that would ordinarily feature in the legislator's decision-making. Nevertheless, it is clear in such circumstances that he preferred a single violation of security to a policy of continued redistribution:

If violent causes, such as a revolution in government, a schism, a conquest, produce the overthrow of property, it is a great calamity; but it is only transitory—it may be softened and even repaired by time. Industry is a vigorous plant, which resists numerous loppings, and in which the fruitful sap rises immediately upon the return of spring. But if property were overthrown with the direct intention of establishing equality of fortune, the evil would be irreparable: no more security—no more industry—no more abundance; society would relapse into the savage state from which it has arisen . . . If equality ought to reign today, for the same reason it ought to reign always. It can only be preserved by the same violences by which it was established. It would require an army of inquisitors and executioners, deaf both to favouritism and complaint—insensible to the seductions of pleasure—inaccessible to personal interest—endowed with every virtue, and engaged in a service which would destroy them all.[61]

In the case of social catastrophe the legislator is faced with balancing the disappointment resulting from his redistributive measures with the likely disappointment resulting from the possible violent overthrow of property. Again he is able to make such a decision on the grounds of the 'disappointment-preventing principle', because he balances like considerations. However, as he is unable to make a precise determination of the degree to which disappointment is felt by the community he is only justified

---

[60] See C. F. Bahmueller, *The National Charity Company* (Berkeley, Calif., 1981), 130–40, and J. Semple, 'Bentham's Haunted House', *Bentham Newsletter*, 11 (1987), 35–44.

[61] Bowring, i. 311–12.

in making such decisions in cases of impending social catastrophe, where the cost of not acting is indisputable.

The second instance in which the 'disappointment-preventing principle' is needed to reconcile the claims of reform with the need to respect the existing pattern of expectations arises directly from constitutional reform. Bentham's position here is similar to that found in the earlier writings on the role of disappointment in the determination of utilitarian policies. He regarded vested rights and sinecures as sources of utility despite the fact that they provide the conditions in which vested interests flourish. Therefore, the legislator's task is to advance the course of reform while respecting the interests of place-holders. This is achieved by remunerating and compensating those place holders in a manner which is sufficient to outweigh the disappointment that results from the violation of those expectations that are derived from these sinecures and superfluous offices.[62] Clearly the legislator has no justification for discounting the expectation utilities of place holders. Bentham expected the 'disappointment-preventing principle' to apply most directly to the case of constitutional reform, and most of the discussion of the principle occurs in the context of his writings on reform. In the early manuscripts referred to above, he argued that reform is only justified if its benefits are great, and, therefore, will outweigh the costs of remuneration and compensation, however expensive they may be.[63] This view is upheld in the case of his later concern with constitutional reform. In determining the course of action, the legislator has to consider the cost of remuneration and compensation against the benefits of such reform. There are ways in which the legislator can attempt to reduce the cost of reform, such as trying to re-employ those deprived of their jobs in the new institutional arrangements.

However, despite the use of compensation to overcome disappointment there does appear to be a problem posed by the need for constitutional reform. The whole notion of compensation is premissed on the idea that the payment of a sum of money can diminish the damage to expectations and prevent the spread of alarm throughout the community of property-holders. Secondly, compensation and remuneration suggest that all values can be given a price, and given the variety of ends that individuals can pursue, this seems an implausible assumption. The exercise of power is in many cases self-rewarding and no sum of money can adequately compensate its loss.

In the first case Bentham was aware that interfering with expectations produced not only a loss on behalf of a particular individual, but also the alarm felt by others at the expectation of suffering a similar loss of property. It is the intention of the legislator, and not compensation which has the effect of diminishing the alarm that results from interference with the existing pattern of expectations. The legislator's aims and his policy of reform will, therefore, have the greatest effect in reducing the alarm that

[62] UC c, 186.
[63] Ibid., 178.

results from interference with the existing pattern of expectations. The provisions of compensation and remuneration reduces the direct disappointment that results from being deprived of an income, and also demonstrates to the wider audience that the legislator is concerned with maintaining respect for the security of property and not unduly violating expectations. Secondly, the legislator can reduce the risk of alarm by confining his attention to a certain class of individuals and only one aspect of their property. He is not concerned with depriving them of all their property nor is he with punishing them for being the beneficiaries of institutional arrangements for which they cannot be held personally responsible.

The second strand of criticism is that the emphasis on compensation and remuneration suggests that all values can be reduced to money values and that money can compensate for loss of power and prestige. This criticism is largely mistaken for the following reasons. Firstly, the Benthamite legislator is largely concerned with the abolition of sinecures and superfluous offices. These offices often carried no power or responsibility. Therefore, monetary compensation was the most appropriate means of preventing disappointment. The fixed expectations derived from these superfluous offices were financial and these could be secured while the offices were abolished by means of pensions and direct financial compensation. In most cases the question of translating the enjoyment of wielding power into a monetary value does not arise. Where these offices did involve the exercise of power Bentham did not try to translate that into a monetary value at all. He suggested instead that disappointment could be reduced in such cases by replacing those displaced office-holders in the new institutions, where they could wield power and exercise authority. The compensation was solely connected to the disappointment that resulted for loss of salaries. Throughout his reform writings the 'disappointment-preventing principle' relates to the disappointment that resulted from direct interference with personal property. This is because personal property is the greatest source of expectation and the primary efficient condition of liberty and interest realization. Indeed, far from attempting to compensate for the loss of power through reform, Bentham argued that a person ought not to be compensated for loss of power. His reason is that compensation is only appropriate in the case of loss of personal property, that is possession, condition in life and reputation. Power can never be an object of personal property. It is always, even in the unreformed constitution, held in trust for the community and not for the benefit of the individual power-holder. Because a power-holder enjoys the exercise of power as a trust, it is not something that he can dispose of at his will. He cannot, therefore, develop expectations about his future disposal of power.

As previously stated, reputation and condition in life are objects of personal property, and the disappointment that results from interference with them should be compensated. However, this again raises the question of whether all values can be translated into monetary terms. In one sense it is clear that loss of reputation cannot be directly compensated. While compensation may make the loss of reputation easier to bear, it does not remove the resulting disappointment. The disappointment at loss of reputation is addressed indirectly in the way compensation is provided. Therefore, the legislator can avoid disappointing expectations by translating sinecures into fixed-term personal pensions which continue to give a material income to the beneficiary. Because they are the object of personal property no loss of reputation need result. However, on the death of the beneficiary instead of the sinecure being bequeathed to the beneficiary's heirs or returned to the government which can then bestow it on another person, the personal pension is abolished. Such an arrangement would serve the end of the reform without causing disappointment either in terms of loss of property or loss of reputation or condition in life. In this example Bentham did not allow direct utilitarian policies to interfere with the expectation utilities derived from property. Therefore, the legislator was able to combine a respect for the expectations derived from property with a policy of constitutional reform, as long as the legislator's intention was made clear by the use of compensation and remuneration. Bentham was unprepared to sacrifice the existing pattern of expectations to incremental gains in utility. Any violation of property rights that has been allowed either in order to finance greater security or in the interest of constitutional reform is a unique measure. Thus, the 'disappointment-preventing principle' only justifies those policies which either contribute directly to the greater security of property and so cancel out any disappointment, or those which interfere with the pattern of property rights, but which leave the underlying distribution of material property unaffected by means of compensation and remuneration. The problem of combining security of expectation with a progressive equalization of property remains. Redistribution in the interests of equality is justified on utilitarian grounds, as Bentham acknowledged,[64] but it is equally clear that he thought the direct pursuit of equality would result in disaster.[65] In order to progress towards the equalization of property, he had to develop a policy which made no direct attack on the security of property.

Bentham's concern with protecting the existing pattern of expectations, when the reform of those institutions from which they are derived was desirable, is reflected in the following passage from an 1828 manuscript entitled 'Law Amendment: Official Aptitude, etc.':

In this case, mischievous as is the institution, no sufficient ground does the mischievousness present for the abolition of the hereditary nuisance except with

[64] BL Add. MS 33550, fo. 136 (Bowring, iii. 320).
[65] Bowring, i. 311–12.
[66] UC lxi, 63.

compensation and that compensation adequate: ground for abolition, yes, and altogether sufficient, ground for refusal of compensation, no.[66]

The requirement to protect expectations was at the heart of Bentham's commitment to justice, and it is precisely this commitment to the security of expectation which appears to undermine progress towards equality. Even compensation is not an adequate solution to Bentham's predicament because the purpose of compensation was to modify the pattern of property rights without actually upsetting the substantive distribution of property. So long as the legislator does not make extreme modifications to the existing pattern of property rights then the pattern of expectations remains stable. Because the Benthamite legislator is aiming at a redistribution of substantive property holdings and not merely a modification of the pattern of property rights, the use of compensation and remuneration is inappropriate. Interferences with the distribution of substantive property has a much more unsettling affect on real expectations and the conditions of interest formation and satisfaction.

However, Bentham believed it was possible to progress towards equality of property without interfering with the existing pattern of expectations by means of the law governing succession. It is for this reason that the law governing succession is discussed within the 'Principles of the Civil Code'.[67] The law governing succession regulates the redistribution of property-holdings after the possessor's death and the cessation of his expectations. In a series of late manuscripts concerned with the problems of pursuing equality Bentham wrote:

In the instance of each individual, a particular point there is at which, without defalcation made from security in his instance, or in the instance of any other individual, his property may be subjected to a distribution or other disposition, whereby, according to the amount of it advance towards absolute equality may be made.

This time is the time of a man's death. In his instance, no such evil is produced, for he is no more. In the instance of no other individual if, sufficient and effective care has been taken to exclude expectation, will evil be produced: for the only evil incident to the case is disappointment, and, by the exclusion of expectation, disappointment has been excluded.[68]

On a person's death his expectations terminate. This is the case even though a person might entertain expectations about the disposal of his property after his death. Those expectations which extend beyond one's natural life are the weakest class of floating expectations because they are not fixed to anything that is within his power once he is dead. A person can take advantage of certain legal practices to secure the performance of his wishes after his death, but in the event of those wishes being ignored, he cannot feel

---

[67] Bowring, i. 334–8.
[68] UC clx, 169.

disappointment. This does not however, give the legislator a free hand to redistribute the fortunes of the deceased, for while he cannot suffer disappointment at the time, he can suffer disappointment at the prospect of his wishes being overridden, but perhaps more important is the real disappointment suffered by his heirs. It is with this group that the legislator is primarily concerned.

The main instrument by which the equalization of property-holdings can be achieved is the system of law governing wills and bequests. Bentham wrote:

On the occasion of a man's death, by the distribution which, according to the natural course of things takes place (abstraction made of arrangements established by positive law, for the express purpose of controlling it), equality, and that without defalcation from security, is promoted.[69]

Bentham saw the redistribution of property from those recently deceased to new generations, as a means of ensuring that all individuals had access to the material conditions of purposive action. Thus, he avoided the problem of having to interfere constantly with the existing distribution of property in order to provide some of its substance for new generations. The end-state principle which prescribes an initial equal distribution of property is premissed on a view of society as being a series of discrete segments which lack any temporal continuity. The law relating to successions provides a temporal unity binding succeeding generations within society and enables all of its members to benefit from the enjoyment of property.

While Bentham saw the system of bequest as the most appropriate means of achieving the redistribution of property without violating expectations, he did not think that the existing rules of succession were those most conducive to the equalization of property-holdings. He advocated a number of reforms which broke up large property-holdings and redistributed them more equally through the community. However, in view of the fact that the existing law of bequest was a source of expectation, he argued that the reform must be gradual in order to take account of existing expectations and to prevent the formation of those that are inconsistent with his proposed reforms. The legislators can achieve the reforms he wishes by giving advance warning of the proposed measures he is to introduce and of allowing a time to lapse between their being announced and coming into effect. Thus if the legislator announces that certain new measures are to come into effect at a certain time in the future, he can prevent the formation of expectations, based on those features of the system that he wishes to abolish. In this way he does not affect those who formed their expectations prior to the announcement, but who do not expect to benefit from inheritance until after the announcement was made. Those who have no

[69] UC clx, 170.

expectations based on the existing system of succession will, therefore, form no subsequent expectations in accordance with the system following the new legislation. Finally, the reform of the existing pattern of expectations will not cause any substantial alarm, because it makes no proposals to do away with a system of bequest altogether. The reform is unique because Bentham recognized that any continual interference with the system would destroy expectations, and thus undermine the practice which he saw as the most appropriate means of pursuing material equality.

The first and most significant reform that Bentham prescribed for the system of bequest in order that it resulted in the greater equalization of property, was the legal equality of men and women, and consequently a woman's right to inherit property on equal terms with a male heir. In a series of manuscripts on the subject of succession, that were later incorporated into the 'Principles of the Civil Code', Bentham wrote:

Article 1st. In point of succession both sexes stand upon the same footing: in relation to children of the same family, though the male only be mentioned, the female shall also be understood. *Principle, Equality.*

Observations. The differences, were there any it ought rather to be in favour of the weaker sex. With more wants it has fewer ways and means: less aptitude for acquiring property, less aptitude for making the most of what it has. So much with regard to propriety: in point of fact it is the stronger sex that has run away with all the preferences. Enquire for the justicative reason, you will find none: ask for the historical reason, the efficient cause, you will find it in the difference in point of force.[70]

Bentham recognized that sexual equality within the law of succession would result in a substantial redistribution of property throughout the community. It would remove a barrier that prevented half of the population from benefiting from the system of succession, and this would inevitably have a significant effect on the pattern of property holdings. Moreover, he also argued that not only should the female sex enjoy practical equality in terms of bequest, but because of inequalities built into the existing system over many generations, there was a prima facie case for positive action in favour of the female sex in order to compensate for their inability to acquire property by other means. This is not quite enough to justify the claim that Bentham was a Feminist.[71] However, it does illustrate how he was prepared to tackle one of the most important sources of female oppression. The inability to inherit property on equal terms with men made it impossible for

[70] Ibid., 152.

[71] For a discussion of Bentham as a Feminist see L. Campos Boralevi, 'In Defence of a Myth', *Bentham Newsletter*, 4 (1980), 33–46, *Bentham and the Oppressed* (Berlin, 1984), and 'Utilitarianism and Feminism', in E. Kennedy and S. L. Mendus (eds.), *Women in Western Political Philosophy* (Brighton, 1987), 159–76. For a criticism of Boralevi's argument see T. Ball, 'Was Bentham a Feminist' and 'Bentham no Feminist: A Reply to Boralevi', both in *Bentham Newsletter*, 4 (1980), (pp. 25–32 and 47–8).

women to have the same economic independence. Bentham acknowledged that in the past there was some ground for inegalitarian rules of succession in order to provide the protection of society from external threats. Without these accumulations of property there would have been no accumulations of abundance sufficient to provide weapons, animals, or the supplies necessary in order to engage in defensive warfare. Therefore, there was a justification for excluding women from the equal title to succession with the first male heir. However, Bentham argued that while in a primitive society such an arrangement might have been beneficial, there was no rational basis for allowing the continuation of that practice.[72] His assertion of equality of rights between men and women is one component of his baseline[73] theory of equality.

The abolition of inequality in the practice of succession would result in a temporary attack on the existing pattern of expectations, but this can be mitigated by a gradual and well-publicized transfer to the new system. While daughters may not have had adequate reasons for forming expectations premissed on the enjoyment of inherited property after a parent's death, they are, nevertheless, able to form expectations based on co-enjoyment of that property while the parent was alive. Co-enjoyment is one of the grounds for the expectations that the law of succession is designed to protect. Thus, there is a case for arguing that the expectations of the female sex to continue in the co-enjoyment of their parents' or husbands' property were disappointed by the existing law of succession. This is so despite the fact that they cannot have expectations to continue enjoying that property once the property holder has died. Despite his recognition of the equal title of women to inherit property with men, Bentham was aware that simply allowing women to inherit property would not necessarily bring about the equalization of property within the community. If the law continued to give discretion to the property-holder as to how he wished his property to be divided, there was the possibility that women would continue to be ignored in cases of succession and inheritance. In order to reconcile this with the desired end of equalizing property-holdings, Bentham proposed some significant changes to the law governing the manner in which a person could dispose of his property, and this shows that Bentham was far more interested in pursuing a radical egalitarian policy by means of the law of succession that either Reeve[74] or Ryan[75] acknowledge in their respective discussions of Bentham's theory of

---

[72] UC clx, 172–3.

[73] For the notion of a baseline theory of Equality see F. R. Berger, 'Mill's Substantive Principles of Justice: a Comparison with Nozick's', *American Philosophical Quarterly*, 19 (1982), 373–8, and *Happiness, Justice and Freedom: The Moral and Political Philosophy of John Stuart Mill* (Berkeley, Calif., 1984), 159–60.

[74] A. Reeve, *Property* (London, 1986), 164.

[75] A. Ryan, *Property and Political Theory* (Oxford, 1984), 98–100 and 108.

property. Bentham maintained that equalization of property was one of the chief ends of the law of succession:

In framing the law relative to successions three objects ought to be kept in view: 1st The necessity of making provision for the rising generation, whose weakness, the companion of infancy retains in a state of indigence. 2. Prevention of disappointment: 3. Equalisation of property.[76]

Though Bentham acknowledged the property-holder's claim to dispose of his property at will, he was more concerned with the effects of such a disposal. He maintained that on the death of a husband all the property was transferred to his wife as she had the greatest expectation based on co-enjoyment. In the case of dividing an estate between children there were two ways of proceeding which Bentham combined. 'As between child and child,' he wrote, 'on the decease of the widower or the widow, equality. This for the general rule is the most obvious, and has the advantages of simplicity.'[77] The direct equalization of property among the deceased's children was the most efficient way of breaking up large property-holdings and redistributing property throughout the community. However, because one of the main grounds for the equalization of property was to provide the material conditions of interest-formation and realization for the 'rising generation', there was a justification for providing a more than equal share to those who had a more urgent need in view of their inability to acquire property by other means. These included young children, those who were unable to work through illness, and women who had no other means of acquiring property. Given these considerations he showed a preparedness to rely on the ordinary prudence of parents to make the appropriate provision for their children. He wrote:

For the solution of these and a host of other difficulties, altogether incapable of being aptly provided for, by general rules, provision being made, and very generally made, by a power of disposition given to the parents or one of them: natural affection, guided by ordinary prudence, being in this case trusted to, for the accomplishment of the universal object—the greatest happiness of the greatest number—interested.[78]

While the natural prudence of parents may have been sufficient to bring about the desired end of the law of succession in many instances, Bentham was still concerned that it may not have been sufficient in all cases. Thus he wrote:

But neither are natural affection nor prudence, in this case, in every instance, what it were to be wished they were. This considered, a course that may naturally enough present itself to the legislator is to divide the thus vacated mass of property into two

---

[76] UC xxxii, 151.
[77] Ibid., clx. 171.
[78] Ibid.

parts: one, the division of which shall be determined by the single consideration of equality: the other in relation to which the care of providing for the differences liable to be made in the proper quantum of allowance by the differences that may have place in respect of the quantity needed, and the correspondent urgency of the demand is left to be provided for by natural affection, guided by ordinary prudence, as above.[79]

By so dividing the vacated mass of property into two parts the legislator was able to ensure provision for the rising generation while also pursuing the equalization of property over time. The question remains, however, as to what discretion this left the property-holder in disposing of his property as he wished. Bentham resolved this problem in two ways. Firstly, given that expectations are the basis of property-titles and that they cease upon the property holder's death, he cannot suffer frustrated expectations nor interference with his property-rights. There are no absolute property rights which could extend to the disposal of property after the death of the property-holder. Secondly, in so far as property-holders do form expectations about the disposal of their property, these are ordinarily concerned with making provision for one's dependents. As we have seen the proposed changes in the rules governing succession do not affect a parent's ability to make provision for his spouse or children. They simply equalize the effects of such provision among all such dependents. Furthermore, on the cessation of the property-holders expectations, those that the legislator has to prevent from disappointment belong to the remaining descendants who have built up expectations on the basis of co-enjoyment of the property, while the property-holder was still alive.

In the case of a property-holder having no descendants or dependents many of the considerations applying in the case of succession are inappropriate, given that there are no expectations based on co-enjoyment. While circumstances in which there are no descendents would suggest the appropriateness of the property reverting to the state and being divided equally among the community, Bentham did not completely accept such a policy. Admittedly there are no expectations based on co-enjoyment so the question of disappointment did not arise. However, Bentham argued that if the law overrides the individual's discretion as to how to dispose of his property, then the law will create a premium on consumption of that property, and thus, a portion of the national capital will be dissolved. He wrote: 'Make his capital of no use to him after his death, he will find himself strongly tempted to convert it into an annuity for his own life. Dissipation will there be encouraged, frugality checked'.[80] Bentham's solution was:

Give then to the proprietor who is without near relations the power of disposing of a certain portion (the half for example) of his property after his death, keeping back

[79] UC clx. 171.
[80] Ibid., xxxii. 149.

the remainder for the benefit of the public purse. Procrastination and so many other chances of intestacy will render the share of the Public, if equal in quantity much superior in value.[81]

Where the legislator comes into possession of a portion of the wealth of a deceased property-holder with no descendents, he has a prima facie reason for distributing the benefits of this wealth equally by using it to supply the cost of government and the administration of justice, thus relieving government from the need to rely on taxation. This policy is most strikingly developed in *Supply without Burthen: or Escheat Vice Taxation.*

The overall object of Bentham's modification of the rules of succession was to facilitate the break-up of large property-holdings and the redistribution of property throughout the community. He argued that the only way to pursue redistribution without overriding the existing pattern of expectations was by means of the rules governing succession. In this respect Bentham's argument preempts that of T. H. Green, who also argued that redistribution based on the law of succession would prevent the accumulation of property in few hands, and thus the inability of the majority to pursue a moral life.[82] Both Bentham and Green go beyond the position of Hume and Smith, who believed that the freedom to dispose of property at will would eventually have a tendency towards equality. Although Green's philosophy is fundamentally at odds with Bentham's utilitarianism, in one important respect Green follows Bentham by arguing that private property has no necessary tendency towards equality and that it needs a redistributive framework if it is to serve as a condition of the moral life. Both theorists recognize the need to maintain the stability of the institution of property while also pursuing some measure of equalization.

Before turning to the role of the 'disappointment-preventing principle' in providing a reason for respecting rights, I will defend Rosen's claim that Bentham was concerned with achieving the substantive equalization of incomes within the community, against the criticism of Postema[83] and others. Despite the claims by Macpherson,[84] Parekh,[85] and Postema, that Bentham sacrificed any substantial commitment to the pursuit of equality to the more important end of securing property, it is now clear that this is not the case. Bentham gave a high priority to securing property and it is clear from his criticisms of 'Levelling Systems'[86] that given the choice between maintaining the given distribution of property and the complete levelling of incomes, security must prevail.[87] However, it is incorrect to infer, as

---

[81] Ibid.

[82] T. H. Green, *Lectures on the Principles of Political Obligation* (London, 1931), 220.

[83] Postema, Review of F. Rosen, *Jeremy Bentham and Representative Democracy*', *Philosophical Review*, 95 (1986), 483–7.

[84] C. B. Macpherson, *The Life and Times of Liberal Democracy* (Oxford, 1977), 29–34.

[85] Parekh, 'Bentham's Theory of Equality', *Political Studies*, 18 (1970), 478–95.

[86] UC lxxxviii (a), 52–81 (Bowring, i. 358–64).

[87] Bowring, i. 311–12.

Postema does, from the priority attached to security that Bentham could have had no serious commitment to the pursuit of equality. Throughout this chapter I have emphasized Bentham's use of the 'disappoinment-preventing principle' as a means of realizing the egalitarian implications of the 'security-providing principle' without violating the pattern of expectations derived from the existing distribution of property. Thus I have given a more sustained treatment of the egalitarian implications of the 'disappointment-preventing principle' to which Rosen rightly draws attention in his study of Bentham's constitutional theory.[88] The reconciliation between the egalitarian implications of Bentham's utilitarian theory of distributive justice and the requirement to secure the existing pattern of expectations, does answer Postema's basic criticism of Rosen. However, Macpherson[89] argues that Bentham's preference for security over equality expresses a substantial commitment to the *laissez-faire* capitalism because he emphasizes Bentham's argument that a regime of equality or a 'Levelling System' is inimical to the progress of industry.[90] What Macpherson fails to recognize is that Bentham's commitment to a commercial or industrial society is based not on any notion of desert, but rather on the commitment to social happiness. It is at the level of the justification of the principles of justice that the ends of equality and security as a means of fostering industry and economic progress are reconciled.

The argument for the equalization of property-holdings is premissed on the judgement that as the distribution of property tends towards equality, the greater the amount of social happiness.[91] The value of property is derived from its function as the basic source of secured expectations, and thus the primary realization condition of interest. Given the importance of property, it is clear that the direct equalization of incomes will not necessarily result in the maximum of social well-being. This is because an equal share in a small sum of social wealth might facilitate less interest-realization then an unequal, but greater share of an alternative distribution of property. The balance that the utilitarian will most favour, is that social arrangement which results in the greatest economic progress, compatible with mechanisms that ensure the eventual distribution of those benefits throughout the community. Bentham's basic position is that distribution must go hand in hand with production. Therefore, the policies towards equalization which he advocates apply most appropriately to a progressive economy. He argued that security of property is an essential component of a successful and progressive economy.[92] Therefore, he was opposed to continual direct interference with the existing distribution of property. This does not imply that Bentham accepted the rules of property acquisition and

---

[88] Rosen, 'Jeremy Bentham and Representative Democracy', p. 224.

[89] Macpherson, *The Life and Times of Liberal Democracy*, p. 31.

[90] Bowring, i. 311–12.   [91] UC clx, 175.

[92] P. J. Kelly, 'Utilitarianism and Distributive Justice: The Civil Law and the Foundations of Bentham's Economic Thought', *Utilitas*, 1 (1989), 62–81.

distribution as unchangeable. He sought instead to redistribute society's wealth in ways that did not sacrifice the expectations of those already enjoying property.

There is no question that Bentham accepted the market as the final arbiter of a fair or just distribution of property, and he acknowledged that utility was the ultimate criterion by which the distribution of property produced by the market should be judged. Nevertheless, he recognized that the system of private property facilitated greater economic prosperity as a result of its being the primary condition of interest realization. Therefore, Bentham modified his direct egalitarian policy in order to take account of the expectations derived from property. The main result of this was that absolute equality of incomes would never be achieved. The policy of equalization resulted in a continual process of breaking up large property-holdings and redistributing them throughout the community to the rising generation. This was what Bentham implied by advocating that the most beneficial distribution is one where the disparities between various property-holdings are most 'regular and insensible'.[93] He saw this tendency to break up large property-holdings and redistribute them throughout the community as a consequence of the commercial economy and the progress of trade. However, he recognized that the egalitarian consequences of this form of economic formation would only be felt if the legal rules concerning succession were modified to ensure the distribution of property throughout the community.

It is therefore clear that Bentham did not subordinate equality to security as a consequence of an ideological commitment to *laissez-faire* capitalism, as Macpherson suggests. Instead, he thought that the pursuit of equality could be achieved without violating security of expectation. Ultimately the dispute between Bentham and Macpherson concerns whether or not the value of equality can be balanced against the benefit of economic progress. Macpherson is in effect rejecting Bentham's utilitarianism. However, while Bentham's utilitarian premises might be open to dispute, it is clear that his reconciliation of equality and security within the framework of a utilitarian theory of justice did not involve any fallacies, as Macpherson suggests. It is also true that abandoning the direct levelling of incomes does not mean that Bentham was unconcerned with the substantive equalization of incomes over time. The pursuit of material equality remained an important component of Bentham's substantive theory of justice throughout his career.

III

The last section was concerned with the 'disappointment-preventing principle' as a criterion of legislative action, but the concept of disappoint-

---

[93] BL Add MS 33550, fo. 137 (Bowring, iii. 230).

ment also plays an important role in grounding rights and in the theory of adjudication, because it provides an objective criterion of pleasure and pain.

Throughout his career Bentham used pleasure and pain as the basic concepts in moral and practical reasoning. Even fictitious entities which are essential in ordinary practical reasoning must be ultimately reducible to the concepts of pleasure and pain. Despite Bentham's attempt to provide criteria for the measurement of the value of pleasure and pain,[94] there is also good reason to believe that he came to realize the matter was more complex than is suggested by *An Introduction to the Principles of Morals and Legislation*, chapter 7. In the 'Principles of the Civil Code'[95] and in later manuscripts[96] Bentham referred to 'value in affection' or 'idiosyncratical value'. These are contrasted with exchange value which could be given a public or objective criterion by monetary means. The distinction between those values of pleasure which could be translated into publicly quantifiable terms and values of pleasure which could not be given an objective or quantifiable value suggests that Bentham was aware of the difficulties of establishing precision in the measurement of pleasure and pain. This is not to suggest that he subscribed to the radical inaccessibility of subjective consciousness, but it does show that he was aware of the practical problems of determining the value of subjective experience. Whenever possible Bentham relied on a publicly accessible criterion for the use of pleasure and pain so that the legislator was not involved in attempting to determine the value of subjective experience. For this reason the legislator's concern is with public sources of pleasure and pain and not with attempts to determine the subjective experience of each individual.

Many objects, actions, and relationships have a subjective value to the individual agent which far exceeds any supposed objective valuation of that object; this is the 'value in affection' or the 'idiosyncratical value'. Concentrating on public criteria of pleasure at the expense of determinate calculations of precise amounts of pleasure does not vitiate Bentham's method for the reason that his whole project is geared toward utilitarian ends. Legislative experimentation in order to determine the precise value of subjective experience would undermine expectations and create significant disutilities. Personal interference and the continuous process of having to modify information would render the costs prohibitive by undermining the ability to form expectations which are themselves a condition of rational action and personal continuity and coherence. Bentham was far more interested in those sources of utility or disutility which were already publicly accessible and which, therefore, provide the grounds for rational deliberation. The concept of disappointment provides such a publicly accessible criterion

---

[94] *IPML* (CW), pp. 38–41.
[95] Bowring, i. 310.
[96] BL Add. MS 33550, fo. 121.

of disutility. This is because pain is the natural concomitant of disappointment, which is the outcome of frustrated expectations.

However, not all frustrated expectations are the subject of Bentham's concern. Some expectations, such as those which result form mere speculations about the future and have no direct causal link with social norms, rules, and practices, invite little disappointment as a result of their frustration. These institutions and practices provide the certainty upon which fixed expectations are premissed. Because of the degree of certainty underlying fixed expectations, they play a significant part in the formation of an individual's goals and projects. Therefore, any frustration of these fixed expectations can be presumed to cause significant disappointment, and thus significant pain. Because these fixed expectations are linked to particular social arrangements and practices, such as property rights, an interference with the practice or right is itself a condition of pain and an objective criterion of disutility.

The sensation of disappointment arises from the frustration of fixed expectations, and these expectations are premissed on institutions and practices such as rights. There is, therefore, a utilitarian reason for respecting those rights and obligations. While Hart is correct to argue that obligations are not based on utility because a necessary condition of obligation is the likelihood of suffering punishment and not the prospect of beneficial consequences,[97] there is, nevertheless, a connection between utility and obligation. This is because any pattern of obligations gives rise to expectations and expectation utilities, and failure to respect them results in disappointment. Moreover, because expectation is a necessary condition of personal continuity, and therefore, of interest formation, there is always a strong utilitarian reason for respecting rights and performing duties. This utilitarian reason to respect rights and perform duties applies in any pattern of rights. There is a utilitarian requirement to respect the property rights of slave-owners and other beneficiaries of unjust social arrangements. The disappointment that would result from the frustration of expectations always provides a weighty objective reason for respecting rights and performing duties. Hart also argues that because obligations depend on the likelihood of sanctions being imposed as a consequence of non-performance, it is the sanctions and not any direct calculation of utility that provide the reason for obedience. While the consequences of obligations may reflect the dictates of utility, this is not always the case.[98] Hart is correct to argue that the obligatoriness of these rights and duties is not directly connected to calculations of utility. However, it is still the case that there is always a utilitarian reason for respecting rights and performing duties. This demonstrates that there is an indirect connection between utility and

---

[97] Hart, 'Natural Rights: Bentham and John Stuart Mill', *Essays on Bentham* (Oxford, 1982), 87.   [98] Ibid., 87 and 128–61.

obligation which holds even in cases where the pattern of rights has originated independently of any utilitarian considerations. Any pattern of obligations has a manifest utilitarian justification because it is the source of expectations, and, therefore, failure to respect these will result in disappointment. Thus, while the criteria for determining legal obligations are independent of considerations of the utility of those practices, there is still a utilitarian reason for respecting them.

This connection between utility and obligation is borne out in Bentham's attitude to received patterns of obligation throughout his works. While he develops a sanction-based criterion for determining what obligations there are, he nevertheless did not allow a utilitarian consideration of what obligations there should be to undermine the obligatoriness of those rights and duties. This is clearly shown in his theory of property, where he developed a strong utilitarian justification for respecting the given pattern of rights and duties despite the possible gains in utility that might result from their modification.

Hart separates utilitarianism and the sources of obligation because the criteria for determining obligations are independent from the dictates of utility.[99] It is possible that the sovereign from whom those obligations are derived could have had reasons wholly opposed to the dictates of utility. While this logical separation between the criteria for obligation and the dictates of utility still creates serious difficulties for Bentham's theory of justice, in particular where there is a utilitarian reason for respecting intuitively unjust institutions, it is the public co-ordination of action provided by those obligations which is the source of the utilitarian reason for respecting them. The utilitarian reason for respecting obligations is not based on the sovereign's intentions in creating them. Instead Bentham is concerned with publicly accessible reasons for respecting obligations, and these are derived from the co-ordination of social action facilitated by a stable pattern of expectations. Underlying his reasoning is the view that individuals are never in a position to make global utility calculations. They never possess sufficient knowledge to make such calculations and are never in a position by their own actions to bring about the maximum of social well-being. This is due to the problems in co-ordinating individual action into a coherent and harmonious public good. While a given distribution of rights might create a system of obligations which is not in accordance with the consequences of a global utility calculations, there is still a publicly accessible utilitarian reason for respecting those rights and duties, whatever their origin. Bentham's concern was with the public accessibility of reasons. In his attack on *ipse dixitism*[100] he was concerned with undermining the claims of individual opinion as a source of reasons for action, arguing that only by providing publicly accessible reasons for action could the maximum

[99] *IPML* (CW), pp. 21–33.
[100] D. Lyons, 'Utility and Rights', *Nomos*, 24 (1982), 107–8.

social well-being be achieved. Therefore, he placed great emphasis on disappointment because it is a source of pain connected to publicly identifiable actions, namely the frustration of expectations and the violation of obligations.

The utilitarian reason for respecting obligations provides a strong ground for rejecting another of Lyons's claims, namely that utilitarianism cannot adequately account for legal rights.[101] Lyons argues that utilitarianism cannot account for the normative force of rights because there is always the possibility of utilitarian calculations providing strong reasons for overriding these rights. According to Lyons, the practice of rights, both moral and legal, requires their functioning as peremptory barriers on the admissibility of consequentialist reasons. Unless the rights provide these peremptory barriers, there is nothing to stop each individual from weighing up the likely consequences of respecting rights on any occasion and determining his actions on the basis of such a calculation. If this sort of reasoning is acceptable on utilitarian grounds, the practice of rights becomes nugatory. At the root of Lyons' argument is the view that rights place peremptory constraints not only on the sorts of reason admissible as a determinant of action, but also on individual practical reasoning. Obligations provide the boundaries within which individual practical reasoning takes place, but they are not themselves subject to individual practical reason. Lyons's criticism was directed primarily at direct utilitarian arguments for the justification of right-conferring institutions. However, in the case of a modified act-utilitarianism much of the appeal of this argument is lost. Lyons's belief that his argument undermines Bentham's commitment to the role of legal rights within his utilitarian system[102] is criticized by Postema.[103] He argues that Lyons's criticism of Bentham's use of legal rights is irrelevant because Bentham explicitly rejected the peremptoriness of rights as overriding utilitarian reasoning.[104] Postema, who maintains that Bentham has a direct utilitarian theory, argues that he was never prepared to rule out utilitarian considerations in determining the obligatoriness of a utilitarian legal right. Thus according to Postema, Bentham was quite prepared to accept changes in the understanding of the practice of rights that would result from subjecting them to direct utilitarian calculations.

There is reason to reject both Postema's argument and Lyons's criticism of Bentham's inability to accommodate legal rights within his utilitarian theory. This is because Bentham was not prepared to allow direct global utility calculations to override the property rights derived from any given distribution of property. As I have already argued Bentham had a strategic act-utilitarian theory, and on the basis of this he was able to account for the normative force of legal rights. Postema's defence of Bentham is therefore

---

[101] Ibid., p. 123.
[102] Postema, *Bentham and the Common Law Tradition*, pp. 321–4.
[103] Ibid., p. 323.   [104] Ibid.

incorrect because he did not base the utilitarian reason for respecting rights on global utility calculations. Instead he established on indirect utilitarian grounds that there is always a prima facie reason for respecting rights by emphasizing the role of disappointment. The efficient reason for respecting rights remains the threat of sanctions, but there is also the indirect utilitarian reason for respecting them in that disappointment will result from not doing so.

Bentham's use of this notion of disappointment enabled him to take seriously the practice of legal rights, because disappointment connects the utilitarian reason for respecting them with the practice of rights. This practice of rights is essentially backward-looking in that the justification for respecting them does not lie with future consequences, but with the pedigree of those rights, that is to say, whether or not they are derived from the accepted rights-conferring institutions. Direct utilitarian considerations are however, forward-looking in that they are not connected to the basis of those rights, but are concerned with the future consequences that are derived from those rights. Bentham managed to connect both the consequentialist consideration with the pedigree reasons for respecting rights. Disappointment is only one of the consequences of violating rights, and thus, frustrating expectations is necessarily connected to the frustrated expectations that are derived from the violated rights. It is the consideration that disappointment will result from violating rights which provides the indirect utilitarian justification for respecting them. This is contrary to Postema's argument that it is direct utilitarian considerations which determine the reason for respecting obligations.

Once again it is the epistemic constraints on direct utility calculations which justify the prevention of disappointment as the sufficient indirect utilitarian reason for respecting rights. According to Bentham, disappointment will result from violating rights and the non-performance of duties. Violating rights and the non-performance of duties provide a publicly available source of pain. However, in the case of direct calculations of the benefits that a particular agent may expect to result from violating a particular right, he can never be certain about the second-order consequences that might originate with his actions and which are beyond his control. Therefore, Bentham rejected direct global utility calculations in favour of the publicly accessible reason provided by disappointment. Bentham's use of the concept of disappointment as the determining criteria for respecting rights, enabled him to respect rights in the way that Lyons's suggests is impossible for a utilitarian.

The final problem arising from contested titles occurs where there is a dispute as to which expectations determine ownership. As I have already argued Bentham accepted the conventional rules of property acquisition.[105]

---

[105] Bowring, i. 326–36.

Therefore, the origin of the title to some object of property is determined by tracing its genealogy and not by calculating who would derive the most utilty from owning it. However, in the case of contested titles there is the problem that the genealogy is inconclusive and that two parties claim to have expectations. In such circumstances, Bentham wrote:

if of a number of competitors, actual or eventually possible, for the objects of desire in question, give it exceptions excepted to that one in whose instance, in the event of his not possessing it, pain of disappointment will be produced in great quantity.[106]

The legislator then determines this by placing:

himself alternately in the situation of the parties on both sides, a question he puts to himself is in which of the two situations would my expectation of success be the strongest, my suffering accordingly in case of disappointment most acute?[107]

This procedure has been compared by Postema[108] to R. M. Hare's role shift test,[109] but there are important differences. The Benthamite legislator is not concerned with the measurement of subjective experience, rather he is trying to establish the sources of each contestant's claim to expectation. This does not involve subjective identification with each contestant's preferences and ideals, as it simply involves determining each individual's relationship with the contested title. The legislator is concerned with providing some public criteria for conferring the title on one or other party. Thus, he will be concerned with whether expectation is based on occupation, co-enjoyment, or some other direct relationship with the contested object. Whoever can demonstrate this public ground for his expectation will be granted the title. If the conflict is irresolvable because the expectations are derived from the opposing sources such as occupation and succession, then the legislator has to resort to compensation and remuneration for the party who will abdicate his claim or else he has the option of dividing the title. In both cases the legislator relies on considerations central to the 'disappointment-preventing principle' as his decision principle and expectations as the publicly accessible reasons for making his decision.

Bentham's use of the two components of his theory of distributive justice, the 'security-providing' and the 'disappointment-preventing' principles enables him to avoid the problems of creating a massive disutility while attempting to institute any ideal utilitarian set of rules. Thus, Bentham is able to reconcile the reformist implications of his utilitarian philosophy with an indirect utilitarian strategy based on the primacy of securing expectations. There is nothing in Mill's discussion of justice which resembles Bentham's account of distributive justice in terms of the 'security-providing' and

---

[106] BL Add. MS 33550, fo. 144.
[107] UC lxxvii, 122.
[108] Postema, *Bentham and the Common Law Tradition*, p. 213.
[109] R. M. Hare, *Freedom and Reason* (Oxford, 1978), 86–111.

'disappointment-preventing' principles. Therefore, while Bentham's theory of distributive justice may remain inadequately developed and defended in the Civil Law writings, it does address an important issue facing any act-utilitarian theory of justice, which is not addressed in Mill's theory of justice.

8

Conclusion

ALTHOUGH the argument of this book is based on unpublished Civil Law manuscripts, reference has been made to some of Bentham's published works, such as *An Introduction to the Principles of Morals and Legislation, A Fragment on Government*, and *Deontology*. Many of these works have been used to support the received interpretation of his moral theory. However, it should be clear that the Civil Law writings give a different perspective to the role of these other works in the development of his political and moral theory. Bentham did not intend the principle of utility to function as a straightforward injunction to maximize social well-being. Therefore, the principle of right which constitutes Bentham's theory of distributive justice provides the formal response to the arguments of Rawls and others, who have claimed that utilitarianism cannot account for individual entitlements or respect for persons.

Rawls's *A Theory of Justice* has been a particular focus of attention in mounting this limited defence of Bentham's utilitarian theory, because it has dominated the contemporary discussion of the theoretical and moral deficiencies of utilitarianism. In the first section of this work it was argued that individual agents are not under a direct obligation to pursue the maximum social well-being in all circumstances, and that a direct utilitarian account of moral and political obligation would undermine the collective enterprise of social life and contradict many of Bentham's own arguments about the nature of obligation and the need to submit to the sovereign's judgement.[1] The abandonment of a direct account of moral obligation enables one to accommodate his strong commitment to property rights in the Civil Law writings with his theory of distributive justice. Although Rawls argued that a utilitarian principle can make some concessions to the importance of liberal values, he maintained that this can only be a contingent commitment which is open to contradiction on the basis of a global utility calculation.[2] Nevertheless, Bentham can avoid the implications of this argument because he does not argue that individuals and the legislator were under a direct obligation to maximize the amount of social well-being. Bentham used a utilitarian principle of right as the source of obligations which are backed by sanctions. This pattern of obligations

---

[1] See Bentham's motto for the good citizen: '*To obey punctually; to censure freely*', *Fragment* (CW), p. 399. I have assumed throughout the argument of this work that this claim would be inconsistent with an individual duty to act upon global utility calculations.

[2] J. Rawls, *A Theory of Justice* (Oxford, 1972), 26.

provides the co-ordinating conditions of social interaction and necessarily results in the maximum of social well-being. Therefore, by doing his duty an individual can at the same time be maximizing the sum of social well-being.

This interpretation of Bentham's utilitarian theory emphasizes the role of rules and principles in constituting the collective good of social well-being. Again these rules are not merely rules of thumb which serve as contingent guides to the maximum of social well-being because they are not subject to constant revision in light of individual utility calculations. Instead they are the necessary components of the collective good. In order to establish this claim it was argued that the purpose of morality was to provide the conditions of social interaction as a means of increasing the communal well-being. This did not involve the legislator in making direct calculations about which motives should be encouraged and discouraged. Rather it simply involved the securing of those conditions within which individuals can form and pursue their own conceptions of well-being. Rule-governed activity, which is the characteristic feature of the social world, not only reduces interpersonal conflicts which frustrate interest satisfaction, it also provides the social conditions within which complex patterns of interest can be formed. Thus rule-governed social interaction provides spheres of personal inviolability within which individual agents are free from the interference of others in the formation and pursuit of their interests. It also provides the ordered social world within which patterns of expectation can develop, which are themselves the necessary basis of personal continuity and coherence. The rules and principles which provide the conditions of social interaction are necessarily of greater utility because they provide the conditions for an enduring conception of the self, and the framework within which the most important class of interests arise.

The class of interests which characterize human nature in modern societies are all premissed on stable patterns of expectation and the conditions of social interaction. It is this acknowledgement of the conditions of social interaction as the conditions of personal continuity and coherence which gives them such a high acceptance utility and which justifies this position as the basis of his system of obligations. Therefore, while the principle of utility as the criterion of moral judgement makes no reference to distributive principles or principles of right, the practical attainment of the maximum of social well-being necessarily entails securing the basic conditions of social interaction. The necessity of these rules and principles in the attainment of the maximum of social well-being is not a logical necessity, for the specification of the criterion of good does not a priori entail a principle of distribution.[3] Rather, the necessity of these rules is a

---

[3] Ayer, Burne, Goldworth, and Werner are all correct in arguing that Bentham's principle of utility does not specify a principle of right or a distributive principle. See A. J. Ayer, 'The Principle of Utility', in *Philosophical Essays* (London, 1954), P. Burne, 'Bentham and the Utilitarian Principle', *Mind*, 58 (1949), 367–8, A. Goldworth, 'The Meaning of Bentham's

natural necessity, in that they follow from a characterization of human nature and purposes. This does not mean that Bentham's whole moral system is premissed on a perfectionist ideal of human nature, but it does mean that underlying his theory is a conception of purposive human agents who form and pursue interests in the context of a social realm. Given this conception of purposive agency it follows that certain conditions must obtain if this is not to be frustrated, and these are the components of Bentham's theory of distributive justice.

The 'security-providing principle' then provides an account of the basic sources of expectation which the legislator ought to secure, and this meant the securing of property in its widest sense. The 'security-providing principle' provides the means for determining how the pattern of rights which make up the utilitarian principle of right ought to be distributed. However, it is clear that Bentham did not intend merely the distribution of negative rights which were concerned with preventing interference, he was also concerned with the distribution of positive rights to the material conditions of interest formation and realization. This means that Bentham was committed to the redistribution of property throughout the community in a way that enables each person to pursue their own conception of well-being. His discussion of justice was not simply confined to commutative justice and the rules for transfer of property by contract. He was primarily concerned with distributive justice because the rules of contract can only have a utilitarian justification in so far as they are based on a prior just distribution. This created two problems which were dealt with by the 'disappointment-preventing principle'. The first problem was posed by new generations constantly coming into existence each with a claim on the material conditions of interest realization. Secondly, given the problem of new generations and the need to extend the distribution of property to all, there is a difficulty in maintaining any fixed expectations within the context of this constant redistribution of wealth in society. Bentham accommodates these difficulties by using the law of bequest as a means of redistributing property to new generations. This means that over time large property-holdings are redistributed among the community in a way which enables each to increase his own well-being. At the same time this redistribution of wealth does not upset the existing pattern of expectation because it takes place after the death of the property-holder. In consequence the transfer from an existing system of right to that which maximizes social well-being is a gradual process and is not achieved in one simple redistribution of wealth. The 'disappointment-preventing principle' recognizes that the conditions of social interaction are embodied in systems of right which do not maximize social well-being. Therefore, the task is to modify the system of right by a

Greatest Happiness Principle', *Journal of the History of Philosophy*, 7 (1969), 315–21, and L. Werner, 'A Note about Bentham on Equality and about the Greatest Happiness Principle', *Journal of the History of Philosophy*, 11 (1973), 237–51.

gradual process of reform which respects existing entitlements rather than overthrowing the system in one revolutionary change. The system of right which is derived from Bentham's principle of distributive justice provides the framework within which individual agents can form and pursue their own interests and at the same time act in a way which maximizes social well-being. The difference between my interpretation and a standard direct-utilitarian interpretation of Bentham's theory is that it accommodates the possibility of the principle of utility providing direct reasons for action within the context of an overall indirect utilitarian strategy. Therefore, the individual agent is not required to act in accordance with a direct utility calculation in each instance nor is he required to forgo acting on utilitarian reasons when these are not outweighed by legal obligations. While these obligations which are derived from the utilitarian principle of right are all based on utilitarian reasons, this status as authoritative reasons for action is based on the sanctions that underwrite them. Thus, in practical decision-making the use of sanctions has the effect of instilling dispositions to acknowledge the bindingness of obligations without subjecting them to direct utilty calculations in each case. These obligations preclude direct consequentialist reasoning in the same way that some modern rights theories attempt to modify the scope of utilitarian reasoning.[4] Bentham's hostility to the language of rights and his rejection of natural-rights theories as the foundation of morality gave the false impression that his theory of justice had nothing in common with recent consequentalist theories of moral rights.[5]

On the basis of this interpretation Bentham's theory of morality can be defended from the form of criticisms advanced by C. L. Ten[6] and Ted Honderich[7] against J. S. Mill's moral theory. Although these criticisms are advanced against Mill's and not Bentham's theory, they must be answered if a successful revisionist defence of Bentham's moral theory is to be advanced. Both Ten and Honderich argue that moral norms cannot be derived from utility which are not themselves subject to the principle of utility. Contrary to Rawls and other critics of utilitarian theories of justice such as Ten and Honderich, it is possible to derive absolute and near-absolute moral principles from utilitarian reasons. Bentham's use of secured expectation as the social condition of personal continuity illustrates that a core of stable social norms are essential in order to bring about the maximum of social well-being. These rules function by creating the social world within which

---

[4] This account of Bentham's theory of distributive justice appears similar to R. Dworkin's theory of justice in *Taking Rights Seriously* (London, 1977). Dworkin uses rights to place significant restraints on utilitarian reasoning by precluding the double counting of preferences.

[5] See D. Lyons, 'Human Rights and the General Welfare', *Philosophy and Public Affairs*, 6 (1977), 113–9.

[6] Ten, *Mill On Liberty* (Oxford, 1980), p. 48.

[7] Honderich, 'The Worth of J. S. Mill on Liberty', *Political Studies*, 22 (1974), 467.

individual practical reasoning takes place. Therefore, they channel individuals into directions which could not obtain without these rules and norms. Apart from a few components of well-being that can be derived from natural motivation and the physiological needs of mankind, most of what counts as distinctively human activity is dependent on this ordering of individual action in accordance with rules and norms. Having given rise to patterns of expectation, the violation of rights and duties, which are derived from these rules and norms, provides a source of disappointment which is a significant disutility. The concept of disappointment is used to connect the occurrence of significant disutilities with the violation of conventionally accepted rights and obligations. Therefore, the acceptance of the utilitarian principle of right can still be justified in terms of utility, even though its functioning as an authoritative reason for action is not derived from a direct utility calculation.[8]

The utilitarian justification of the principle of right is actually dependent on its not being subject to continual revision by means of direct utility calculations. The centrality of security of expectation and the conditions of social interaction within Bentham's account of social well-being suggests that the principle of utility entails a theory of distributive justice. And the principle of right which underlies the theory of distributive justice is only a contingent outcome of applying the principle of utility in so far as the conditions of ordered social interaction are contingent. However, given that Bentham argued that the conditions of social interaction were a necessary condition of personal continuity, the principle of right must be a necessary consequence of the principle of utility.

In this work I have maintained a distinction between the principle of utility as the criterion of moral judgement or the standard of the good from a utilitarian principle of moral obligation. However, in arguing against Hart's indirect utilitarian interpretation of the principle, the claim that the principle of utility cannot be action-guiding was rejected. Some recent revisionist interpretations of Mill's moral theory have tried to maintain that the principle of utility is a standard of the good and not the criterion of what

---

[8] R. Sartorius advances the same argument in *Individual Conduct and Social Norms* (Belmont, Calif., 1975). He writes: 'The act-utilitarian is therefore in fact able to give an account of social norms which bar direct appeals to utility as more than mere rules of thumb in a two fold sense. Firstly, they perform the central function of directing human behaviour into channels that it would not otherwise take by restructuring the sets of considerations of consequences of which utilitarian moral agents must take account. Secondly, they provide reasons for action in that their controversial acceptance is tantamount to the existence of systems of warranted expectations the disappointment of which is a disutility according to standard or normal cases of their violation' (pp. 70–1). Sartorius's work has been of importance in developing this interpretation of Bentham's theory of distributive justice. However, it is clear that these arguments which Sartorius refers to are to be found in Bentham's reliance on expectation and in the operation and purpose of the 'disappointment-preventing principle'.

is right or wrong and what one ought to do.[9] Such a claim is difficult to sustain in the case of Mill and implausible in Bentham's case, but the implausibility can be avoided by acknowledging that the principle of utility can function as a direct reason for action in Bentham's thought as it does in Mill, while at the same time distinguishing between a utilitarian reason for action and an obligation based on utility. Bentham argued that human motivation was such that few would act for purely benevolent reasons, and that most individuals would only act on direct utilitarian reasons when there was a correspondence of interest or an authoritative external reason such as a sanctioned obligation. It is Bentham's rejection of the view that the principle of utility gives rise to direct moral obligations, which frees his theory from Rawlsian criticisms of utilitarian moral reasoning.

There are three questions remaining to be considered in this concluding chapter. Firstly, the constitutive function of rules and norms in Bentham's theory of obligation has been emphasized throughout the argument and given that rule-governed activity is essential in order to maximize social well-being, the question for the legislator is not what action maximizes social well-being, but what distribution of rights and titles. However, there remains the problem of how far Bentham's modified act-utilitarian theory will result in an arrangement of rights and titles that is essentially liberal. If despite the role of rules and norms in constructing the collective good the maximum of utility is best pursued by limiting the liberty of the majority of tyrannizing a minority that he has not answered the challenge of deontological theories of justice.

Bentham's theory entails an extensive sphere of personal inviolability as a consequence of his conception of human motivation and the purposive character of human nature. The wider the sphere of personal inviolability the greater the realm of individual liberty, so Bentham's concern to distribute to each person the most extensive sphere of personal inviolability provides the grounds for the claim that he had a significant commitment to liberty. The reason this extensive realm of personal inviolability is required as a necessary condition of interest formation and realization is derived from his conception of motivation. Although he argued that all action is caused by the perception of pleasure, his psychological theory makes no claims about the necessary uniformity of individual motivation. While Bentham may have thought that there was a significant degree of uniformity among human motivations this is an empirical matter. Therefore, if the legislator is to maximize social well-being by distributing the conditions of social interaction in a way which facilitates the greatest amount of interest

---

[9] John Gray attempts to make this sort of separation in order to defend his indirect utilitarian interpretation of Mill's moral theory; see his *Mill On Liberty: A Defence* (London: 1983), 12–16, Gray's argument is criticized by F. R. Berger in *Happiness, Justice and Freedom* (Berkeley, Calif., 1984) (pp. 110–12).

satisfaction, this entails an extensive distribution of liberty. There is no perfectionist element in Bentham's thought. He acknowledged that there are only quantitative distinctions between different individuals' conceptions of well-being and the good, unlike J. S. Mill who argued that there are qualitative distinctions. The legislator has no reason for excluding any particular conception of well-being expect on the procedural grounds that it is inconsistent with the interests of others in that its satisfaction depends on the violation of the rights of others. Therefore, apart from cases where a conception of interest is procedurally inconsistent with the interests of others, the legislator has no reason to favour the satisfaction of some conceptions of well-being over others. His only concern is to provide the conditions within which each individual is able to secure the satisfaction of his own goals and projects in his own way, and this entails a wide degree of liberty. It could be argued that the maximum social well-being could be achieved if the legislator were able to determine that conception of interest which the majority favoured. However, given the argument that human nature is purposive, and that the most significant class of interests is dependent on the conditions of social interaction, the legislator can provide a greater degree of social well-being by providing the conditions within which individuals are free to develop and pursue their own conceptions of interest.

The second problem facing Bentham's theory of distributive justice is that it provides a utilitarian system of moral obligations, but still recognizes the bindingness of obligations which have no utilitarian justification and are contrary to the rights set out by the utilitarian principle of right. This difficulty is clearest in the case of Bentham's attitude to slavery. He acknowledges that the institution of slavery cannot be justified on the grounds of utility. However, he is unwilling to claim that the absence of utilitarian justification for this institution is sufficient to warrant its immediate destruction. He argued instead that the straightforard rejection of the rights of slave-owners would result in a significant disutility. Although Bentham clearly has no sympathy with the institution of slavery he can only argue that it should be abolished gradually so as not to disappoint the expectations of slave-owners. It is at this point that Bentham's theory of justice is at its weakest. Contractarian theories of rights such as Rawls's do not acknowledge the legitimacy of any conception of the good which is inconsistent with the principle of right. Any such institution or practice has no normative force and ought not to be considered in practical decision-making. One of the main points of Rawls's critique of utilitarianism is that it does not rule out of account those institutions such as slavery which involve the violation of rights. While the maintenance of the institution of slavery until such a time as it can be abolished without violating expectations creates intuitive difficulties for Bentham's theory, it is at least true that he was hostile to the institution of slavery and the slave trade. However, coupled with this hostility and a concern not to upset the general pattern of expectations derived from property-rights by interfering with this category of property, Bentham was also concerned with the immediate plight of the freed slaves. While his concern may seem misplaced, it is at least consistent with a concern for the expectations of slaves who may also suffer general disappointment in the first instance, following the abolition of the institution. All that Bentham need have acknowledged is that the legislator should compensate the slave-owner for the loss of his property for this would retain the property-value which was the initial source of expectation, while at the same time refusing to enforce the rights and claims of those who refuse compensation.

The final question concerns the role of equality within Bentham's theory of distributive justice. It has been consistently maintained throughout this work that equality was a major component of Bentham's theory of justice despite the claim of Parekh that 'the way that Bentham understands the greatest happiness principle has profound anti-liberal and anti-egalitarian implications.'[10] Parekh's criticism of Bentham's failure to take seriously the value of equality within his theory is based on the view that a distributive principle cannot simply be derived from the principle of utility.[11] He also reasons that Bentham's argument fails because it cannot take seriously the role of equality as a value distinct from utility. However, as I have argued, the principle of utility was the criterion of value, and equality can only be a value in that it can be given a utilitarian justification. Bentham's attitude to the value of equality is similar to his understanding of liberty as a distinct and self-subsistent value. If equality is distinct from utility then the pursuit of equality becomes anarchical, because the acceptance of equality as a value does not entail any criteria of application which determine the acceptable application of the concept.[12] To argue that he did not separate the values of utility and equality does not constitute an important criticism of Bentham unless it is coupled with an attack on his monistic conception of value. It is possible for a utilitarian to incorporate the intuitive appeal of the values of liberty and equality within a utilitarian framework. The main difference between a utilitarian account of liberal values and pluralistic account is that the criterion for determining the value and application of these concepts is provided by the principle of utility.

At the end of his discussion of Bentham's theory of equality, Parekh argues that: 'Bentham simply fails to see that equality and fairness and

[10] B. Parekh, 'Bentham's Theory of Equality', *Political Studies*, 18 (1970), 478–95.

[11] Tom Regan has argued that even if Bentham held what Mill describes as 'Bentham's Dictum' that everybody should count for one and nobody should count more than one, there is still the problem that this cannot be derived from the principle of utility; see T. Regan, 'Utility and Equality: Some Neglected Problems', *Journal of Value Inquiry*, 17 (1983), 33–52.

[12] See 'Of the Levelling System', Bowring, i. 358–64 (UC lxxxviii(a), 52–81), for Bentham's critique of the unrestricted pursuit of equality.

justice have each a *prima facie* claim on our moral attention, independently of whether or not they promote general happiness', and later that: 'Equality thus is not reducible to utility but has an independent status, and when it comes into conflict with utility, the latter does not have automatic precedence.'[13] In these passages it is clear that Parekh fails to recognize that Bentham presented an integrated theory of justice which combined liberty, equality, and justice within a utilitarian framework. Utility was not a value that could conflict with equality unless equality was interpreted in such a way that its intuitive appeal collapses. A more important criticism advanced in his paper is the claim that Bentham's commitment to equality was reducible to the equalization of property and did not involve any substantial commitment to equality of right or respect for the separateness of persons. Parekh's argument is given plausibility by Bentham's concentration on questions of equalizing incomes in his manuscript discussion of equality. However, he is wrong to maintain that Bentham had no concern with the substantive equality of right.

Bentham did not attempt to derive a conception of equality or a distributive principle from the criterion of value, but this does not prevent equality functioning as an essential component of his utilitarian system of obligation. Equality follows from the utilitarian principle of right in that the legislator has no ground for prefering the interest of one individual over that of another. This argument does not depend on the claim that the legislator cannot determine among conceptions of interest to find those who contribute most to the maximum of social well-being. Bentham certainly thought that the legislator did not have the knowledge to make such judgements,[14] but it is unclear that he believed such knowledge was not in principle possible. However, the Benthamite legislator is not under a direct obligation to act on the dictates of a direct utility calculation in all circumstances. Therefore, he is not under an obligation to determine the subjective value of each conception of interest unless it is procedurally inconsistent with the interests of others. Instead the legislator ought to proceed by assuming an equal distribution of right will maximize social well-being and only limiting that equal title when a conception of individual well-being becomes procedurally inconsistent with others. This initial commitment to equality is based not on the claim that individuals' existing conceptions of interest are of equal value, for it is in principle possible to determine whether this is so or not. Rather, Bentham begins from the position of distributing the rights necessary for interest formation and realization and this is not determined by appealing to the existing interests of the community. However, once the distribution of rights and titles is made by Bentham's principle of distributive justice it is possible that some conceptions of interest are procedurally inconsistent and must be discouraged.

---

[13] Parekh, 'Bentham's Theory of Equality', p. 494.   [14] *IPML* (CW), p. 290.

Thus the thief and the murderer are not given an equal title to pursue their interests of robbery and murder. But it could might be argued that any conception of interest which makes little contribution of social well-being could also be precluded in favour of another which makes a greater contribution to the collective good. If this is allowed then Bentham's commitment to equality of right can be abandoned in favour of an unequal distribution of right which would make a greater contribution to overall well-being.

Bentham did have a conclusive reason not to interfere with the equal distribution of rights and titles because to do so in order to bring about a marginal increase in utility would undermine the stability of expectation and create disappointment among those whose rights are violated. In the same way that security requires the equalization of property-holdings in the long term, equality of right is also dictated by the need to secure a stable pattern of expectations. By distributing equal patterns of rights, the legislator creates the conditions within which the security of each is dependent on the security of all. If some individuals were not guaranteed equality of respect in the distribution of rights, then they would have an incentive not to see the maintenance of the stable social order as a condition of their own security.

Bentham was also concerned with the equality of right to the positive conditions of interest-formation and realization. This resulted in his plans for the redistribution of income and wealth through a reform of the law of bequest and succession. This second aspect of Bentham's theory of equality explains Parekh's view that Bentham was primarily concerned with equalization rather than equality of right. However, the positive right to the material conditions of interest formation and satisfaction are derived from his prior commitment to equality of right based on the utilitarian principle of distributive justice. The last chapter was concerned with the means by which he intended to provide this positive provision of the conditions of subsistence while maintaining stability of expectation.

The theory of equality that can be derived from Bentham's theory of right involves components of the 'baseline' theory which Berger attributes to Mill.[15] Bentham acknowledged that substantive inequalities of wealth, power, and education are wrong unless they can be given some utilitarian justification. Thus the burden of proof rests with those who wish to maintain inequalities of wealth, power, and education. Also Bentham argued that even substantive inequalities of wealth, which are justified on the ground that they are necessary for the furtherance of economic activity and abundance, cannot permit others to starve. Therefore, Bentham was committed to securing the basic provision of subsistence for all. Less

---

[15] Berger, *Happiness, Justice and Freedom*, pp. 159–60, and 'Mill's Substantive Principles of Justice: A Comparison with Nozick', *American Philosophical Quarterly*, 19 (1982), 373–8.

emphasis is given to the other two components of Berger's 'baseline' theory, which claims that:

Inequalities must not undermine the status of persons *as equals*. In concrete terms this means that inequalities must not result in some gaining complete power over the lives of others, or in some persons being degraded,

and

Only *certain* kinds of grounds serve to justify inequality—that the inequality will make no one worse off, or that it is the result of rewarding according to desert. Advantages must be earned through voluntary effort.[16]

However, it is possible to derive these components of a 'baseline' theory of equality from Bentham's constitutional theory and his acceptance of labour as one of the conditions for conferring property rights.

Berger's 'baseline' theory of equality incorporates some of the positions adopted by non-consequentialists within a utilitarian normative framework. Bentham and Mill both reject the strong notion of equality derived from an absolutist conception of personal integrity. This is not because they lack commitment to the substantive position adopted by many deontological theories, but rather that the justification of such values depends upon appeals to *external* reasons,[17] that is reasons which are derived from an autonomous morality and not the interest philosophy on which utilitarianism is premissed. However, because utilitarian theory abandons one important way of grounding a substantive notion of moral equality does not entail that the notion disappears from utilitarian thought, as Parekh seems to imply. Equality does not function as the starting-point from which moral discourse begins, therefore imposing limits on the outcome of moral decision-making. Yet, equally, neither is it confined merely to the progressive equalization of income, as Parekh implies, although this is an important implication of Bentham's commitment to substantive equality. Instead the individual's claim to equality of consideration is derived from his position as an equal location of value, and from the formal rules of social interaction which provide the conditions of personal continuity and coherence. The formal element of equality is derived from the fact that social stability entails conferring rights equally, or at least minimizing inequality, as it does with equalizing wealth and property holdings.

However, the substantial element of the commitment to equality which might be redistributed as the equality of respect for the integrity or separateness of persons is derived from the function these formal conditions of social organization have in providing the conditions of separateness and personal continuity. By conferring on each person the protection of their person, property, condition in life, and reputation, along with the

[16] Berger, *Happiness, Justice and Freedom*, pp. 159–60.
[17] See B. Williams, 'Internal and External Reasons', *Moral Luck* (Cambridge, 1981), 101–13.

progressive equalization of property-holdings over time, the legislator is protecting the conditions which provide for the development of a separate sense of identity and worth. When this commitment is coupled with rejection of any qualitative distinctions between individual conceptions of well-being it is clear that there is a prima facie case for acknowledging the equal value of all individuals. Thus, Bentham is able to build a significant commitment to equality as a major component within his utilitarian theory of justice without making appeal to reasons external to an interest-based moral psychology.

Bentham's commitment to equality of right along with his commitment to substantial material equality over time, provides further support for the claim that Bentham had a liberal theory of justice which respects individual entitlements and the separateness of persons. His principle of right embodies a commitment to the most extensive equal liberty and his theory is free from any perfectionist conception of the person. On the basis of the defence of Bentham's utilitarian theory of distributive justice advanced in this work, and despite attempts to criticize him as an authoritarian and emphasize the darker side of enlightenment thinking within his moral theory,[18] there is good reason to see Bentham as an important thinker within early liberal theory who was concerned with reconstructing a foundationalist liberal theory in the absence of a Christian natural law framework of the sort presupposed by Locke.

The contemporary criticism of utilitarianism which has flourished since Rawls's *A Theory of Justice*, has obscured the significance of the utilitarian tradition within the development of liberalism in the nineteenth and twentieth centuries. By developing the utilitarian theory of distributive justice embodied in Bentham's Civil Law writings it is possible to show that Classical utilitarianism, at least as it is found in the writings of Bentham and J. S. Mill, is not inimical to considerations of justice, and that theory of utilitarianism as it was used by both writers provided a powerful argument in favour of liberalism.

---

[18] The supposed authoritarian character of Bentham's theory of law is emphasized by all those who reflect the received interpretation of his thought, in particular C. F. Bahmueller, *The National Charity Company* (Berkeley, Calif., 1981), S. R. Letwin, *The Pursuit of Certainty* (Cambridge, 1965), D. G. Long, *Bentham on Liberty* (Toronto, 1977), and Parekh, 'Bentham's Theory of Equality', *Political Studies*, 18 (1970), 478–95. The darker side of Enlightenment thinking is emphasized in Michel Foucault, *Discipline and Punish: The Birth of the Prison*, trans. A. Sheridan (Harmondsworth, 1979).

Bibliography

A comprehensive bibliography of works on Bentham and his ethical theory can be found in *The Bentham Newsletter*, 1978–88, and *Utilitas: A Journal of Utilitarian Studies*, 1989 onwards. The following is a list of all those works referred to in the text and those used in developing the argument of this book.

MANUSCRIPT SOURCES

Bentham manuscripts in the University College London Library.
Bentham manuscripts in the British Library, Add. MSS 33537–64.

BENTHAM'S WORKS

The Collected Works of Jeremy Bentham, general eds., J. H. Burns, J. R. Dinwiddy, and F. Rosen (London and Oxford, 1968–):
Chrestomathia, ed. M. J. Smith and W. H. Burston (Oxford, 1983).
A Comment on the Commentaries and A Fragment on Government, ed. J. H. Burns and H. L. A. Hart (London, 1977).
Constitutional Code, i, ed. F. Rosen and J. H. Burns (Oxford, 1983).
The Correspondence of Jeremy Bentham, i–ii, ed. T. L. S. Sprigge (London, 1968), iii, ed. I. Christie (1971); iv–v, ed. A. T. Milne (1981); vi-vii, ed. J. R. Dinwiddy (1984, 1988); viii–ix, ed. Stephen Conway (1988, 1989).
Deontology together with A Table of the Springs of Action and Article on Utilitarianism, ed. A. Goldworth (Oxford, 1983).
An Introduction to the Principles of Morals and Legislation, ed. J. H. Burns and H. L. A. Hart (London, 1970).
First Principles Preparatory to Constitutional Code, ed. Philip Schofield (Oxford, 1989).
Of Laws in General, ed. H. L. A. Hart (London, 1970).
Jeremy Bentham's Economic Writings, ed. W. Stark (3 vols., London, 1952–4).
Traités de législation, civile et pénale, ed. P. E. L. Dumont (3 vols., Paris, 1802). Trans. by R. Hildreth as *The Theory of Legislation*, by Jeremy Bentham, ed. with an introduction by C. K. Ogden (London, 1931).
The Works of Jeremy Bentham, Published under the Superintendence of his Executor, John Bowring (11 vols., Edinburgh, 1838–43).

SECONDARY SOURCES

ACKERMAN, B., *Social Justice in the Liberal State* (New Haven, Conn., 1980).
ALBEE, E., *A History of English Utilitarianism* (New York, 1902).
APPLEBY, J. O., *Economic Thought and Ideology in Seventeenth Century England* (Princeton, NJ, 1978).

ARBLASTER, A., *The Rise and Decline of Western Liberalism* (Oxford, 1984).

ATIYAH, P. S., *The Rise and Fall of Freedom of Contract* (Oxford, 1979).

ATKINSON, C. M., *Jeremy Bentham: His Life and Work* (London, 1905).

AYER, A. J., 'Freedom and Morality', in G. W. Keeton and G. Schwartzenberger (eds.), *Jeremy Bentham and the Law* (London, 1948).

—— 'The Principle of Utility', in *Philosophical Essays* (London, 1954).

BAHMUELLER, C. F., *The National Charity Company: Jeremy Bentham's Silent Revolution* (Berkeley, Calif., 1981).

BAILEY, R. R., 'The Hedonism of Jeremy Bentham', Ph.D. thesis (London, 1938).

BALDWIN, T., 'MacCallum and the Two Concepts of Freedom', *Ratio*, 26 (1984), 124–42.

BALL, T., 'Bentham no Feminist: A Reply to Boralevi', *Bentham Newsletter*, 4 (1980), 47–8.

—— 'Was Bentham a Feminist', *Bentham Newsletter*, 4 (1980), 25–32.

BARRY, B., *Political Argument* (London, 1965).

BAUMGARDT, D., *Bentham and the Ethics of Today* (Princeton, NJ, 1952).

BECKER, L. C., *Property Rights: Philosophic Foundations* (London, 1977).

BEDAU, H. A., 'Justice and Classical Utilitarianism', *Nomos*, 6 (1963), 284–305.

BENN, S. I., 'Freedom, Autonomy and the Concept of a Person', *Proceedings of the Aristotelian Society*, 76 (1976), 109–30.

—— and PETERS, R. S., *Social Principles and the Democratic State* (London, 1959).

—— and WEINSTEIN, W. L., 'Being Free to Act and Being a Free Man', *Mind*, 80 (1971), 194–211.

BERGER, F. R., *Happiness, Justice and Freedom: The Moral and Political Philosophy of John Stuart Mill* (Berkeley, Calif., 1984).

—— 'Mill's Substantive Principles of Justice: A Comparison with Nozick', *American Philosophical Quarterly*, 19 (1982), 373–8.

BERLIN, I., *The Age of Enlightenment* (Oxford, 1979).

—— 'Equality', *Proceedings of the Aristotelian Society*, 56 (1956), 301–26.

—— 'Two Concepts of Liberty', in *Four Essays on Liberty* (Oxford, 1969).

BLACKBURN, S., *Spreading the Word: Groundings in the Philosophy of Language* (Oxford, 1984).

BORALEVI, L. CAMPOS, *Bentham and the Oppressed* (Berlin, 1984).

—— 'In Defence of a Myth', *Bentham Newsletter*, 4 (1980), 33–46.

—— 'Utilitarianism and Feminism', in E. Kennedy and S. L. Mendus (eds.), *Women in Western Political Philosophy* (Brighton, 1987).

BRADLEY, F. H., *Ethical Studies* (Oxford, 1935).

BRANDT, R. B., *Ethical Theory* (Englewood Cliffs, NJ, 1959).

—— *A Theory of the Good and the Right* (Oxford, 1979).

BREBNER, J. B., 'Laissez-faire and State Intervention in Nineteenth Century Britain', *Journal of Economic History* (suppl.), 8 (1948), 59–73.

BROCK, D., 'Recent Work in Utilitarianism', *American Philosophical Quarterly*, 10 (1973), 241–69.

BUCHANAN, A., 'Distributive Justice and Legitimate Expectations', *Philosophical Studies*, 28 (1975), 419–25.

BUCHANAN, J., 'The Justice of Natural Liberty', *Journal of Legal Studies*, 5 (1976), 1–16.

BURNE, P., 'Bentham and the Utilitarian Principle', *Mind*, 58 (1949), 367–8.
—— 'The Moral Theory of Jeremy Bentham and William Paley', MA thesis (London, 1949).
CAMPBELL, T., *Justice* (London, 1988).
CASSIRER, E., *The Philosophy of the Enlightenment* (Princeton, NJ, 1951).
CHRISTIE, I. R., *Wars and Revolutions: Britain 1760–1815* (London, 1982).
COATES, W. H., 'Benthamism, Laissez-faire and Collectivism', *Journal of the History of Ideas*, 11 (1950), 357–63.
COLLINI, S., 'The Tendencies of Things: John Stuart Mill and Philosophic Method', in J. Burrow, S. Collini, and D. Winch (eds.), *That Noble Science of Politics: A Study in Nineteenth Century Intellectual History* (Cambridge, 1983).
COLMAN, J., *John Locke's Moral Philosophy* (Edinburgh, 1983).
CONNOLLY, W. E., *The Terms of Political Discourse* (Oxford, 1983).
COPELSTON, F., *A History of Philosophy*, viii, *Bentham to Russell* (New York, 1967).
CRANSTON, M., *Freedom* (London, 1967).
—— *Philosophers and Pamphleteers: Political Theorists of the Enlightenment* (Oxford, 1986).
—— *What are Human Rights?* (London, 1973).
CROMPTON, L., *Byron and Greek Love: Homophobia in Nineteenth Century England* (Berkeley, Calif., 1985).
—— 'Jeremy Bentham's Essay on "Pederasty": An Introduction', *Journal of Homosexuality*, 3 (1978), 383–7.
—— 'Jeremy Bentham's Essay on "Pederasty": Part 2', *Journal of Homosexuality*, 4 (1978), 91–107.
CROPSEY, J., 'On the Relation of Political Science and Economics', *American Political Science Review*, 54 (1960), 3–64.
CUMMING, R. D. G., *Human Nature and History: A Study of the Development of Liberal Political Thought* (2 vols., Chicago, Ill., 1969).
DALGARNO, M. T., 'The Contemporary Significance of Bentham's Anarchical Fallacies: A Reply to William Twining', *Archive für Rechts- und Sozialphilosophie*, 61 (1975), 357–67.
DAY, J. P., 'Individual Liberty', in A. Phillips-Griffiths (ed.), *Of Liberty*, Royal Institute of Philosophy Lecture Series, 15 (1983), 17–29.
—— 'Locke and Property', *Philosophical Quarterly*, 16 (1966), 207–20.
DEMSETZ, H., 'Some Aspects of Property Rights', *Journal of Law and Economics*, 9 (1966), 61–70.
—— 'Toward a Theory of Property Rights', *American Economic Review*, 57 (1967), 61–70.
DEVLIN, P., *The Enforcement of Morals* (Oxford, 1965).
DICEY, A. V., *Lectures on the Relation between Law and Public Opinion in England during the Nineteenth Century* (London, 1905).
DICKINSON, H. T., *Liberty and Property: Political Ideology in Eighteenth-Century Britain* (London, 1977).
DICKSON, P. G. M., *The Financial Revolution in England: A Study in the Development of Public Credit, 1688–1756* (London, 1970).
DINWIDDY, J. R., *Bentham* (Oxford, 1989).
—— 'Bentham and the Early Nineteenth Century', *Bentham Newsletter*, 8 (1984), 15–33.

DINWIDDY, J. R., 'Bentham on Private Ethics and the Principle of Utility', *Revue Internationale de Philosophie*, 36 (1982), 278–300.

—— 'Bentham's Transition to Political Radicalism', *Journal of the History of Ideas*, 36/4 (1975), 683–700.

—— 'The Classical Economists and the Utilitarians', in E. K. Bramsted and K. J. Melhuish (eds.), *Western Liberalism: A History in Documents From Locke to Croce* (London, 1978).

DUBE, A. D., 'The Theme of Acquisitiveness in Bentham's Political Thought', Ph.D. thesis (London, 1989).

DUNN, J., 'The Identity of the History of Ideas', *Philosophy*, 43 (1968), 85–104.

—— 'Liberalism', in *Western Political Theory in the Face of the Future* (Cambridge, 1979).

—— *The Political Thought of John Locke* (Cambridge, 1969).

—— *Rethinking Modern Political Theory* (Cambridge, 1985).

DWORKIN, R., 'Liberalism', in *A Matter of Principle* (Oxford, 1986).

—— Taking Rights Seriously (London, 1977).

ELSTER, J., *Ulysses and the Sirens: Studies in Rationality and Irrationality* (Cambridge, 1979).

EVERETT, C. W., *The Education of Jeremy Bentham* (New York, 1931).

—— *Jeremy Bentham* (London, 1966).

FEINBERG, J., 'Harm and Self-Interest', in P. M. S. Hacker and J. Raz (eds.), *Law, Morality and Society* (Oxford, 1977).

—— 'The Interest in Liberty on the Scales', in A. I. Goldman and J. Kim (eds.), *Values and Morals* (Dordrecht, 1978).

—— *The Moral Limits of the Criminal Law* (4 vols., Oxford, 1984–8).

—— *Social Philosophy* (Englewood Cliffs, NJ, 1973).

FINNIS, J., *Natural Law and Natural Rights* (Oxford, 1980).

FISHKIN, J., 'Utilitarianism Versus Human Rights', in E. Frankel Paul, F. D. Miller, Jr., and J. Paul (eds.), *Human Rights* (Oxford, 1984).

FOOT, P., *Virtues and Vices* (Oxford, 1978).

FOUCAULT, M., *Discipline and Punish: The Birth of the Prison*, trans. A. Sheridan (Harmondsworth, 1977).

FRANKENA, W. K., *Ethics* (Englewood Cliffs, NJ, 1963).

—— 'The Naturalistic Fallacy', *Mind*, 48 (1939), 464–77.

FRANKFURT, H. G., 'Freedom of the Will and the Concept of a Person', *Journal of Philosophy*, 68 (1971), 5–20.

FREEMAN, M. D. A., 'Jeremy Bentham: Contemporary Interpretations', in R. Faucci (ed.), *Gli italiani e Bentham dalla 'felicità pubblica' all'economia del benessere*, i (Milan, 1982), 19–48.

FREY, R. G., 'Act-Utilitarianism, Consequentialism and Moral Rights', in R. G. Frey (ed.), *Utility and Rights* (Oxford, 1985).

—— 'Act-Utilitarianism: Sidgwick or Bentham and Smart', *Mind*, 86 (1977), 95–100.

—— 'Can Act-Utilitarianism be Put into Practice', *Journal of Value Inquiry*, 11 (1977), 49–58.

—— 'Consequences in Act-Utilitarianism', *Journal of Value Inquiry*, 15 (1981), 79–83.

—— 'Introduction: Utilitarianism and Persons', in R. G. Frey (ed.), *Utility and Rights* (Oxford, 1985).

—— 'Moral Experts', *Personalist*, 59 (1978), 47–52.

FULLER, L. L., *The Morality of Law* (New Haven, Conn., 1964).

GEWIRTH, A., 'Starvation and Human Rights', in *Human Rights: Essays on Justification and Applications* (Chicago, Ill., 1982).

GIBBARD, A., 'Natural Property Rights', *Nous*, 10 (1976), 77–85.

—— 'Utilitarianism vs Human Rights', in E. Frankel Paul, F. D. Miller, Jr., and J. Paul (eds.), *Human Rights* (Oxford, 1984).

GILL, E. R., 'Property and Liberal Goals', *The Journal of Politics*, 45 (1983), 675–95.

GODWIN, W., *Enquiry Concerning Political Justice*, ed. F. E. L. Priestley (Toronto, 1946).

GOLDWORTH, A., 'Bentham's Concept of Pleasure and its Relation to Fictitious Terms', *Ethics*, 82 (1972), 334–42.

—— 'Jeremy Bentham on the Measurement of Subjective States', *Bentham Newsletter*, 2 (1979), 2–17.

—— 'The Meaning of Bentham's Greatest Happiness Principle', *Journal of the History of Philosophy*, 7 (1969), 315–21.

—— 'The Sympathetic Sanction and Sinister Interest in Bentham's Utilitarianism', *History of Philosophy Quarterly*, 4 (1987), 67–78.

GOSLING, J. C. B., *Pleasure and Desire: The Case for Hedonism Reviewed* (Oxford, 1969).

GRAHAM, J. F., 'The Political and Moral Thought of Jeremy Bentham: A Revaluation', Ph.D. thesis (London, 1978).

GRAMPP, W. D., *Economic Liberalism* (2 vols., New York, 1965).

—— 'On the Politics of the Classical Political Economists', *Quarterly Journal of Economics*, 62 (1948), 714–47.

GRAY, J., 'Indirect Utility and Fundamental Rights', in E. Frankel Paul, F. D. Miller, Jr., and J. Paul (eds.), *Human Rights* (Oxford, 1984).

—— *Liberalism* (Milton Keynes, 1986).

—— *Mill On Liberty: A Defence* (London, 1983).

GREEN, T., *An Examination of the Leading Principle of the New System of Morals in Mr Godwin* (London, 1798).

GREEN, T. H., *Lectures on the Principles of Political Obligation* (London, 1931).

GREENAWALT, K., *Conflicts of Law and Morality* (Oxford, 1987).

GRIFFIN, J., 'Are There Incommensurable Values?' *Philosophy and Public Affairs*, 7 (1977), 39–57.

—— 'Is Unhappiness Morally More Important than Happiness?' *Philosophical Quarterly*, 29 (1979), 47–55.

—— 'Modern Utilitarianism', *Revue Internationale de Philosophie*, 36 (1982), 331–75.

—— 'Towards a Substantive Theory of Rights', in R. G. Frey (ed.), *Utility and Rights* (Oxford, 1985).

—— *Well-Being* (Oxford, 1986).

GUTMANN, A., *Liberal Equality* (Cambridge, 1980).

HAAKONSSEN, K., *The Science of the Legislator* (Cambridge, 1981).

HACKER, P. M. S., 'Bentham's Theory of Action and Intention', *Archiv für Rechts- und Sozialphilosophie*, 62 (1976), 89–109.

HACKER, P. M. S., 'Sanction Theories of Duties', in A. W. E. Simpson (ed.), *Oxford Essays in Jurisprudence*, 2nd ser. (Oxford, 1973).

HAKSAR, V., *Liberty, Equality and Perfectionism* (Oxford, 1979).

HALÉVY, E., *The Growth of Philosophic Radicalism*, trans. M. Morris (London, 1972).

HAMPSHIRE, S., 'Morality and Pessimism', in *Morality and Conflict* (Oxford, 1983).

HARE, R. M., *The Language of Morals* (Oxford, 1952).

—— *Freedom and Reason* (Oxford, 1963).

—— *Moral Thinking: Its Levels, Method and Point* (Oxford, 1981).

HARRISON, J., *Hume's Theory of Justice* (Oxford, 1981).

—— 'Utilitarianism, Universalization, and our Duty to be Just', *Proceedings of the Aristotelian Society*, 53 (1952), 105–13.

HARRISON, R., *Bentham* (London, 1983).

—— 'The Only Possible Morality', *Proceedings of the Aristotelian Society* (suppl.), 50 (1976), 21–42.

HARROD, R. F., 'Utilitarianism Revised', *Mind*, 45 (1936), 137–56.

HART, H. L. A., 'Are There any Natural Rights', *Philosophical Review*, 64 (1955), 175–91.

—— 'Bentham: Lecture on a Master Mind', *Proceedings of the British Academy*, 48 (1962), 299–320.

—— 'Between Utility and Rights', in A. Ryan (ed.), *The Idea of Freedom* (Oxford, 1979).

—— *The Concept of Law* (Oxford, 1961).

—— *Essays on Bentham* (Oxford, 1982).

—— 'Introduction', in J. H. Burns and H. L. A. Hart (ed.), *An Introduction to the Principles of Morals and Legislation* (London, 1982).

—— *Law, Liberty and Morality* (Oxford, 1963).

—— 'Natural Rights: Bentham and John Stuart Mill', *Essays on Bentham* (Oxford, 1982).

—— 'Rawls on Liberty and its Priority', in N. Daniels (ed.), *Reading Rawls* (Oxford, 1975).

HAVARD, W. C., *Henry Sidgwick and Later Utilitarian Philosophy* (Gainesville, Fla., 1959).

HAY, D., 'Property, Authority and the Criminal Law', in D. Hay, *et al.*, *Albion's Fatal Tree* (London, 1975).

HAYEK, F. A., *The Constitution of Liberty* (London, 1960).

—— 'Individualism: *True and False?' Individualism and Economic Order* (London, 1949).

—— *Law, Legislation and Liberty* (3 vols., London, 1973–9).

HELD, V., 'Property Rights and Interests', *Social Research*, 46 (1979), 550–79.

HIMMELFARB, G., 'Bentham's Utopia: The National Charity Company', *Journal of British Studies*, 10 (1970), 80–125.

—— 'The Haunted House of Jeremy Bentham', in *Victorian Minds* (New York, 1968).

—— 'On Reading Bentham Seriously', *Studies in Burke and his Times*, 14 (1972), 179–86.

HOBBES, T., *Leviathan* (Harmondsworth, 1968).

HODGSON, D. H., *The Consequences of Utilitarianism* (Oxford, 1967).

HOLLANDER, S., *The Economics of John Stuart Mill* (2 vols., Oxford, 1985).

HONDERICH, T., 'The Problem of Well-Being and the Principle of Equality', *Mind*, 90 (1981), 481–504.

—— 'The Worth of J. S. Mill on Liberty', *Political Studies*, 22 (1974), 463–70.

HONORÉ, A. M., 'Ownership', in A. G. Guest (ed.), *Oxford Essays in Jurisprudence* (Oxford, 1961).

—— 'Property, Title and Redistribution', in C. Wellman (ed.), *Equality and Freedom: Past, Present and Future, Archiv für Rechts- und Sozialphilosophie*, 10 (1977), 107–16.

—— 'Social Justice', in R. S. Summers (ed.), *Essays in Legal Philosophy* (Oxford, 1970).

HONT, I., and IGNATIEFF, M. (eds.), *Wealth and Virtue: The Shaping of Political Economy in the Scottish Enlightenment* (Cambridge, 1983).

HORTON, J., 'Toleration, Morality and Harm', in J. Horton and S. L. Mendus (eds.), *Aspects of Toleration: Philosophical Studies* (London, 1985).

HOSPERS, J., *Libertarianism* (Los Angeles, Calif., 1971).

—— 'The Nature of the State', *Personalist*, 59 (1978), 398–404.

HUME, D., *Enquiries Concerning Human Understanding and Concerning the Principles of Morals*, ed. L. A. Selby-Bigge, 3rd edn., rev. P. H. Nidditch (Oxford, 1979).

—— *Essays, Moral, Political and Literary*, ed. T. H. Green and T. H. Grose (2 vols., Oxford, 1963).

—— *A Treatise of Human Nature*, ed. L. A. Selby-Bigge, 2nd edn., rev. P. H. Nidditch (Oxford, 1978).

HUME, L. J., *Bentham and Bureaucracy* (Cambridge, 1981).

—— 'Revisionism in Bentham Studies', *Bentham Newsletter*, 1 (1978), 3–20.

HUTCHINSON, T. W., 'Bentham as an Economist', *Economic Journal*, 66 (1956), 288–306.

HUTT, W. H., *Economists and the Public: A Study of Competition and Opinion* (London, 1936).

IRVINE, W., 'Shaw, the Fabians and the Utilitarians', *Journal of the History of Ideas*, 8 (1947), 218–31.

JAMES, M. H., 'Bentham's Democratic Theory at the Time of the French Revolution', *Bentham Newsletter*, 10 (1986), 5–16.

—— 'Bentham on the Individuation of Laws', *Northern Ireland Legal Quarterly*, 24 (1973), 91–116.

JAMES, P., *Population Malthus* (London, 1979).

JONES, P., 'Toleration, Harm and Moral Effect', in J. Horton and S. L. Mendus (eds.), *Aspects of Toleration: Philosophical Studies* (London, 1985).

KELLEY, D., 'Life, Liberty and Property', in E. Frankel Paul, F. D. Miller, Jr., and J. Paul (eds.), *Human Rights* (Oxford, 1984).

KELLY, P. J., 'Utilitarianism and Distributive Justice: The Civil Law and the Foundations of Bentham's Economic Thought', *Utilitas*, 1 (1989), 62–81.

—— 'Utilitarian Strategies in Bentham and J. S. Mill', *Utilitas* (forthcoming).

KENNY, A., *Action, Emotion and Will* (London, 1963).

—— 'Happiness', *Proceedings of the Aristotelian Society*, 66 (1965), 93–102.

KYMLICKA, W., 'Rawls on Teleology and Deontology', *Philosophy and Public Affairs*, 17 (1988), 173–90.

LAWSON, F. H., *An Introduction to the Law of Property* (Oxford, 1958).

LETWIN, S. R., *The Pursuit of Certainty* (Cambridge, 1965).

LIEBERMAN, D., 'Political Economy and Jeremy Bentham', unpub. paper, Seminar in the History of Political Ideas, Institute of Historical Research (London, 1986).

—— 'The Province of Legislation Determined: Legal Theory in Eighteenth-Century Britain', Ph.D. thesis (London, 1980).

LIVELY, J., *The Enlightenment* (London, 1966).

—— and REES, J. C. (eds.), *Utilitarian Logic and Politics* (Oxford, 1978).

LOCKE, J., *An Essay Concerning Human Understanding*, ed. P. H. Nidditch (Oxford, 1975).

—— *Two Treatises of Government*, ed. P. Laslett (New York, 1965).

LOEVINSOHN, E., 'Liberty and the Redistribution of Property', *Philosophy and Public Affairs*, 6 (1977), 226–239.

LONG, D. G., *Bentham on Liberty: Jeremy Bentham's Idea of Liberty in Relation to his Utilitarianism* (Toronto, 1977).

—— 'Bentham on Property', in A. Parel and T. Flanagan (eds.), *Theories of Property: Aristotle to the Present* (Waterloo, 1979).

LUCAS, J. R., 'Against Equality', *Philosophy*, 40 (1965), 296–307.

—— *On Justice* (Oxford, 1980).

LYONS, D., 'Benevolence and Justice in Mill', in H. B. Miller and W. H. Williams (eds.), *The Limits of Utilitarianism* (Minneapolis, Minn., 1982), 42–70.

—— *Ethics and the Rule of Law* (Cambridge, 1984).

—— *Forms and Limits of Utilitarianism* (Oxford, 1965).

—— 'Human Rights and the General Welfare', *Philosophy and Public Affairs*, 6 (1977), 113–29.

—— *In the Interest of the Governed: A Study in Bentham's Philosophy of Utility and Law* (Oxford, 1973).

—— 'Mill's Theory of Justice', in A. I. Goldman and J. Kim (eds.), *Values and Morality* (Dordrecht, 1978), 1–20.

—— 'Mill's Theory of Morality', *Nous*, 10 (1976), 101–20.

—— 'On Reading Bentham', *Philosophy*, 47 (1972), 74–9.

—— 'Utility and Rights', *Nomos*, 24 (1982), 107–38.

—— 'Was Bentham a Utilitarian?' in G. N. A. Vesey (ed.), *Reason and Reality*, Royal Institute of Philosophy Lecture Series, 5 (1971), 196–221.

LYSAGHT, L. J., 'Bentham on the Aspects of a Law', *Northern Ireland Legal Quarterly*, 24 (1973), 117–32.

MACCALLUM, G. C., 'Negative and Positive Freedom', *Philosophical Review*, 76 (1967), 312–34.

MACINTYRE, A., 'Pleasure as a Reason for Action', *Monist*, 49 (1965), 215–33.

MACK, M. P., 'The Fabians and Utilitarianism', *Journal of the History of Ideas*, 16 (1965), 76–88.

—— *Jeremy Bentham: An Odyssey of Ideas, 1748–1792* (London, 1962).

MACKIE, J. L., 'The Disutility of Act-Utilitarianism', *Philosophical Quarterly*, 23 (1973), 289–300.

—— *Ethics: Inventing Right and Wrong* (Harmondsworth, 1977).

—— *Hume's Moral Theory* (London, 1980).

MACKINTOSH, SIR, J., *Dissertations on the Progress of Ethical Philosophy* (Edinburgh, 1830).

MacPherson, C. B., *Democratic Theory: Essays in Retrieval* (Oxford, 1973).

—— *The Life and Times of Liberal Democracy* (Oxford, 1977).

—— 'On the Concept of Property', in C. Wellman (ed.), *Equality and Freedom: Past, Present and Future, Archiv für Rechts- und Sozialphilosophie*, 10 (1977), 81–5.

—— *The Political Theory of Possessive Individualism: Hobbes to Locke* (Oxford, 1962).

—— *The Rise and Fall of Economic Justice and other Essays* (Oxford, 1985).

Malthus, T. R., *Essay on the Principle of Population* 6th edn. (2 vols., London, 1826); new edn. (London, 1973).

Manning, D. J., *The Mind Of Jeremy Bentham* (London, 1968).

Mavrodes, G. I., 'Property', *Personalist*, 53 (1972), 245–62.

Melden, A. I., *Rights and Persons* (Oxford, 1977).

Mendus, S. L., *Toleration and the Limits of Liberty* (London, 1989).

Mill, J. S., *Essays on Ethics, Religion and Society*, ed. John M. Robson (Toronto, 1969) (The Collected Works of John Stuart Mill, x).

—— *Essays on Politics and Society*, ed. John M. Robson (2 vols., Toronto, 1977) (The Collected Works of John Stuart Mill xviii and xix).

Miller, D., 'Arguments for Equality', in P. A. French, T. E. Uehling, Jr., and H. K. Wettstein (eds.), Midwest Studies in Philosophy, 7, *Social and Political Philosophy* (Minneapolis, Minn., 1982).

—— 'Justice and Property', *Ratio*, 22 (1980), 1–14.

—— 'The Macpherson Version', *Political Studies*, 80 (1982), 120–7.

—— *Philosophy and Ideology in Hume's Political Thought* (Oxford, 1981).

—— *Social Justice* (Oxford, 1976).

Milne, A. J. M., 'Bentham's Principle of Utility and Legal Philosophy', *Northern Ireland Legal Quarterly*, 24 (1973), 275–304.

—— 'Coleridge and Bentham as Political Thinkers' in Ph.D. thesis (London, 1952).

Milne, A. Taylor, *Catalogue of the Manuscripts of Jeremy Bentham in the Library of University College London* (London, 1962).

Milo, R. D., 'Bentham's Principle', *Ethics*, 84 (1974), 128–39.

Montesquieu, C. L. De Secondat, Baron De., *The Spirit of The Laws* (New York, 1949).

Moore, G. E., *Principia Ethica* (Cambridge, 1903).

Moore, J., 'A Comment on Pocock', in A. Parel and T. Flanagan (ed.), *Theories of Property Aristotle to the Present* (Waterloo, 1979).

Narveson, J., *Morality and Utility* (Baltimore, Md., 1967).

Nozick, R., *Anarchy, State, and Utopia* (Oxford, 1974).

Oakshott, M., *On Human Conduct* (Oxford, 1975).

—— *Rationalism in Politics* (London, 1962).

O'Brien, D. P., *The Classical Economists* (Oxford, 1975).

O'Neill, O., 'The Most Extensive Liberty', *Proceedings of the Aristotelian Society*, 80 (1980), 45–59.

Oppenheim, F., *Political Concepts* (Oxford, 1981).

Parekh, B., 'Bentham's justification of the Principle of Utility', in id. (ed.), *Jeremy Bentham: Ten Critical Essays* (London, 1974).

—— *Bentham's Political Thought* (London, 1973).

—— 'Bentham's Theory of Equality', *Political Studies*, 18 (1970), 478–95.

PAREKH, B., (ed.), *Jeremy Bentham: Ten Critical Essays* (London, 1974).

PARFIT, D., *Reasons and Persons* (Oxford, 1984).

PERRY, D., *The Concept of Pleasure* (The Hague, 1967).

PETRELLA, F., 'Benthamism and the Demise of Classical Economic *Ordnungspolitik*', *History of Political Economy*, 9 (1977), 215–36.

PLAMENATZ, J. P., 'Bentham and his School', in *Man and Society* (2 vols., London, 1963).

—— *The English Utilitarians* (Oxford, 1966).

POCOCK, J. G. A., 'The Mobility of Property and the Rise of Eighteenth Century Sociology', in A. Parel and T. Flanagan (eds.), *Theories of Property Aristotle to the Present* (Waterloo, 1979).

—— *Politics, Language and Time: Essays on Political Thought and History* (New York, 1971).

POSNER, R., 'Blackstone and Bentham', *Journal of Law and Economics*, 19 (1979), 569–606.

—— 'Utilitarianism, Economics, and Legal Theory', *Journal of Legal Studies*, 8 (1979), 103–40.

POSTEMA, G. J., *Bentham and the Common Law Tradition* (Oxford, 1986).

——'Bentham and Dworkin on Positivism and Adjudication', *Social Theory and Practice*, 5 (1979), 347–76.

—— 'Bentham's Early Reflection on Law, Justice and Adjudication', *Revue Internationale de Philosophie*, 36 (1982), 219–41.

——'The Expositor, the Censor and the Common Law', *Canadian Journal of Philosophy*, 9 (1979), 643–70.

——'Facts, Fictions and the Law: Bentham on the Foundations of Evidence', *Archiv für Rechts- und Sozialphilosophie*, 16 (1983), 37–64.

——'The Normativity of Law', in R. Gavison (ed.), *Issues in Contemporary Legal Philosophy: The Influence of H. L. A. Hart* (Oxford, 1987).

—— 'The Principle of Utility and the Law of Procedure: Bentham's Theory of Adjudication', *Georgia Law Review*, 11 (1977), 1393–423.

—— Review of F. Rosen, *Jeremy Bentham and Representative Democracy: A Study of the Constitutional Code*, *Philosophical Review*, 95 (1986), 483–7.

POYNTER, J. R., 'Benthamite Utopias', in E. Kamenka (ed.), *Utopias* (Melbourne, 1986).

—— *Society and Pauperism: English Ideas on Poor Relief, 1795–1834* (London, 1969).

PRIOR, A. N., *Logic and the Basis of Ethics* (Oxford, 1949).

QUINTON, A., *Utilitarian Ethics* (London, 1989).

RAPHAEL, D. D., 'Bentham and the Varieties of Utilitarianism', *Bentham Newsletter*, 7 (1983), 3–14.

—— (ed.), *British Moralists: 1650–1800* (2 vols., Oxford, 1969).

—— *Justice and Liberty* (London, 1980).

RAWLS, J., 'Distributive Justice', in P. Laslett and W. G. Runcimann (eds.), *Philosophy, Politics and Society*, 3rd ser. (Oxford, 1967).

—— 'Distributive Justice: Some Addenda', *Natural Law Forum*, 13 (1968), 51–71.

—— 'Justice as Fairness', *Philosophical Review*, 67 (1958), 164–94.

—— 'Kantian Constructivism in Moral Theory', *Journal of Philosophy*, 77 (1980), 515–72.

—— *A Theory of Justice* (Oxford, 1972).

—— 'Two Concepts of Rules', *Philosophical Review*, 64 (1955), 3–32.

RAZ, J., *The Authority of Law* (Oxford, 1979).

—— *The Concept of a Legal System*, 2nd edn. (Oxford, 1980).

—— 'Liberalism, Autonomy, and the Politics of Neutral Concern', in P. A. French, T. E. Uehling, Jr., and H. K. Wettstein (eds.), *Midwest Studies in Philosophy*, 7, *Social and Political Philosophy* (Minneapolis, Minn., 1982).

—— *The Morality of Freedom* (Oxford, 1986).

—— 'On the Nature of Rights', *Mind*, 93 (1984), 194–214.

—— 'Principles of Equality', *Mind*, 87 (1978), 321–42.

—— 'Rights Based Moralities', in R. G. Frey (ed.), *Utility and Rights* (Oxford, 1985).

REES, J. C., *Equality* (London, 1971).

—— *John Stuart Mill's* On Liberty (Oxford, 1985).

REEVE, A., *Property* (London, 1986).

REGAN, D. H. *Utilitarianism and Co-operation* (Oxford, 1980).

REGAN, T., 'Utility and Equality: Some Neglected Problems', *Journal of Value Inquiry*, 17 (1983), 33–52.

REICH, C. A., 'The New Property', *Yale Law Journal*, 73 (1964), 733–87.

RESCHER, N., *Distributive Justice: A Constructive Critique of the Utilitarian Theory of Distributive Justice* (New York, 1966).

ROBBINS, L. C., *The Theory of Economic Policy in English Classical Political Economy*, 2nd edn. (London, 1978).

ROBERTS, W., 'Behavioural Factors in Bentham's Conception of Political Change', *Political Studies*, 10 (1962), 163–79.

—— 'Bentham's Conception of Political Change: A Liberal Approach', *Political Studies*, 9 (1961), 254–66.

—— 'Bentham's Poor Law Proposals', *Bentham Newsletter*, 3 (1979), 28–44.

ROBSON, J. M., *The Improvement of Mankind* (Toronto, 1968).

ROSEN, F., 'Basic Needs and Justice', *Mind*, 86 (1977), 88–94.

—— 'Bentham on Democratic Theory', *Bentham Newsletter*, 3 (1979), 46–61.

—— 'Bentham and Mill on Liberty and Justice', in F. Rosen and G. Feaver (eds.), *Lives, Liberties and the Public Good* (London, 1987).

—— 'Jeremy Bentham', in D. Miller, J. Coleman, W. Connolly, and A. Ryan (eds.), *The Blackwell Encyclopaedia of Political Thought* (Oxford, 1987).

—— 'Jeremy Bentham: Recent Interpretations', *Political Studies*, 30 (1982), 575–81.

—— *Jeremy Bentham and Representative Democracy* (Oxford, 1983).

—— 'Legitimacy: A Utilitarian View', in A. Moulakis (ed.), *Legitimacy/Légitimité* (Berlin, 1986).

—— 'Utilitarianism and Justice: A Note on Bentham and Godwin', *Enlightenment and Dissent*, 4 (1985), 47–52.

RYAN, A. (ed.), *John Stuart Mill and Jeremy Bentham: Utilitarianism and other Essays* (Harmondsworth, 1987).

—— *J. S. Mill* (London, 1974).

—— *The Philosophy of John Stuart Mill* (London, 1970).

—— *Property* (Milton Keynes, 1987).

—— 'Property, Liberty and On Liberty', in A. Phillips-Griffiths (ed.), *Of Liberty*, Royal Institute of Philosophy Lecture Series, 15 (1983), 217–31.

RYAN, A. *Property and Political Theory* (Oxford, 1984).

—— 'Utility and Ownership', in R. G. Frey (ed.), *Utility and Rights* (Oxford, 1985).

RYAN, C. C., 'Yours, Mine, and Ours: Property Rights and Individual Liberty', in J. Paul (ed.), *Reading Nozick* (Oxford, 1982).

RYLE, G., *The Concept of Mind* (Harmondsworth, 1963).

—— 'Pleasure', *Proceedings of the Aristotelian Society* (suppl.), 28 (1954), 135–46.

SARTORIUS, R., *Individual Conduct and Social Norms* (Belmont, Calif., 1975).

SCHAPIRO, I., *The Evolution of Rights in Liberal Theory* (Cambridge, 1986).

SCHAPIRO, J. S., 'Utilitarianism and the Foundations of English Liberalism', *Journal of Social Philosophy*, 4 (1939), 121–37.

SCHLATTER, R. B., *Private Property: The History of an Idea* (London, 1951).

SCHNEEWIND, J. B., *Sidgwick's Ethics and Victorian Moral Philosophy* (Oxford, 1977).

SCHOEMAN, F., 'Bentham's Theory of Rights', *Personalist*, 56 (1975), 109–28.

SCHUMPETER, J. A., *History of Economic Analysis* (New York, 1954).

SCHWARTZ, P., 'Jeremy Bentham's Democratic Despotism', in R. D. Collinson-Black (ed.), *Ideas in Economics* (London, 1986).

—— *The New Political Economy of J. S. Mill* (London, 1972).

SEMMEL, B., *John Stuart Mill and the Pursuit of Virtue* (New Haven, Conn., 1984).

SEMPLE, J., 'Bentham's Haunted House', *Bentham Newsletter*, 11 (1987), 35–44.

SEN, A., 'Equality of What?', in *Choice, Welfare and Measurement* (Oxford, 1982).

—— 'Utilitarianism and Welfarism', *Journal of Philosophy*, 76 (1979), 463–89.

SHACKLETON, R., 'The Greatest Happiness of the Greatest Number: The History of Bentham's Phrase', *Studies in Voltaire and the Eighteenth Century*, 90 (1972), 1461–81.

SIDGWICK, H., *The Elements of Politics*, 3rd edn. (London, 1908).

—— *The Methods of Ethics*, 7th edn. (London, 1907).

SIMONS, H. C., *Economic Policy for a Free Society* (Chicago, Ill, 1948).

SINGER, P., 'Is Act-Utilitarianism Self-Defeating', *Philosophical Review*, 81 (1972), 94–104.

—— 'The Triviality of the Debate over "Is-Ought" and the Definition of "Moral" ', *American Philosophical Quarterly*, 10 (1973), 51–6.

SKINNER, Q., 'Conventions and the Understanding of Speech Acts', *Philosophical Quarterly*, 20 (1970), 118–38.

—— 'The Idea of Negative Liberty: Philosophical and Historical Perspectives', in R. Rorty, J. B. Schneewind, and Q. Skinner (eds.), *Philosophy in History* (Cambridge, 1984).

—— 'Meaning and Understanding in the History of Ideas', *History and Theory*, 8 (1969), 3–53.

—— 'Some Problems in the Analysis of Political Thought and Action', *Political Theory*, 2 (1974), 277–303.

SMART, J. J. C., 'Hedonistic and Ideal Utilitarianism', in P. A. French, T. E. Uehling, Jr., and H. K. Wettstein (eds.), *Midwest Studies in Philosophy*, 3, *Studies in Ethical Theory* (Minneapolis, Minn., 1978).

—— 'An Outline of a System of Utilitarian Ethics', in id. and B. Williams (eds.), *Utilitarianism For and Against* (Cambridge, 1973).

SMITH, C. I., 'Bentham's Second Rule', *Journal of the History of Ideas*, 31 (1970), 462–3.

SNARE, F., 'The Concept of Property', *American Philosophical Quarterly*, 9 (1972), 200–6.

STARK, W., 'Bentham as an Economist II: Bentham's Influence', *Economic Journal*, 56 (1946), 583–608.

—— 'Liberty and Equality, or: Jeremy Bentham as an Economist', *Economic Journal*, 51 (1941), 56–79.

STEARNS, J. B., 'Bentham on Public and Private Ethics', *Canadian Journal of Philosophy*, 5 (1975), 583–94.

STEINER, H., 'The Concept of Justice', *Ratio*, 16 (1974), 206–25.

—— 'How Free: Computing Personal Liberty', in A. Phillips-Griffiths (ed.), *Of Liberty*, Royal Institute of Philosophy Lecture Series, 15 (1983), 73–90.

——'Individual Liberty', *Proceedings of the Aristotelian Society*, 76 (1975), 33–50.

——'Liberty and Equality', *Political Studies*, 29 (1981), 555–69.

——'The Structure of a Set of Compossible Rights', *Journal of Philosophy*, 74 (1977), 767–75.

STEINTRAGER, J., *Bentham* (London, 1977).

—— 'Language and Politics: Bentham on Religion', *Bentham Newsletter*, 4 (1980), 4–20.

—— 'Morality and Belief: The Origin and Purpose of Bentham's Writings on Religion', *Mill Newsletter*, 6 (1971), 3–15.

STEPHEN, J. F., *Liberty, Equality and Fraternity*, ed. R. J. White (Cambridge, 1967).

STEPHEN, L., *The English Utilitarians* (3 vols., London, 1900).

—— *History of English Thought in the Eighteenth Century* (2 vols., London, 1876).

SUMNER, L. W., *The Moral Foundation of Rights* (Oxford, 1987).

—— 'Rights Denaturalised', in R. G. Frey (ed.), *Utility and Rights* (Oxford, 1985).

TAWNEY, R. H., *Equality*, 5th edn. (London, 1964).

TAYLOR, C., 'What is Human Agency?', *Philosophical Papers* (2 vols., Cambridge, 1985).

—— 'What's Wrong with Negative Liberty', in A. Ryan (ed.), *The Idea of Freedom* (Oxford, 1979).

TEN, C. L., *Mill On Liberty* (Oxford, 1980).

THOMAS, W., *The Philosophic Radicals: Nine Studies in Theory and Practice 1817–1841* (Oxford, 1979).

TULLY, J., *A Discourse on Property: Locke and his Adversaries* (Cambridge, 1980).

TWINING, W. L., 'The Contemporary Significance of Bentham's Anarchical Fallacies', *Archiv für Rechts- und Sozialphilosophie*, 61 (1975), 325–56.

—— *Theories of Evidence: Bentham and Wigmore* (London, 1985).

VINER, J., 'Bentham and J. S. Mill the Utilitarian Background', in *The Long View and the Short* (Glencoe, Ill., 1958).

WALDRON, J., *Nonsense upon Stilts: Bentham, Burke and Marx on the Rights of Man* (London, 1987).

—— *The Right to Private Property* (Oxford, 1988).

—— 'Theoretical Foundations of Liberalism', *Philosophical Quarterly*, 37 (1987), 127–50.

—— 'Two Worries about Mixing One's Labour', *Philosophical Quarterly*, 33 (1983), 37–44.

WALLAS, G., 'Bentham as Political Inventor', *Contemporary Review*, 129 (1926), 308–19.

WARNOCK, G. J., *The Object of Morality* (London, 1971).

WEINSTEIN, W. L., 'The Concept of Liberty in Nineteenth Century English Political Thought', *Political Studies*, 13 (1965), 145–62.

WENER, L., 'A Note about Bentham on Equality and about the Greatest Happiness Principle', *Journal of the History of Philosophy*, 11 (1973), 237–51.

WHELAN, F. G., 'Property as Artifice: Hume and Blackstone', *Nomos*, 22 (1980), 102–25.

WHITELEY, C. H., 'On Duties', *Proceedings of the Aristotelian Society*, 53 (1953), 97–104.

WILLIAMS, B., 'Conflicts of Values', in *Moral Luck* (Cambridge, 1981).

—— 'A Critique of Utilitarianism', in J. J. C. Smart and B. Williams (eds.), *Utilitarianism For and Against* (Cambridge, 1973).

—— 'The Idea of Equality', in P. Laslett and W. G. Runciman (eds.), *Philosophy, Politics and Society*, 2nd ser. (Oxford, 1962).

—— 'Internal and External Reasons', in *Moral Luck* (Cambridge, 1981).

—— *Morality: An Introduction to Ethics* (Cambridge, 1972).

WILLIFORD, M., *Jeremy Bentham on Spanish America: An Account of his Letters and Proposals to the New World* (Baton Rouge, 1980).

WINCH, D., *Adam Smith's Politics* (Cambridge, 1978).

—— *Classical Political Economy and Colonies* (London, 1965).

WINCH, P., 'Nature and Convention', in *Ethics and Action* (London, 1972).

WOLIN, S. S., *Politics and Vision: Continuity and Innovation in Western Political Thought* (London, 1961).

WOLLHEIM, R., 'Equality', *Proceedings of the Aristotelian Society*, 56 (1956), 281–300.

ZAGDAY, M. I., 'Bentham and the Poor Law', in G. W. Keeton and G. Schwartzenberger (eds.), *Jeremy Bentham and the Law* (London, 1948).

Index